I0793012

IMAGES
of America

GOLIAD

On the Cover: Goliad's place in the heritage of the Texas Revolution was recognized in 1906, when the Daughters of the Texas Revolution held their annual meeting in Goliad on the 70th anniversary of the revolution. At that meeting, the last surviving veterans of the Texas Revolution and their wives gathered and were photographed at Mission Espiritu Santo on April 21, 1906. Shown here from left to right are S. F. Sparks (Rockport), Alonso Steele (Mexia), W. P. Zuber (Austin), L. T. Lawer (Florence), and J. W. Darlington (Taylor). Their wives are unidentified. (Courtesy of the Goliad County Historical Commission's Market House Museum Collection.)

IMAGES
of America

GOLIAD

Raymond Starr

ARCADIA
PUBLISHING

ISBN 978-0-7385-7873-6

Published by Arcadia Publishing
Charleston, South Carolina

Printed in the United States of America

Library of Congress Control Number: 2009930217

For all general information contact Arcadia Publishing at:
Telephone 843-853-2070
Fax 843-853-0044
E-mail sales@arcadiapublishing.com
For customer service and orders:
Toll-Free 1-888-313-2665

Visit us on the Internet at www.arcadiapublishing.com

This book is a project of the Goliad County Historical Commission, designed to help preserve and disseminate the history of Goliad. All profits from this book will be used for the conservation and promotion of Goliad's history.

Contents

ACKNOWLEDGMENTS

The bulk of the photographs in this book are from the Goliad County Historical Commission's Market House Museum Collection. That collection consists of 950 images covering many aspects of Goliad's history. Many of the pictures are old, and some are not very clear, but they are a priceless record of Goliad's past. Unless noted otherwise, all photographs in this book are from that collection; those from other sources are acknowledged in the picture captions.

No book like this is based on extensive primary research; it is mostly drawn from the work of others. The books by Beth White, Nell White, Joe Tom Davis, and the Goliad County Historical Commission's *The History and Heritage of Goliad County*—the basic reference book for Goliad-area history—have been the most frequently used sources of information for this book. Full citations for these authors can be found in the bibliography.

Many people helped in many ways with this project. They include Bob Allen, Joyce Baecker, Cristy Billo, Erika Bochat, Kyle Boyd-Robertson, Beth Ellis, Mona Foust, Harold Gleinser, Myra Heard, Melissa Gonzales, Kathy Johnson, James Johnson, Patsy Light, Bennie Martinez, Louise O'Connor, Debbie Parsons, Randel Scott, Tom Shelton, Tommy Tijerena, Rhonda Todd, Janie von Dohlen, John C. von Dohlen Jr., Jim Walker, Newton Warzecha, Carolyn Williams, and Estella Zermeno.

John C. von Dohlen III provided valuable technical assistance with computer and photography matters. The editorial staff of Arcadia Publishing—particularly Kristie Kelly, Hannah Carney, and Hunter Byrd—have been very helpful.

INTRODUCTION

"Remember Goliad!" was the cry that fixed Goliad's place as a major icon of the Texas Revolution and which made the name Goliad one that resonates with most Texans, and even many visitors from other parts of the country and the world, and draws them to visit the place where the cry was born. It is also an excellent theme for a book on the history of Goliad. This book will show the origins of the term and how, for nearly two centuries, that cry has remained alive in the community. References to that fatal day in March 1836, as well as Goliad's mission past and the origins of ranching, have been continual themes in the town's history, celebrated in many monuments, historical sites, programs, parades, and institutions. Coupled with the preservation of many centuries-old buildings in the town, this process has kept history in the foreground of Goliad's life and appearance. It has made it easy to "remember Goliad."

There is also much else to remember about Goliad. Even without its Spanish roots and its role in the Texas Revolution, Goliad has been a memorable small town worthy of reflection. It began in 1749, when the Spanish relocated a mission and presidio (which had originally been built to discourage foreign invaders) to their present-day site on the San Antonio River. The mission (soon joined by a sister institution, the Rosario Mission) tried to convert and "civilize" the Native Americans; in the process, the misson raised cattle, originating the Texas ranching industry. At the same time, the presidio was a military and administrative center for the whole area. A town called "La Bahia" grew up around the presidio, and by the late 18th century, the area was the second most populated in the Spanish colonies in Texas.

After the successful Mexican Revolution of 1821, the Spanish colonial outpost became a Mexican one and soon changed its name from Bahia to Goliad. The presidio and the town were the site of several military engagements culminating in the capture of the presidio by the Texans in the Texas Revolution. They renamed it "Fort Defiance," declared independence (prematurely, as it turned out) and created the now-famous "bloody arm" flag. After the Mexican army defeated the Texans at the nearby Battle of Coleto Creek in 1836, the Mexicans executed 342 hostages, which became the largest loss of Texan life in the Texas Revolution—more than all other casualties of the war combined. It is no wonder "Remember Goliad" (along with "Remember the Alamo") became a battle cry at the Battle of San Jacinto, and has remained part of Texas culture ever since.

After the Texas Revolution, Goliad embarked on a difficult road. The Goliad town site was moved north of the river in the 1840s, although many Tejanos (citizens of Hispanic origin) remained in the area around the now-abandoned presidio. That neighborhood, still called "La Bahia," has remained a cohesive community to present times. During the 1840s and 1850s, the town suffered Native American raids as well as Mexican efforts to regain Texas, including the Mexican War. As the town began to emerge, the Civil War further disrupted things. In the aftermath of that conflict there were the difficult Reconstruction years, with gratuitous violence, cattle rustling, and official corruption. The violence was so severe that vigilante organizations were formed that themselves became sources of killing and disorder. In time, Texas Rangers helped calm the situation. By the end of the 1870s, Goliad was ready to take off as a ranching, agricultural, and neighborhood trading community, and with the help of the railroad, which arrived in 1889, it did. In the generation that followed, the town visitors see today came into being.

The peak of town growth was from 1880 to 1930, when the economy flourished. It developed its commercial center around the courthouse square, developed services such as electricity, telegraph, telephones, gas, public water, and sewer. Schools, churches, clubs, and service organizations emerged, and many forms of recreation and entertainment were enjoyed. While the town of Goliad was the center of this growth, a series of smaller communities—Ander, Weesatche, Cologne, Fannin, Berclair, Charco, Schroeder, and others—flourished in the rural areas of the county. As a list of the number of hotels, banks, grocery stores, and cotton gins indicates, Goliad was a successful town catering to almost all the needs of its citizens.

Goliad's decline began somewhat with the Depression but increased dramatically in the years after World War II as the resulting economic distress made the 1930s more difficult. That distress was balanced with the energetic efforts of county judge James A. White, who succeeded in obtaining state and federal aid from Depression relief agencies and the Texas Centennial celebrations of the 1930s to establish Goliad State Park, reconstruct Mission Espiritu Santo within that park, build the municipal auditorium, and erect a large monument to Col. James Fannin and his men, who had been slaughtered by the Mexican army in 1836.

After World War II, the town prospered for a while, but as was true all across the nation, good roads and better jobs caused many to abandon Goliad and it fell into a downturn, becoming a somewhat shabby ghost of its past self. In time, the community began to fight back. The old presidio was restored, creating a major site to celebrate Goliad's past. In the 1970s, citizens established a historical district to preserve the old buildings around the square, and in the 1980s, they entered the Main Street program and spruced up the community. Since that time, the community has continually revisited its heritage of Spanish-colonial roots, ranching, the Texas Revolution, and its history as a rural Texas town that still has much of the feel of its mostly lost past. As such, heritage tourism has emerged as the town's major economic base, and many visitors come to experience and remember Goliad.

One

Colonial Beginnings 1749–1836

Modern Goliad began with Spain's efforts to protect its northern frontier from possible foreign intrusion. In 1749, Spain relocated the Mission Nuestra Señora del Espiritu Santo de Zuniga and its accompanying presidio, usually referred to as Presidio La Bahia, to a spot on the San Antonio River.

The mission was designed to convert Native Americans to Christianity and to make them Spanish citizens. The mission built a nearly self-sufficient community, including the addition of a huge herd of longhorn cattle, which became the foundation for the cattle ranching industry in Texas.

The Presidio La Bahia played a large role as a military and administrative center of the area. As such, the presidio formed a key link in the transportation network that tied Texas to Spain in the Colonial period—the El Camino Real de los Tejas. La Bahia was so important to Spain that, in the latter 18th century, 25 percent of Texans lived in that area.

Around the fort, a settlement grew, originally called La Bahia, which renamed itself Goliad in 1829. The name is an anagram of Hidalgo, one of the heroes of the Mexican Revolution against Spain, with the "H" dropped.

There was considerable military action at the presidio. In addition to continual conflict with Native Americans, the fort itself was the focus of a number of events, including captures by revolutionaries and filibusters in 1812 and 1821. When the conflict between the Texas province and central Mexico began in 1835, a Texan group occupied the fort and declared independence from Mexico two months before the official Texas Declaration of Independence. Later, as Mexico sought to regain its revolting province, Mexico defeated a Texan army in the Battle of Coleto, about 10 miles from the presidio. The surrendered Texans were taken to the presidio and on March 27, 1936, the Mexican army executed 342 Texan prisoners. This became known as the Goliad Massacre, and "Remember Goliad" became a chant along with the cry "Remember the Alamo" in motivating Texans to continue the fight for independence. This secured Goliad's place in history and became the focal point of the community's identity.

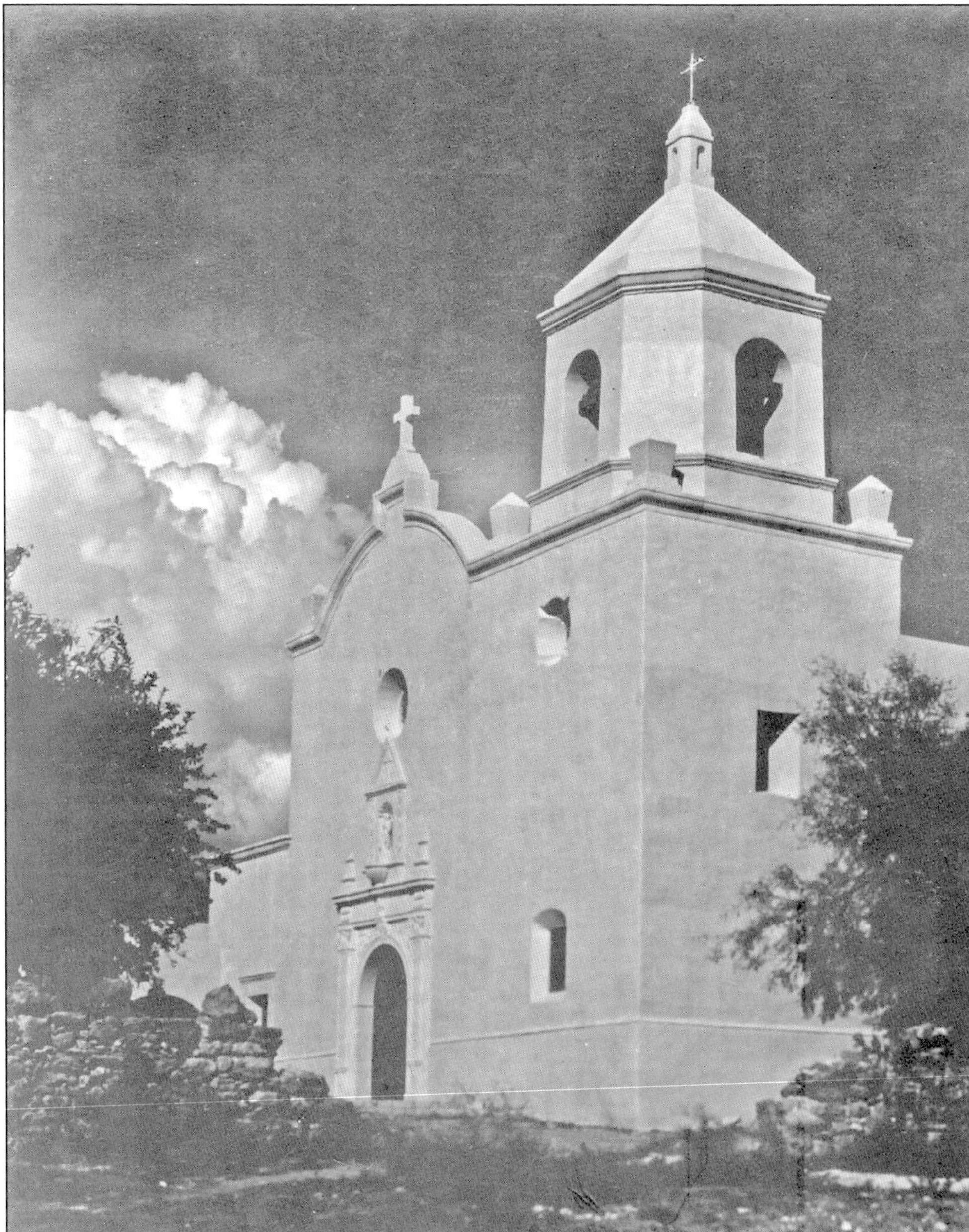

This picture of the reconstructed chapel portrays the Mission Nuestra Señora del Espiritu Santo de Zuniga where Goliad began. It was originally established in 1722 near Matagorda Bay but was relocated several times before being moved to the San Antonio River in 1749. It, along with the accompanying Presidio La Bahia, became the core of the settlement, which was named Goliad in 1829. The mission served the native peoples until secularization in 1830. After secularization, the mission was abandoned, and the buildings were used by several schools—like the Hillyer Female College and Aranama College—and by both Confederate and Union troops during the Civil War. Afterwards, it fell into ruins; some of its building materials were used for new buildings in town. The mission was finally restored and made the centerpiece of a state park in the 1930s. (Courtesy of Texas Department of Parks and Wildlife.)

This painting of a Native American (note the markings on the cheeks) illustrates the people the mission was established to serve. The Native Americans—mostly Aranama Indians—were brought to the mission for religious instruction and to convert them into Spanish citizens. They learned European building trades and agricultural, ranching, and domestic skills. Their life was highly regulated and they were generally not very receptive, so the population of the mission was never very large. (Painting by Nola Davis; courtesy of Texas Department of Parks and Wildlife.)

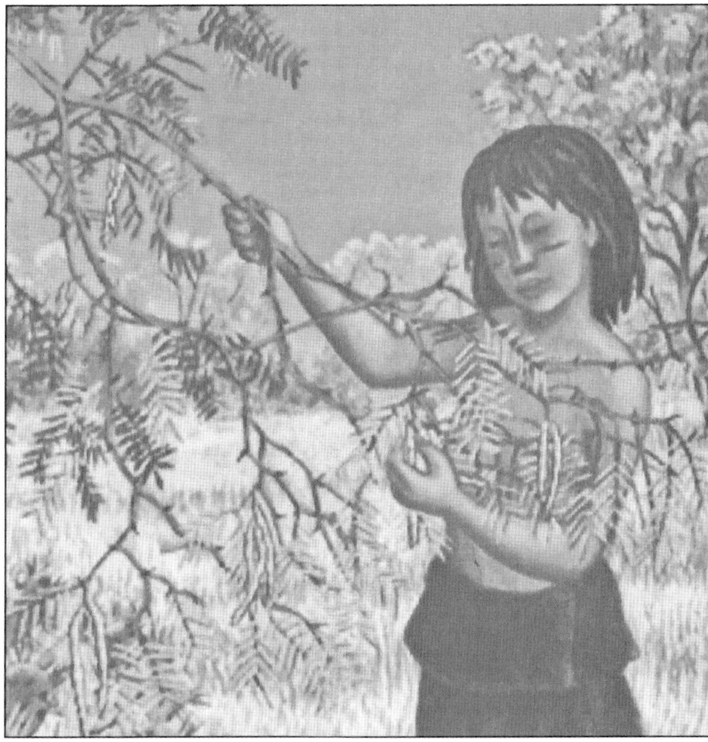

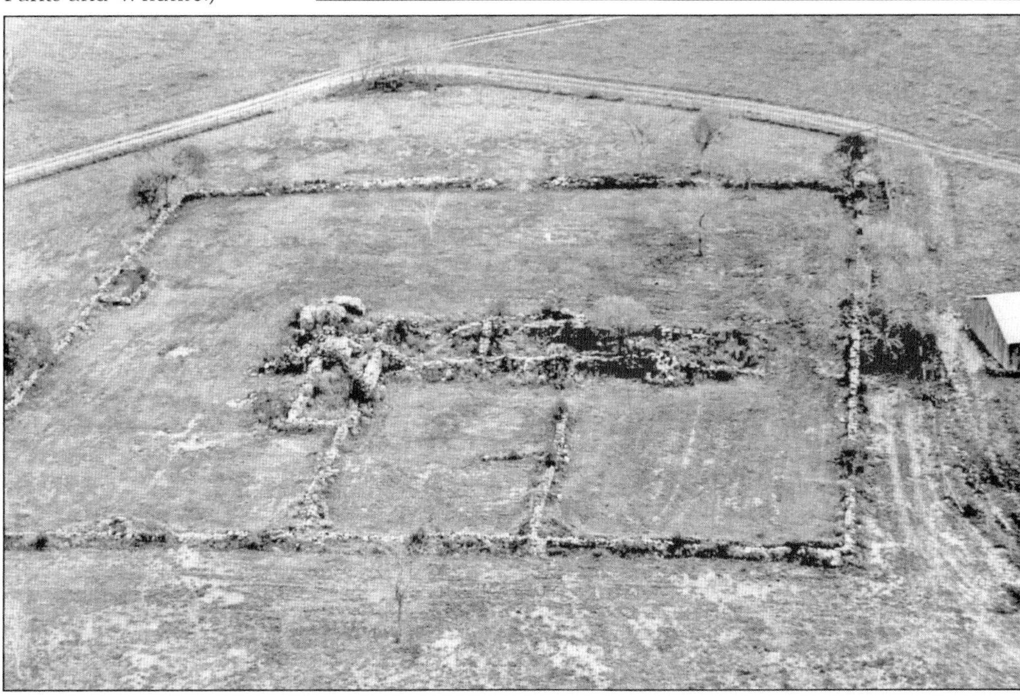

In 1754, the Spanish established a second mission, Neustra Señora del Rosario, whose ruins are shown here in a 1930s aerial view, to try to convert the very difficult Karankawa Indians. It prospered for a while, but in time Comanche raids and the independent nature of the Karankawas caused it to be suspended, and eventually it closed in 1807.

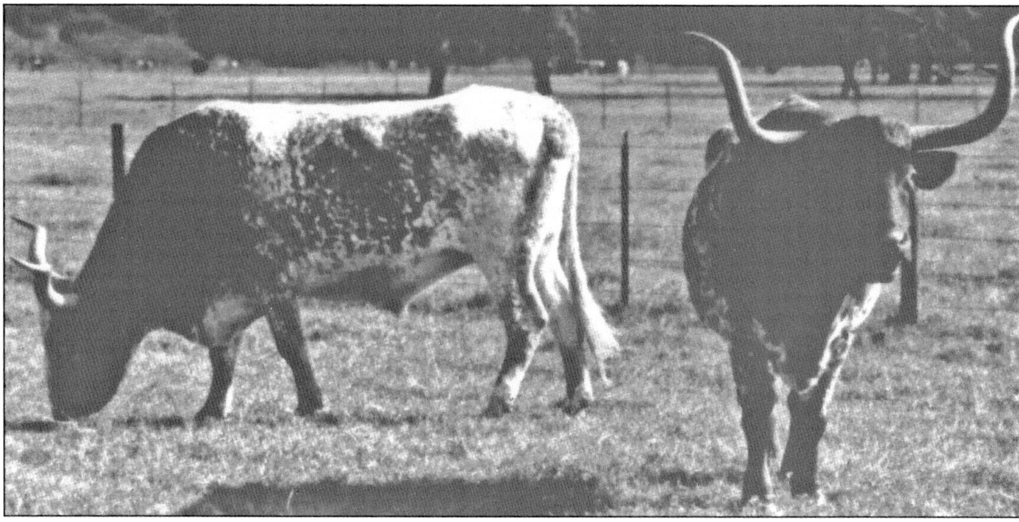

To feed their charges, the missions established herds of cattle, which numbered 40,000 over time. These animals were the roots of the cattle ranching industry in Texas. The cattle raised were longhorns. They were a unique Texas breed that evolved in the area from cattle brought over from Spain. The longhorns were superbly adapted to the region; they have long been used by Goliad as a defining symbol.

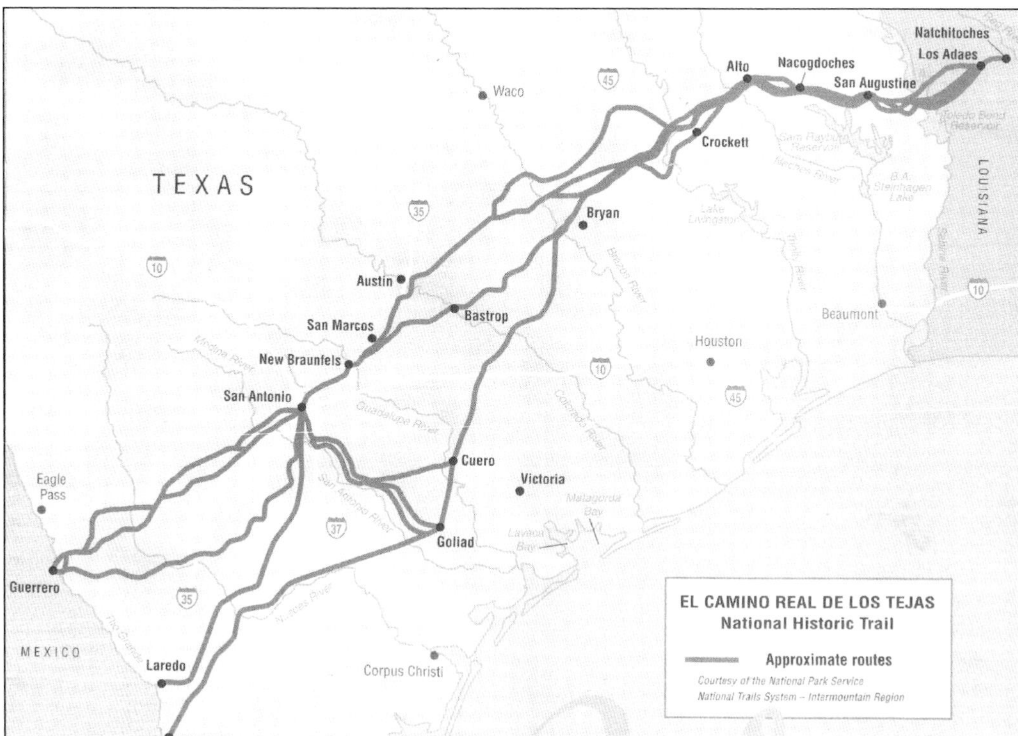

Goliad's situation as the only Spanish presidio along the Texas coast can clearly be seen in this modern map of the El Caminio Real de los Tejas—the system of roads the Spanish created to serve their colony. Many of the roads continue to be used today and are now being developed into a historic trail by the National Park Service. (Courtesy of National Park Service.)

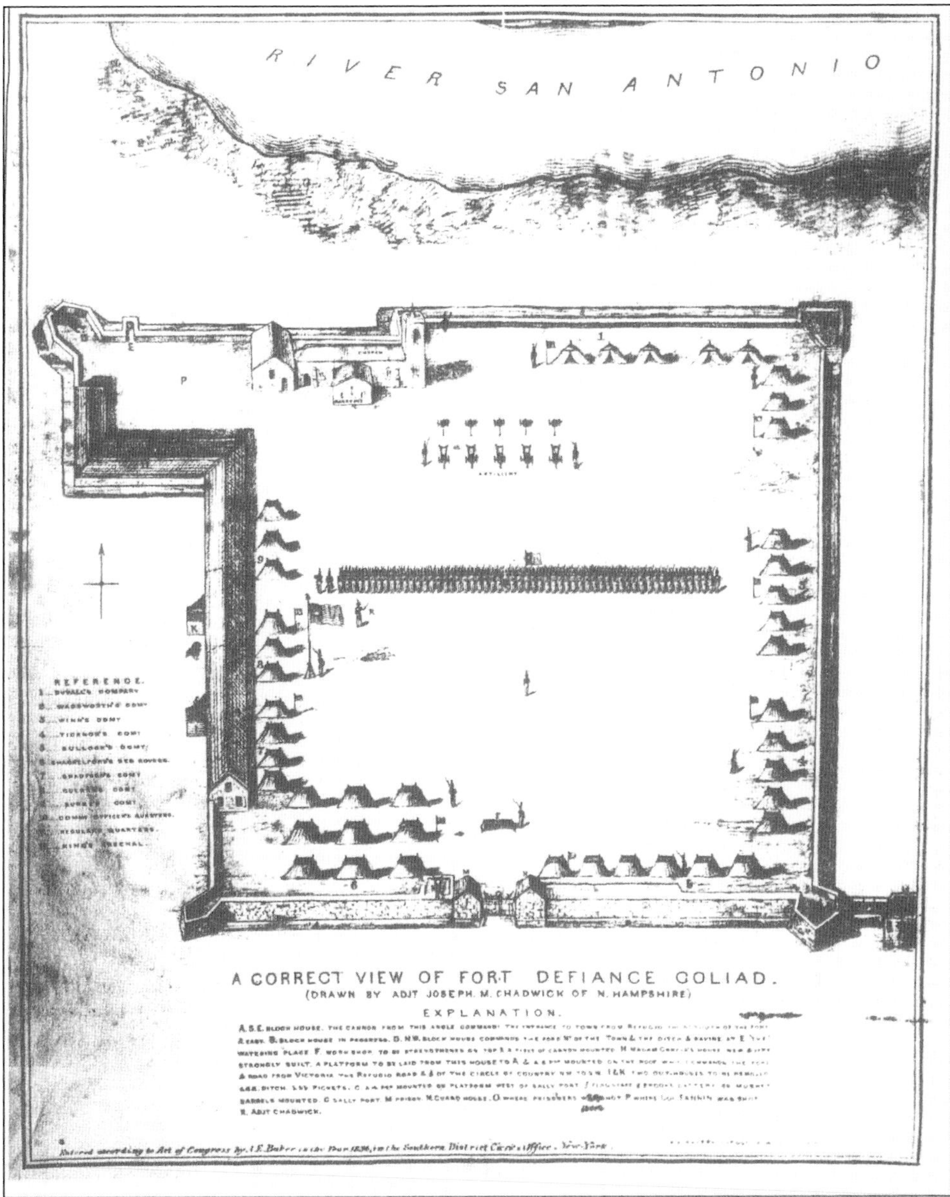

Map 2: "A Correct View of Fort Defiance Goliad." This drawing was used by Raiford Stripling during the restoration of Presidio La Bahía. It was an 1836 copy by a New York lithographer based on the small drawing made by Captain Joseph M. Chadwick seventeen days before the battle.

This photograph of an 1836 lithograph, based on a map made by Capt. Joseph Chadwick 17 days before the Battle of Coleto, shows what Presidio La Bahia looked like (except for a small error in the placement of the chapel). The presidio was a major Spanish military and administrative center that, according to a 1767 Spanish official's account, was in a "commanding [location] on a hill in which they have found a vein of stone that offers great advantage for construction." It was also noted that the 50 soldiers stationed there were the best-dressed in the province, although there was scurvy and malaria. Because of its strategic location, there was considerable military action here; current presidio director Newton Wazecha says it was the most fought-over site in colonial Texas. (Courtesy of Kathryn Stoner O'Connor Foundation.)

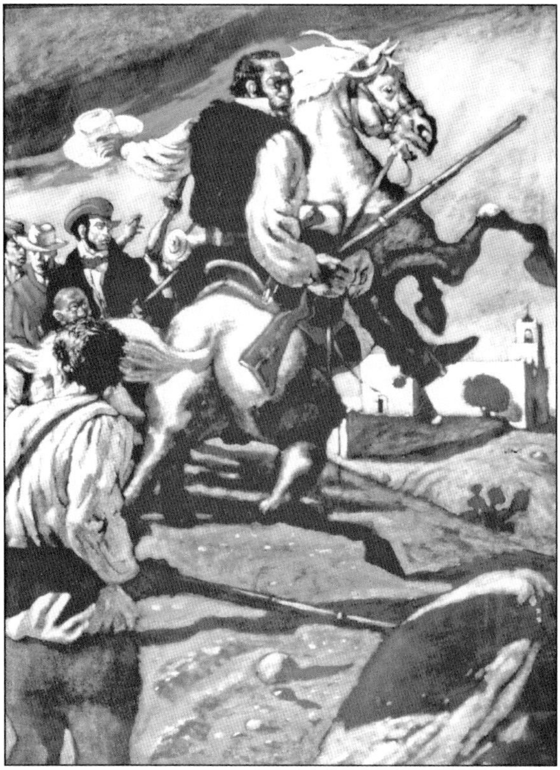

On October 10, 1835, a Texan army under George Collingsworth's leadership attacked Presidio La Bahia, quickly capturing it. This secured the strategic site for the revolutionaries but also made the presidio a major target for the Mexican army. During the attack, freedman Sam McCullogh was wounded in the shoulder, becoming, according to many, the first Texan casualty of the revolution. Artist Kermit Oliver presents McCullogh's role in the attack in dramatic form. (Courtesy of UTSA Institute of Texan Cultures.)

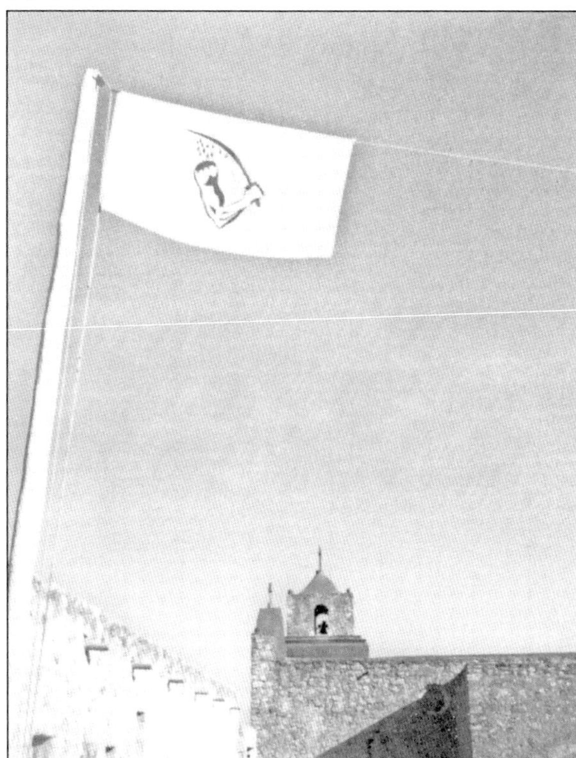

After capturing the presidio, the Texans produced the first Texas Declaration of Independence on December 20, 1835, and created a flag that was raised "amidst rapturous hurrahs." The flag featured a red arm grasping a drawn sword on a white background and symbolized the Texan's sentiment that they would rather lose an arm than live under the rule of Mexican despot Antonio Lopez de Santa Ana. This has become Goliad's unofficial flag. (Courtesy of Kathryn Stoner O'Connor Foundation.)

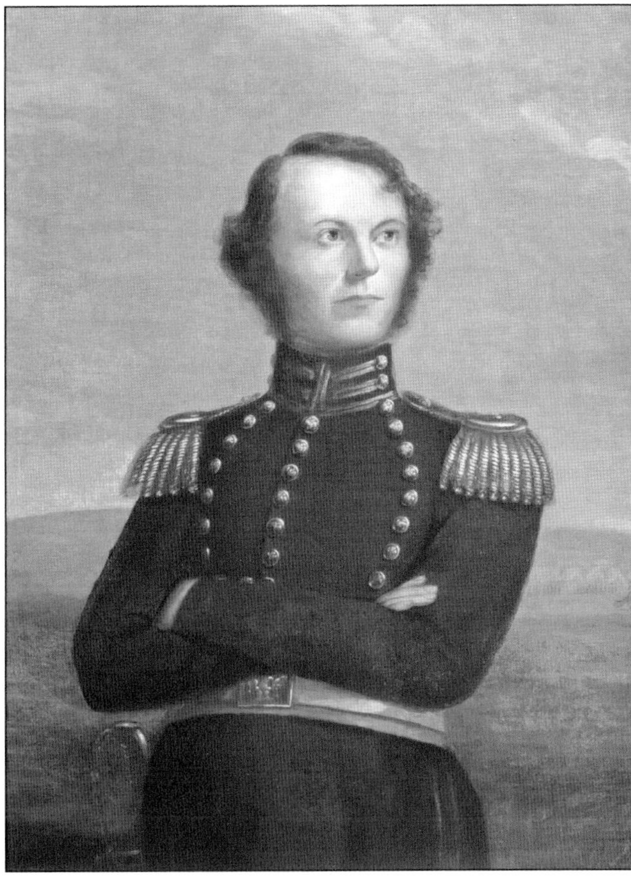

James W. Fannin was a young soldier from Georgia who came to Texas and became a slave trader. Because he had two years at West Point, he was made commander of the troops at Goliad. A reluctant and very incompetent commander, he made a number of mistakes when ordered to abandon the presidio in March 1836 in the face of a large, advancing Mexican army. Those mistakes set the stage for the Goliad Massacre. (Courtesy of Dallas Historical Society.)

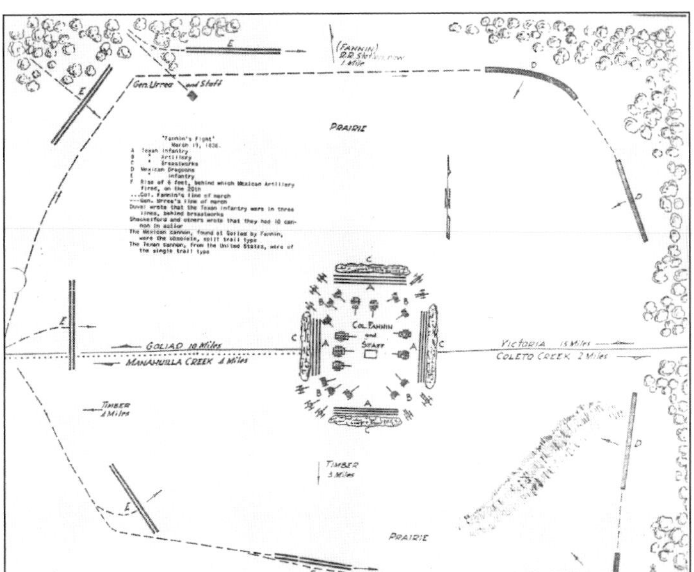

On March 19, 1836, Colonel Fannin began a retreat in the face of a large, advancing Mexican army under Gen. José de Urrea. After allowing themselves to be caught in an open field (see map at left), Colonel Fannin's Texan army was forced to engage in a ferocious battle. Fannin recognized the hopelessness of the situation and surrendered to the Mexican army the next morning. The prisoners were then moved back to Presidio La Bahia. (Courtesy of Kathryn Stoner O'Connor Foundation.)

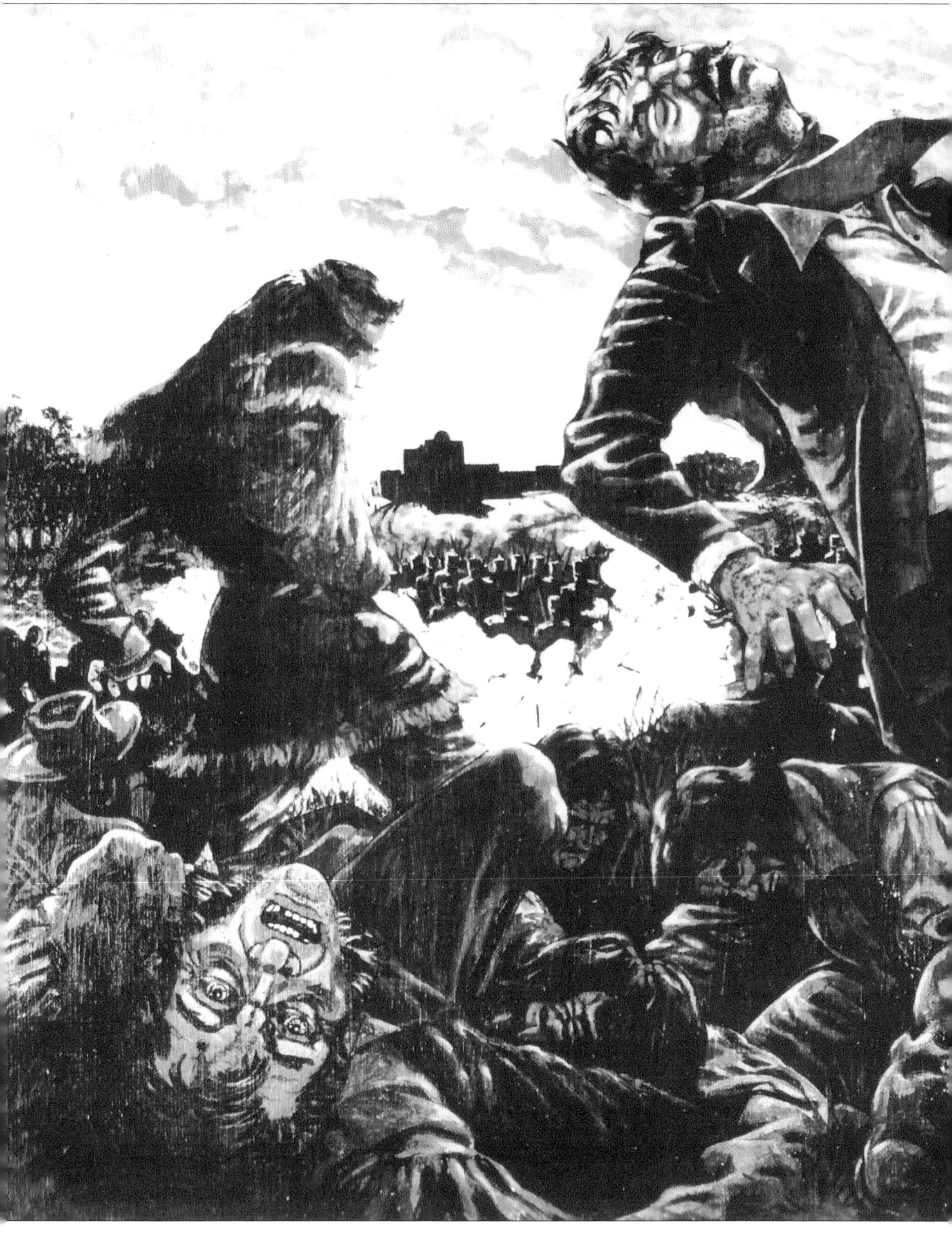

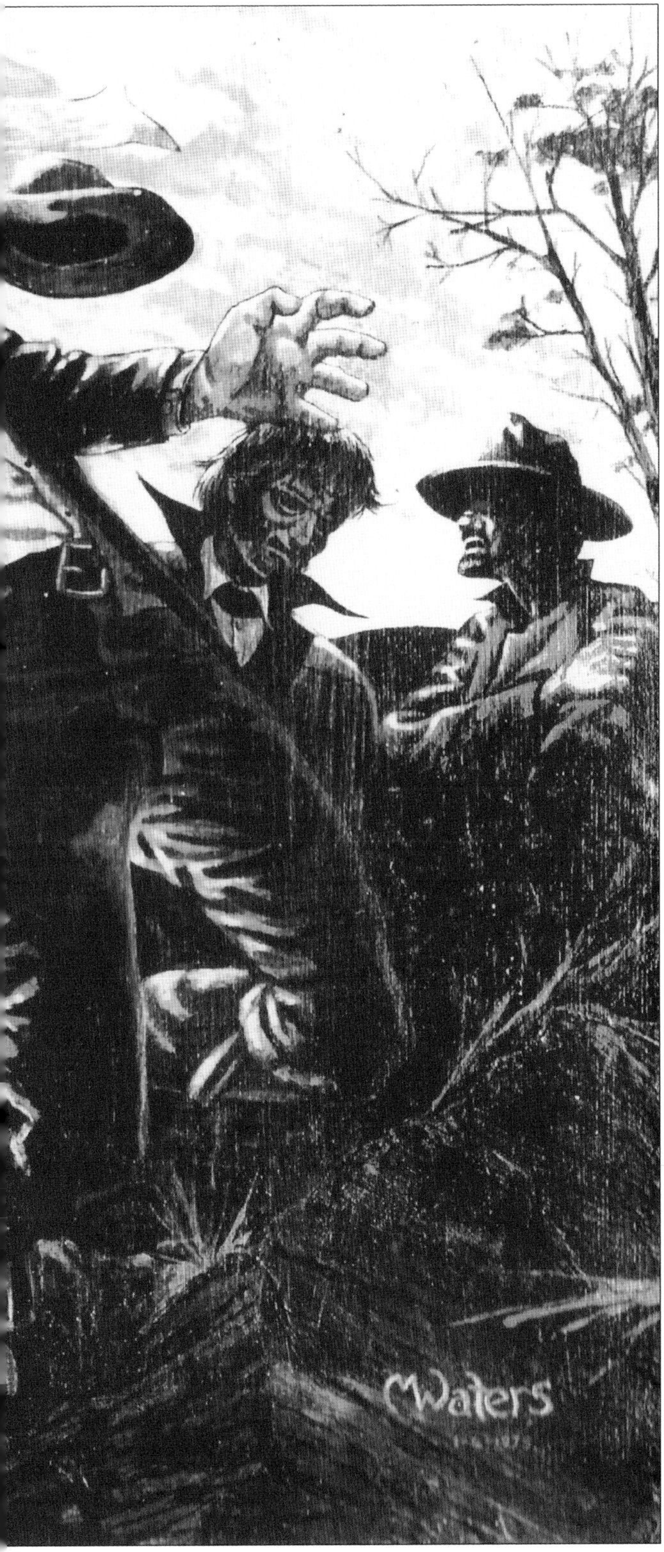

This highly dramatized watercolor by Edward Johnson illustrates the most fateful day in Goliad history—the slaughter of Fannin and his men on March 27, 1836. Acting on orders from General Lopez de Santa Ana and over the strenuous objections of General Urrea and the Mexican officers and soldiers in Goliad, Mexican soldiers marched the prisoners out of the fort and shot them; Fannin was killed within the presidio walls. Although as many as 25 men might have escaped that day, at least 342 were killed. This has become known as the Goliad Massacre. (Some find the title "massacre" prejudicial against Mexico and prefer the word "execution.") The cry "Remember Goliad" became a rallying cry for Texan patriots for the remainder of the revolution along with "Remember the Alamo." It also forever marked Goliad as a major shrine of Texas history. (Courtesy of UTSA Institute of Texan Culture.)

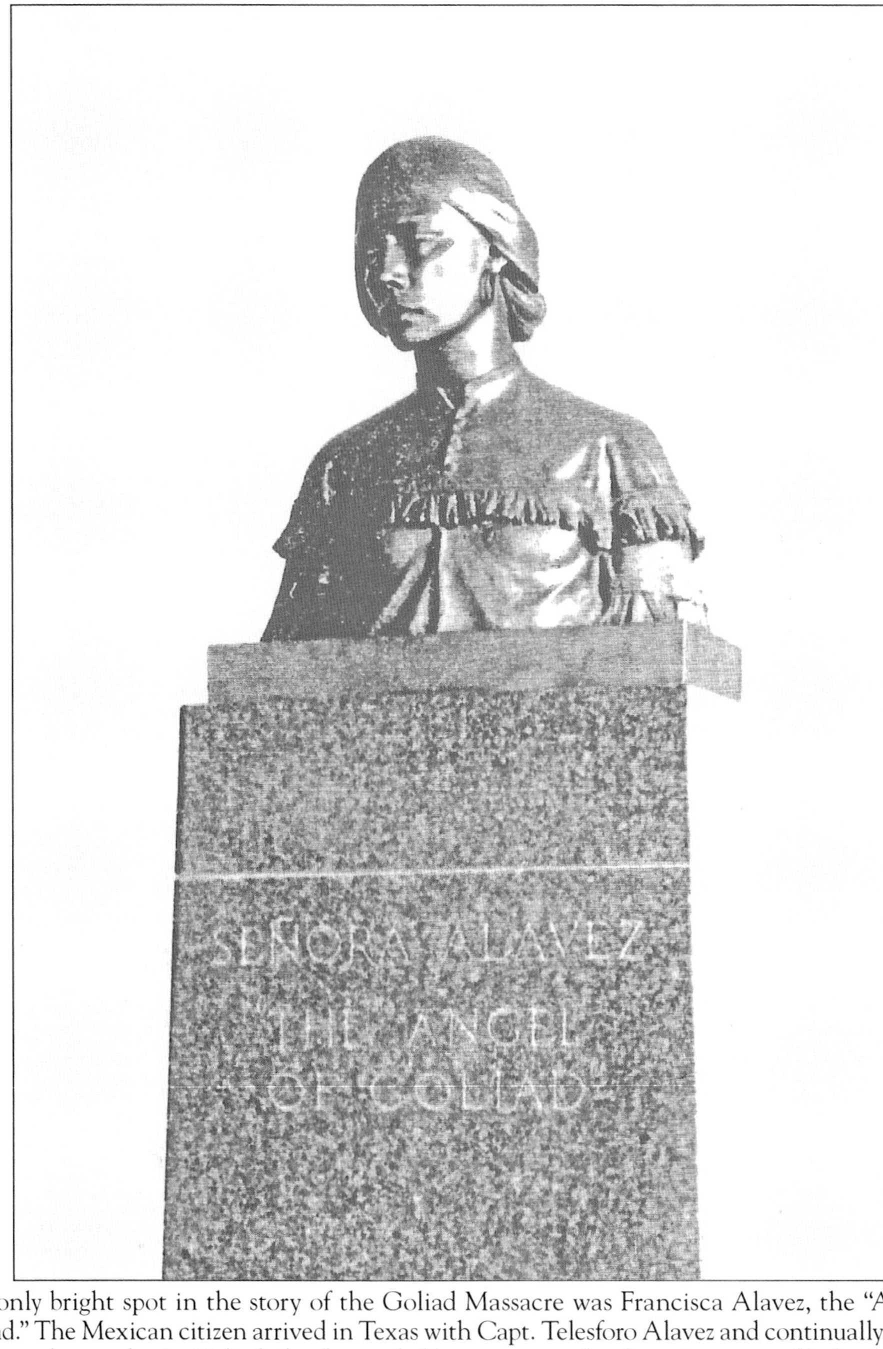

The only bright spot in the story of the Goliad Massacre was Francisca Alavez, the "Angel of Goliad." The Mexican citizen arrived in Texas with Capt. Telesforo Alavez and continually showed mercy to the needy. At Goliad, she demanded humane care for the prisoners and helped some of them hide and escape death. She also later intervened on behalf of Texan prisoners at Copano, Victoria, and Matamoros. Alavez has long been honored in Goliad with this statue (originally in the Centennial Auditorium), a mural, a Texas Historical Commission marker, and a statue on a hike-and-bike trail named after her. Massacre survivor Dr. J. H. Barnard wrote, "Her name deserves to be recorded in letters of gold among those angels who have from time to time been commissioned . . . to relieve the sorrows and cheer the hearts of men."

Two

Goliad in the New Nation 1837–1880

The years between the Texas Revolution and the end of Reconstruction after the Civil War were years of turmoil and violence. There was the disorder after the Revolution, including several efforts by Mexico to regain Texas. There were continual Indian raids, especially by the feared Comanches, into the 1850s. In 1857, there was the Cart War, when locals attacked Mexicans who entered the cartage trade at lower costs than the longtime Anglo cart drivers. This led to violence, including the inauguration of the Hanging Tree as a place for public executions. Then there was the Civil War. There were no military engagements in Goliad during the war, but the town was much affected as many local men went off to war and commerce was disrupted by the Yankee blockade. After the war, there were the hostilities and unpleasant experiences of the Reconstruction and beyond, which included almost unlimited cattle rustling, random killing and robbing, and the rise of the Ku Klux Klan attacks. Part of the violence was caused by the famous Taylor-Sutton feud, which featured general outlawry but also continued the resistance of former Confederates against Unionists and Union sympathizers. The peaceable citizens of Goliad County finally retaliated with vigilantism with the formation of Regulators. At times, the state sent Texas Rangers to the area, and eventually peace came to the region.

Despite the turmoil of the period, the town leaders moved the town to a new site north of the San Antonio River. The county of Goliad was created, one of the original counties in the Republic of Texas. The town grew into a typical rural Texas community. It established a courthouse, a number of schools and community institutions such as churches, a Masonic lodge, a town cemetery, and a wide array of businesses and services. In the countryside, ranching continued with some agriculture. Goliad, located at the points of origin for the Chisholm and other trails, participated heavily in the cattle drives of the 1860s and 1870s. In addition, a number of smaller communities grew up in the rural areas of the county. By the end of the period, the county's population had grown from a few hundred to 5,800 people. Goliad was well-rooted and ready for the railroad and significant growth and development during its second generation.

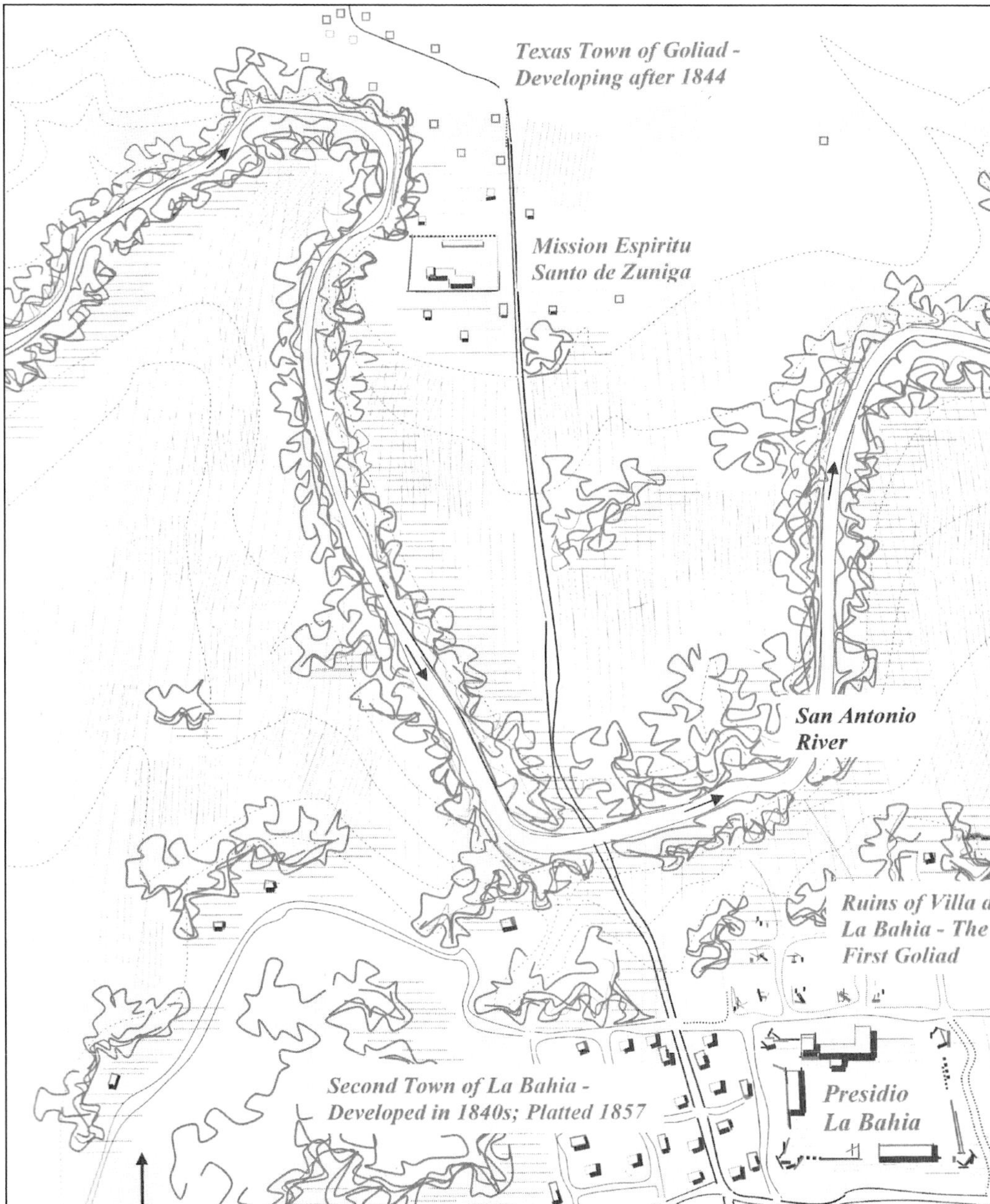

After the Texas Revolution, the Anglo residents moved the site of Goliad north from the presidio to its present site. That became the Goliad that evolved into the present-day town. Many Tejanos remained around the presidio in the area called La Bahia. Often alienated from the Anglo majority, partly because most lost their land to them, many Tejanos remained south of the river, and that area has remained home to much of the town's Spanish-speaking population. The new town north of the river grew gradually during that period from a desolate handful of people after the Revolution to a town of several thousand by the beginning of the 19th century. (Map by Daniel Fox; courtesy of Presidio La Bahia.)

The house built in 1840 by English immigrant Lloyd Vivian is of local stone quarried at the site, with walls 18 inches thick. The house was built with protection in mind; there are no windows on the west side, making it easier to defend against Native American raids, which were still occurring into the 1850s.

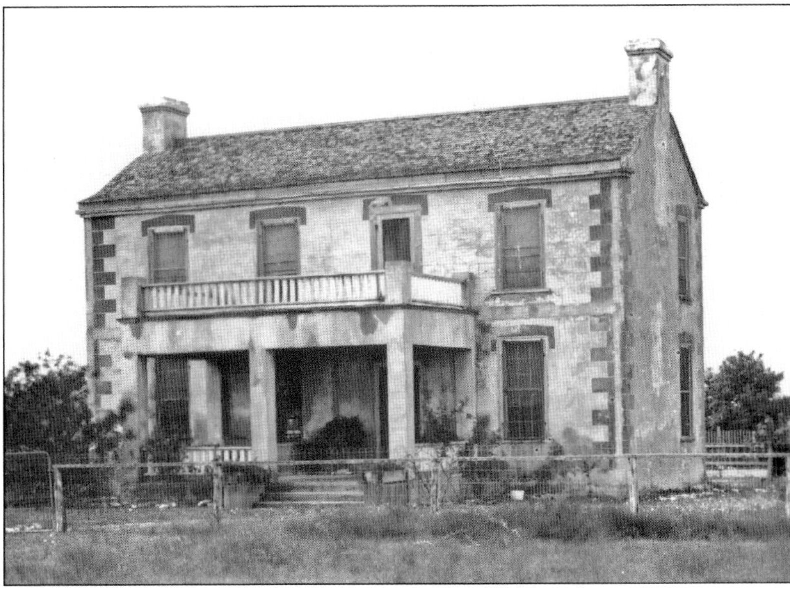

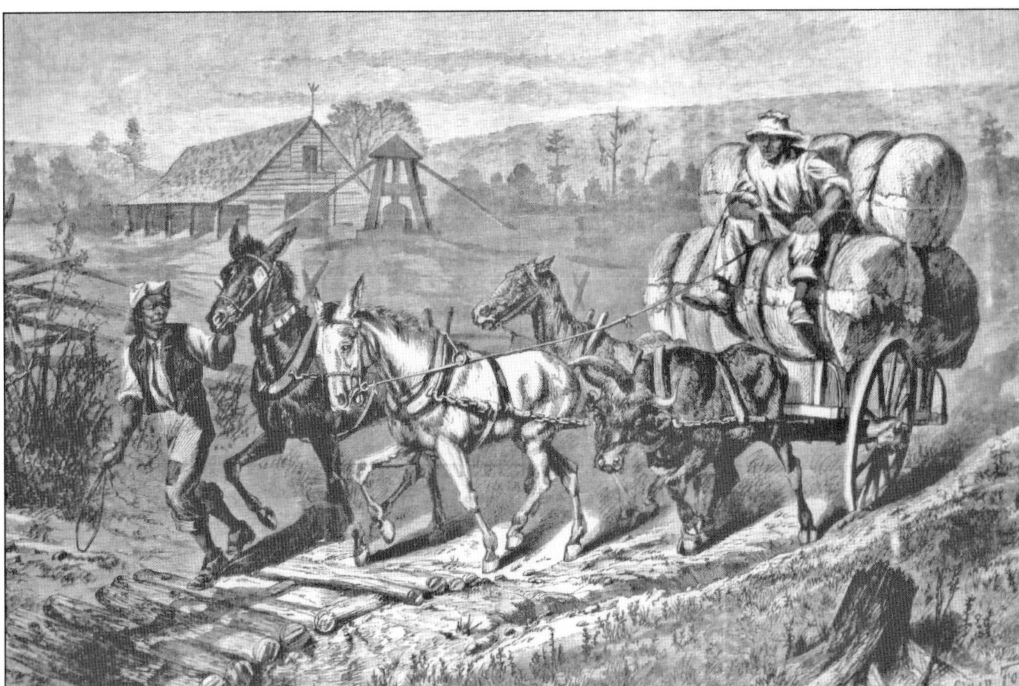

This etching of slaves with a cotton wagon reflects slavery's significance in Goliad. The 1860 census indicated there were 843 slaves out of a population of 3,384. There was enough fear concerning the size of this number that, in 1858, the city passed an ordinance forbidding nonresident slaves to remain in town after sundown, unless they had wives in town. (Courtesy of UTSA Institute of Texan Culture.)

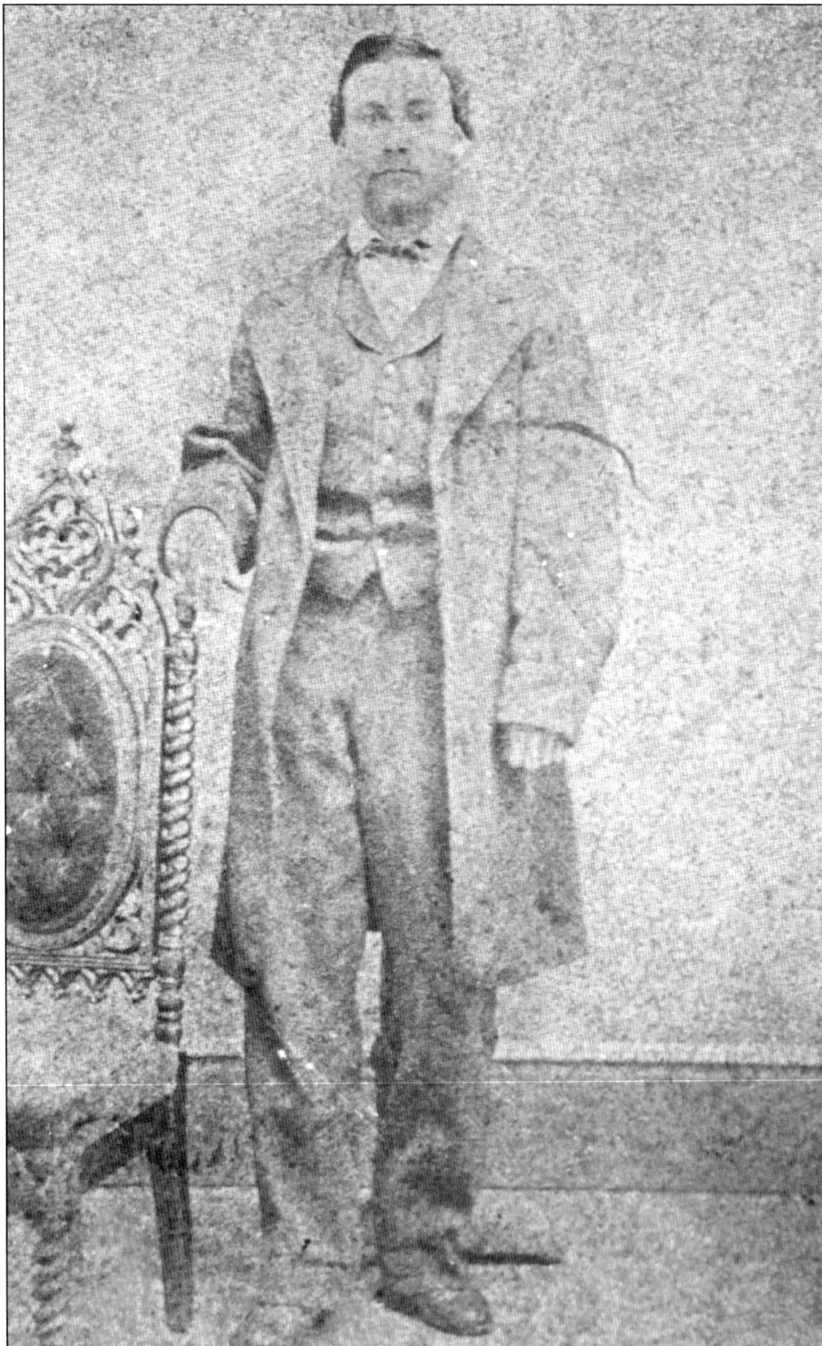

Many Goliad men served in the Civil War, including Juan Elias Lozano, shown here in 1863. He was an example of the 9,900 Mexican Americans who participated in the Civil War, mostly on the Confederate side. Lozano fought in West Texas and Mississippi before returning home to marry Trinadad de la Garza. After the war, he co-owned the Alamito Ranch on Copano Bay until he was murdered by land-grabbers in 1877—an example of the lawlessness of the 1870s. Lozano is buried in La Bahia Cemetery with an appropriate Confederate veteran's memorial.

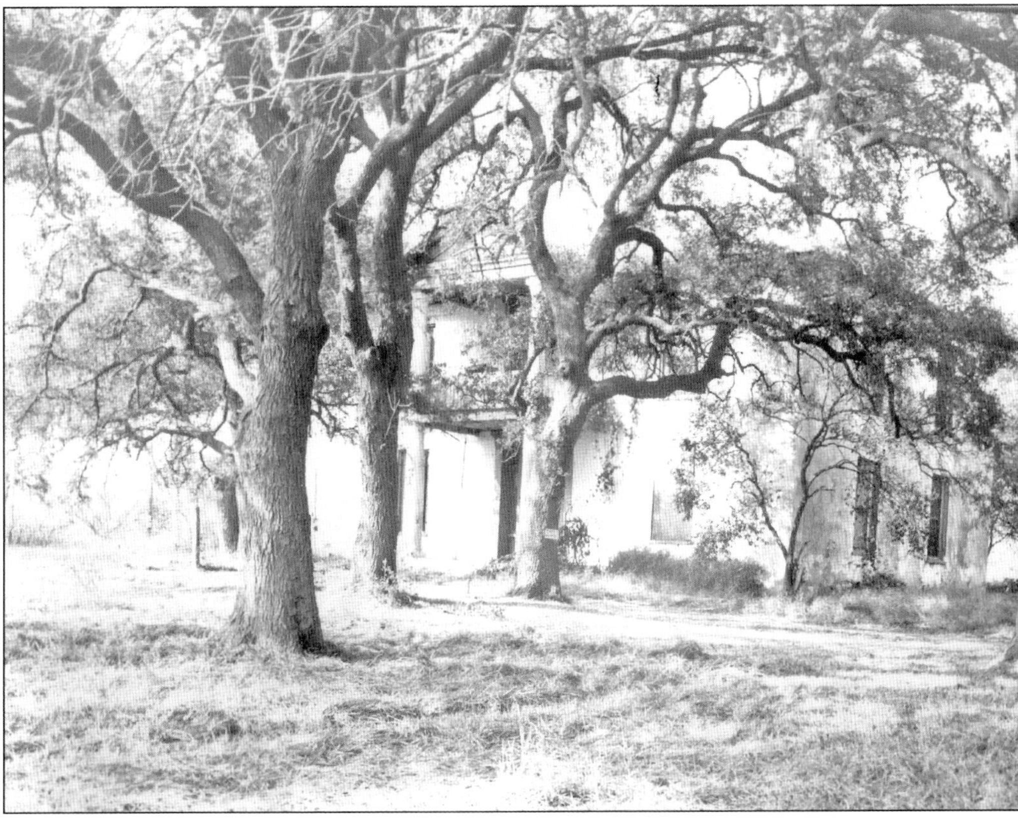

Barton Peck came to Texas in 1838 with 2,000 cattle to become a very successful Goliad rancher. When he died, his widow, Frances "Fannie" Peck (née Menefee), became an important rancher in her own right. In 1842, the Pecks began a large stone home (above) built with rock quarried on the banks of the San Antonio River. Built in the Greek Revival–style favored at that time, the house was two stories and featured an elegant interior staircase in the main hall, shown in the photograph at right. The Peck house has been restored and is now occupied by John Claus von Dohlen III and his family. His children are the family's seventh generation to live in the house, making it one of the oldest buildings in Texas continually occupied by its original family. (Above, courtesy of Kyle Boyd-Robertson; right, courtesy of John Claus von Dohlen, Jr.)

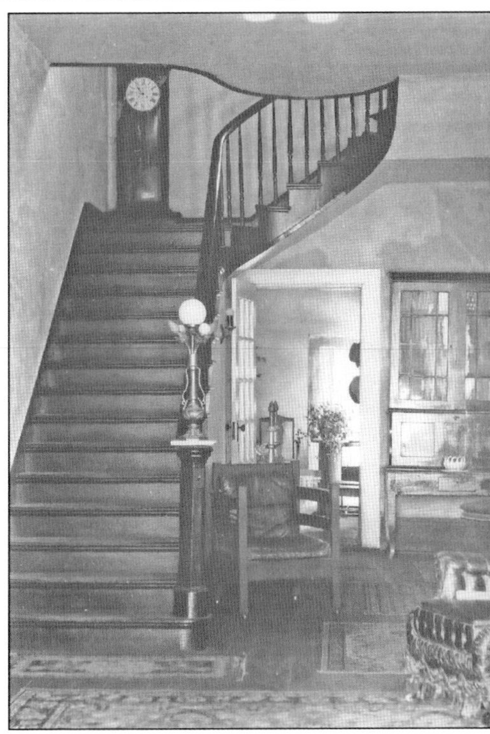

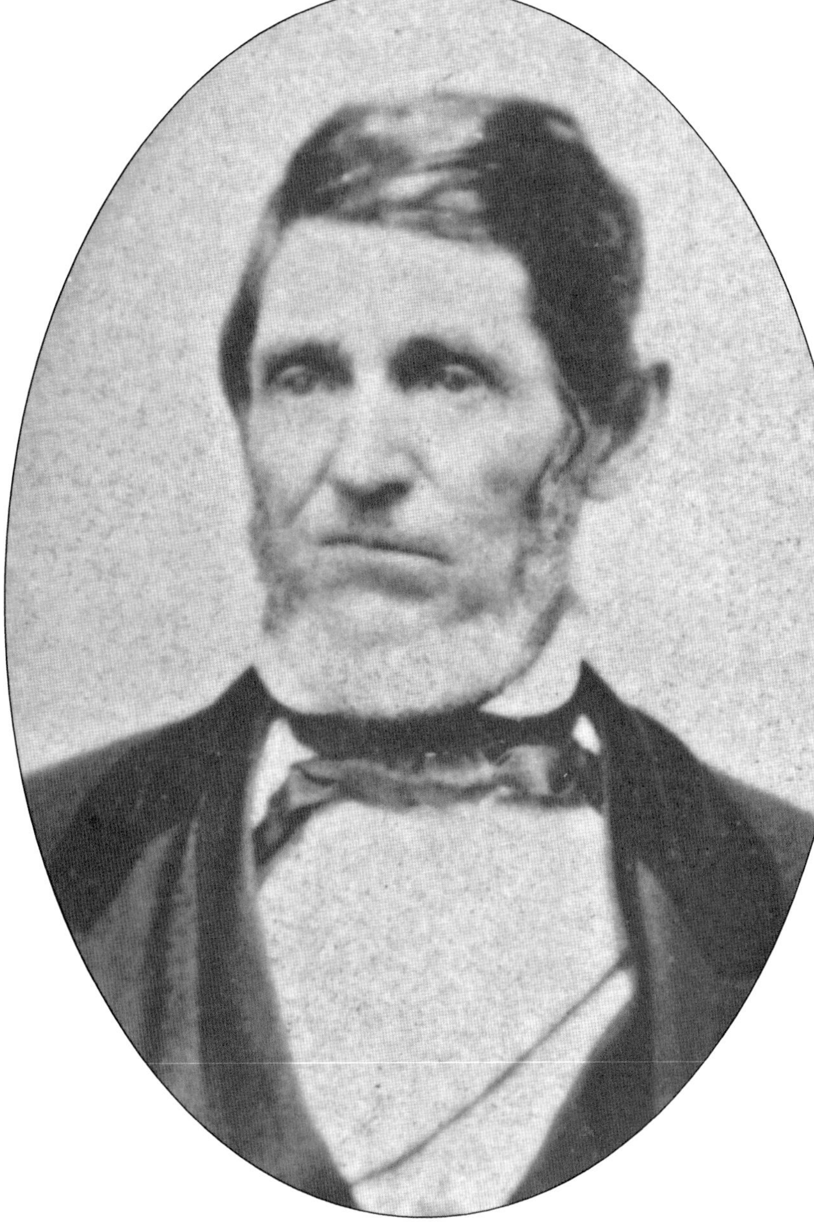

Another prominent citizen of the period was Pryor Lea, shown here in the 1860s. He came to Goliad in 1846 to promote roads and a railroad. He lived in the chapel at the Presidio La Bahia until the property was returned to the Roman Catholic Church in 1853. Lea was prominent in business and public affairs until his death in 1879. He served in the 1861 Secession Convention, the state senate, and as state superintendent of education. Lea also played a large role in establishing the first Baptist church west of the Guadalupe. This happened on May 7, 1849, when a dozen people met under a live oak to form the church.

An indication of the maturing of Goliad as a community came in 1852, when several prominent citizens established a Masonic lodge. Two years later, they began construction of this two-story rock building on Commercial Street. Lodge meetings have been held on the upper floor of the building ever since; the downstairs has been used as a post office, a residence, a city hall, the Red Cross headquarters, and is currently the office of the *Texan Express*.

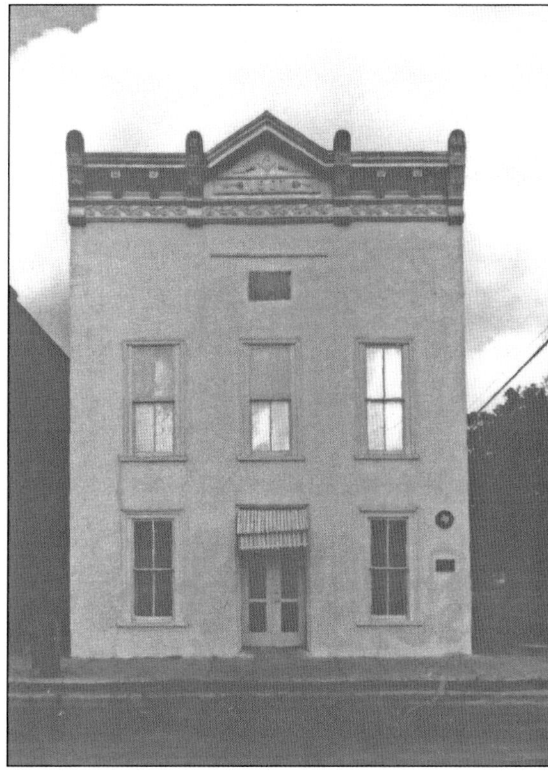

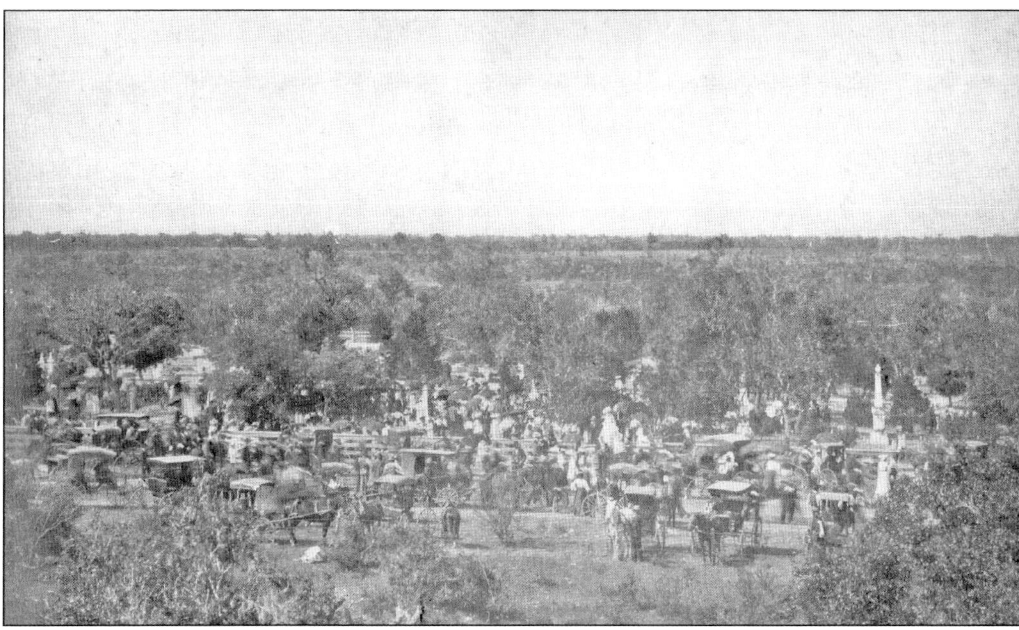

Another sign of the development of Goliad in the years after the Texas Revolution was the establishment of a cemetery. In 1853, the city authorized creation of the cemetery, which was named Oak Hill. The city maintained it until 1882, when women formed the Oak Hill Cemetery Association to care for the facility. The oldest gravestone is dated 1843; the remains of 19 Confederate veterans are buried there.

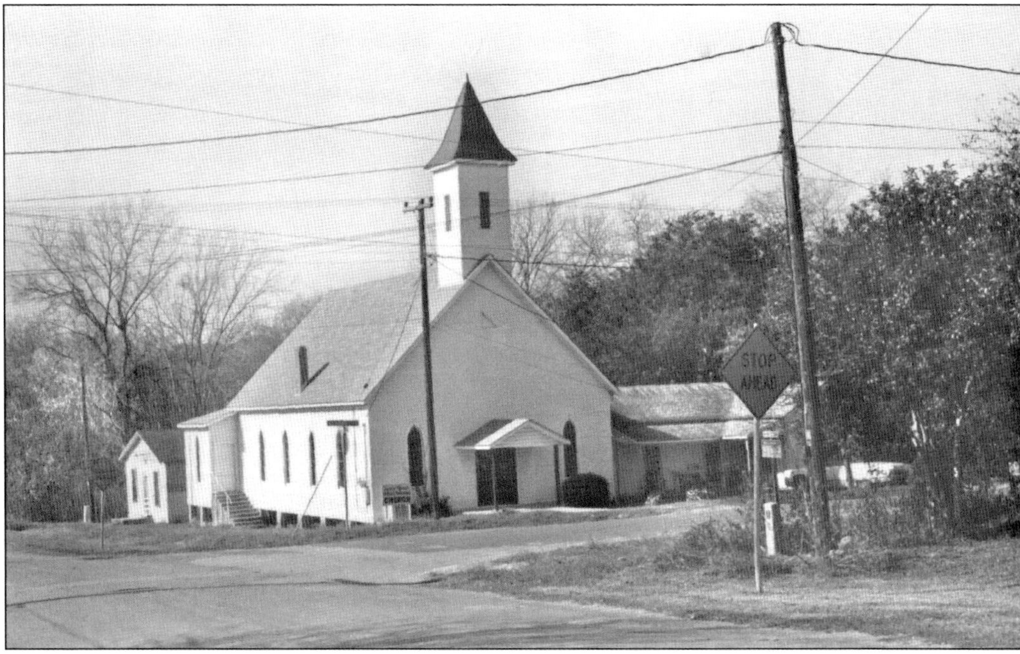

In 1872, African Americans in Goliad founded the Fannin Street United Methodist Church; later, in 1884, the Mount Moriah Baptist Church was established. These two churches have been the social center of African American life in Goliad ever since. The building pictured here is not the original Fannin Street Methodist Church structure because it was destroyed in the 1902 tornado, with heavy losses of life.

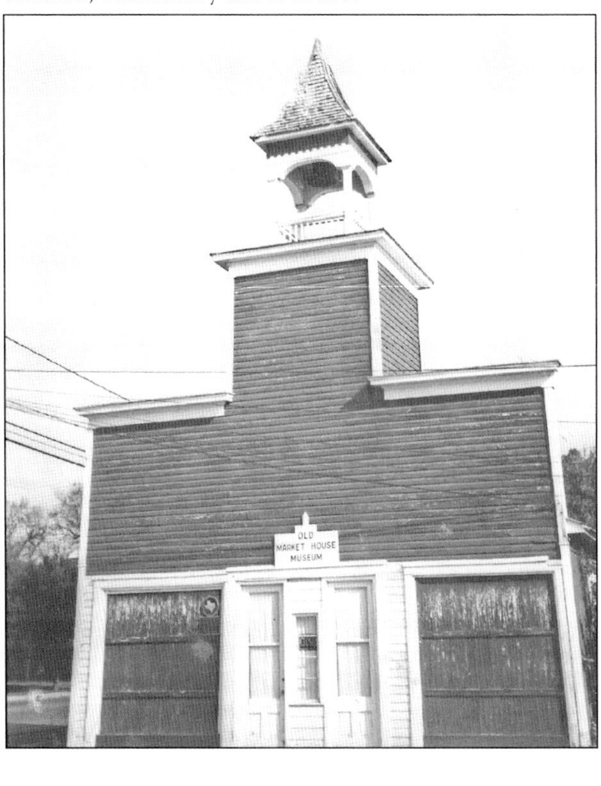

Another sign of the maturing of Goliad was the setting aside of a public market space in 1853, followed by the construction of a market house building in 1871. The building contained stalls, which were rented for the sale of meat and other goods. In 1886, the building was enlarged with space for firefighting equipment, and in 1888, the tower was added. Since the 1960s, it has been the Goliad County Historical Commission's museum.

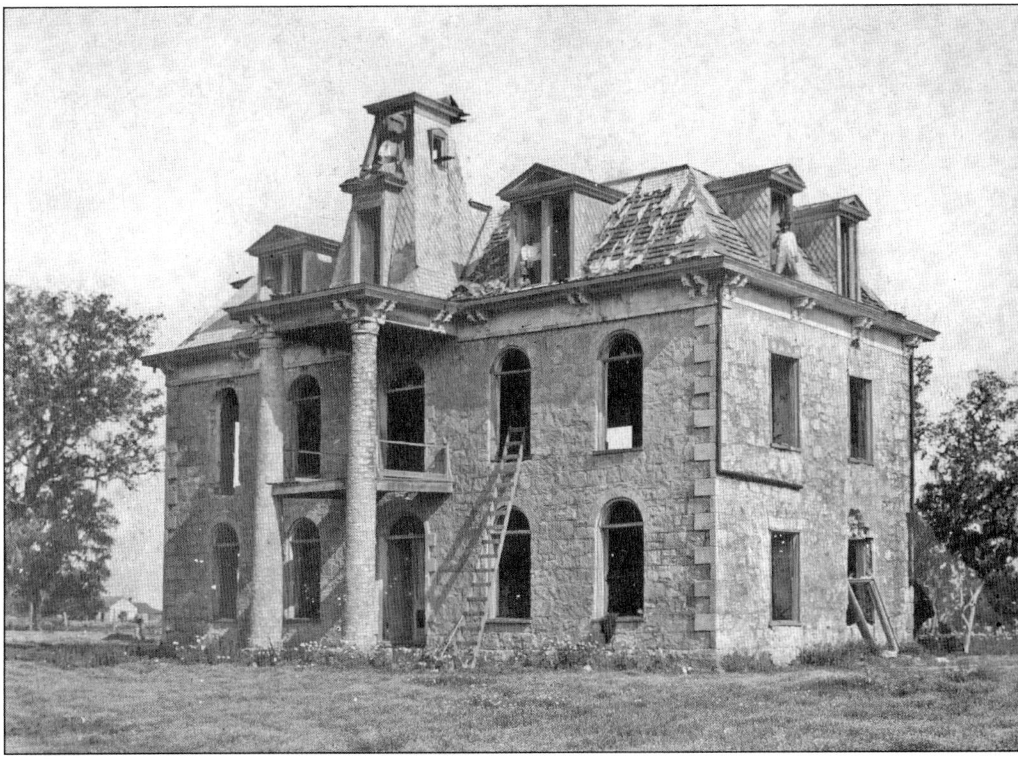

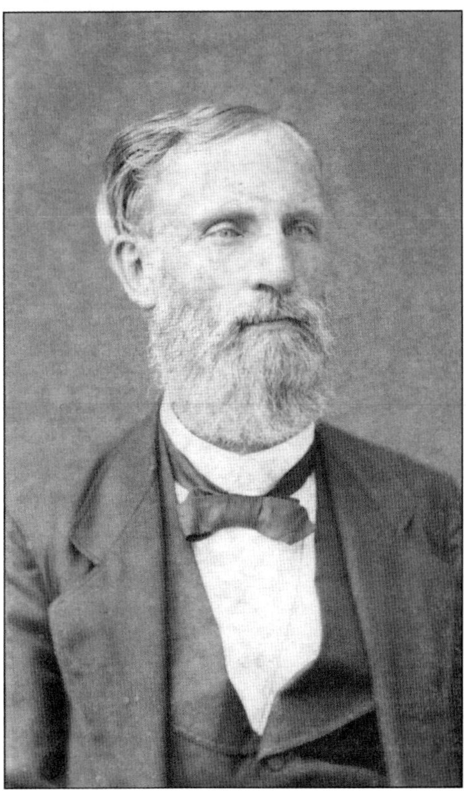

Starting with Hillyer Female College (founded at the old mission in 1848), Goliad has hosted a number of colleges. Aranama College succeeded Hillyer, and in 1852, the Paine Female Institute was established. Although called colleges, they essentially offered secondary school–level education. This 1913 photograph of the decaying Paine Institute building shows the demise of these schools with the development of public education.

A number of significant educational leaders were involved with the various colleges, none more distinguished than Prof. A. A. Brooks, whose educational leadership in the 1870s caused some to call Goliad the "Athens of Texas." He possessed one of the first doctorates in Texas, and led Goliad College (the successor to Paine Institute) from 1872–1877. His presence was so dominant that most people referred to the school as "Brooks College."

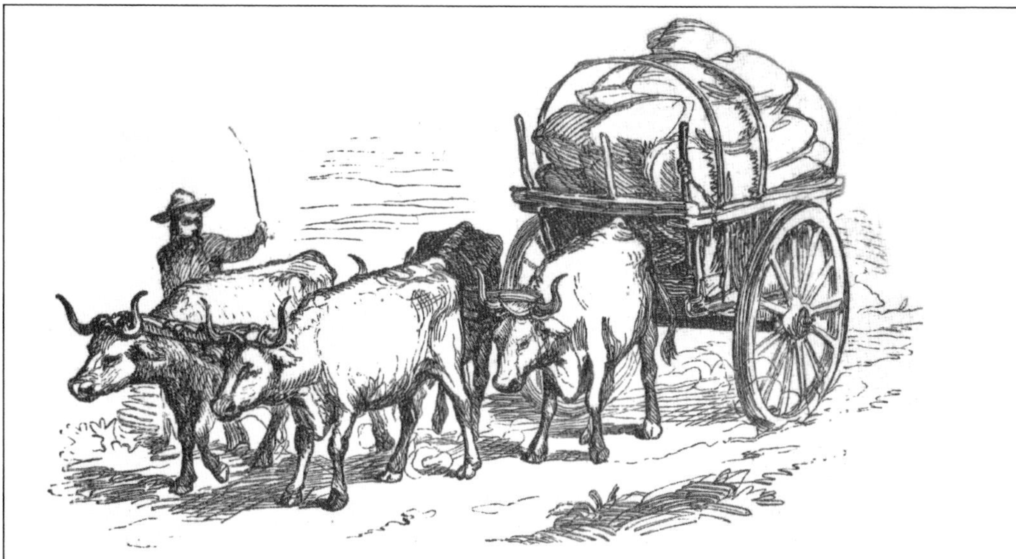

"We encounter wagons drawn by oxen."

In the 1850s, Goliad was a major stop for large American ox-drawn freighters carrying heavy traffic from the Gulf Coast to San Antonio. They were expensive, and in 1857, Mexicans began to compete with two-wheeled carts (as pictured above), cutting the price of shipping from Indianola to San Antonio from $3 per 100 pounds to 50¢ or even less. American freighters retaliated, leading to extensive violence, deaths, and a surge of anti-Mexican sentiment, much of it centered on Goliad. In time, Goliad created a Vigilante Committee that captured two of the killers, tried them in a vigilante court, and hung them on a live oak in the courthouse lawn. That tree (or one like it) was used for hangings for years to come, making the Hanging Tree another Goliad icon. (Above, courtesy of UTSA Institute of Texan Culture; below, courtesy of Texas Department of Parks and Wildlife.)

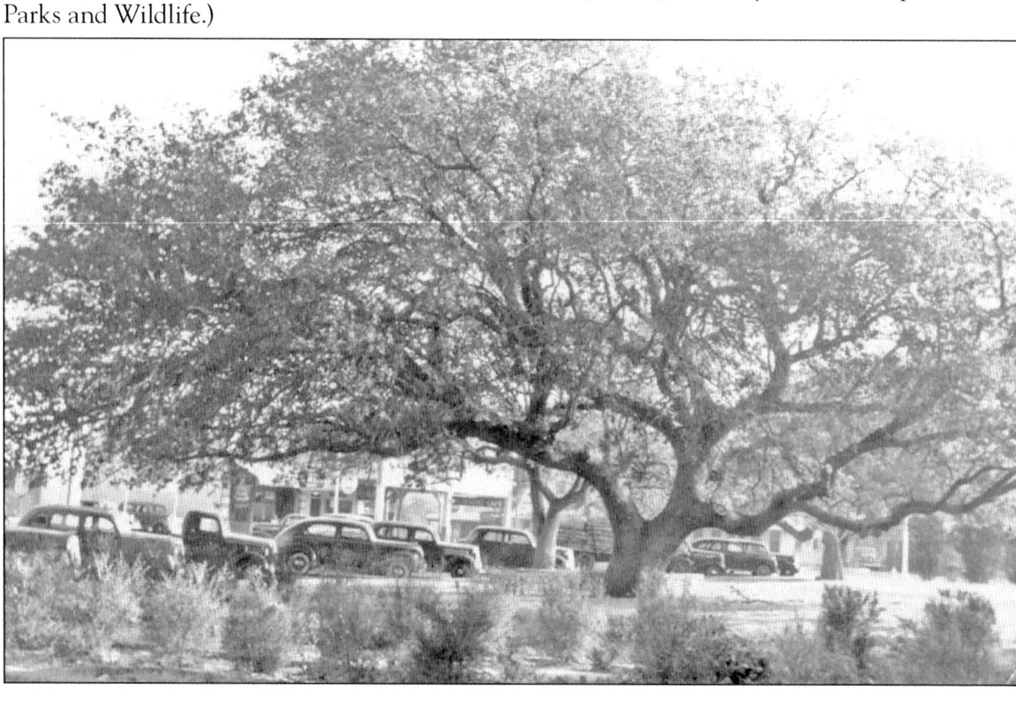

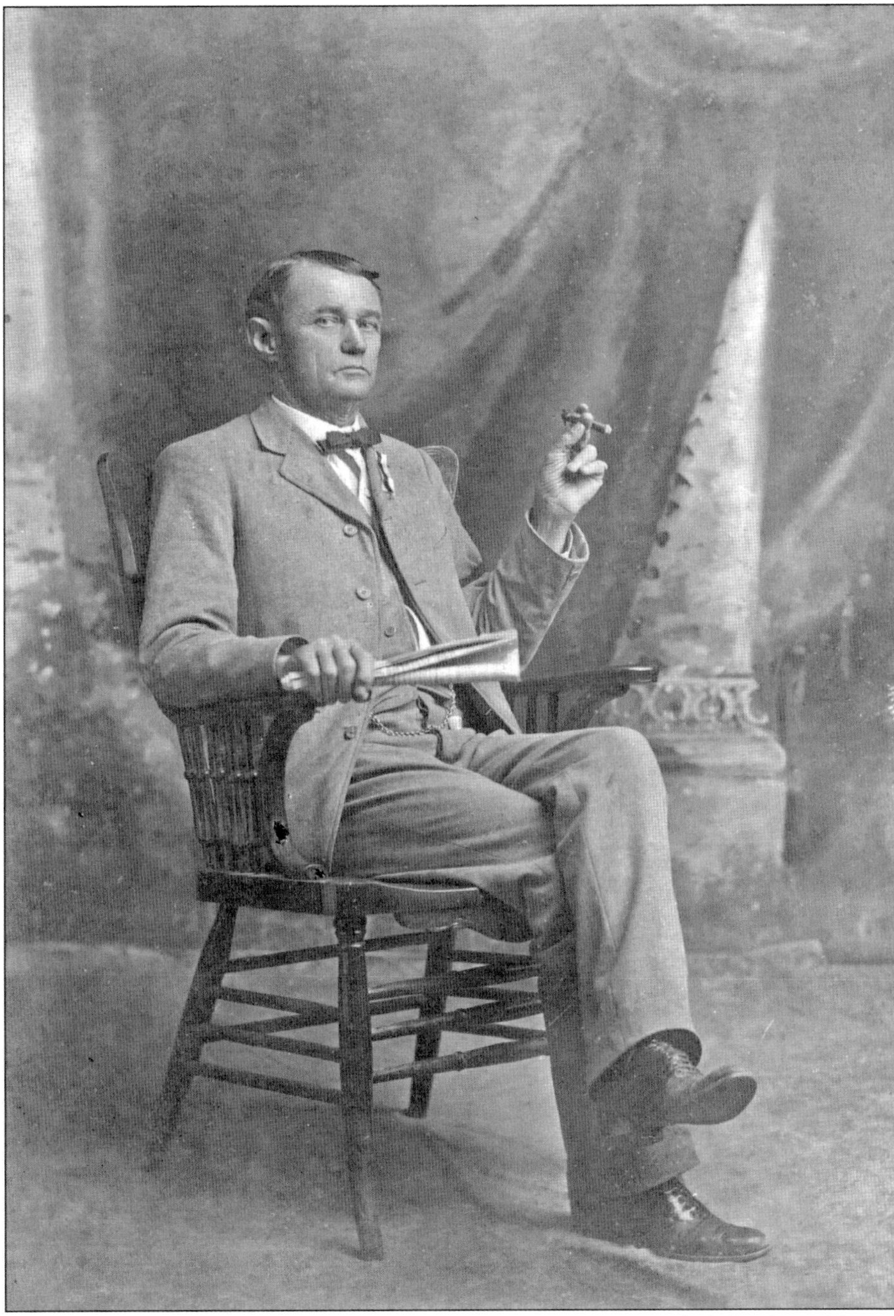

Gus Patton was one of Goliad's most distinguished citizens. He guarded the Cart War prisoners in the courthouse before their inauguration of the Hanging Tree; served in the Confederate army; married Sue Peck, daughter of Barton Peck; and became a leading lawyer, county attorney, county judge, and businessman. All his life he remained a staunch defender of the Confederacy and the justness of its cause. These sentiments got him in trouble when two African-American soldiers stationed in Goliad after the Civil War arrested him for wearing his Confederate buttons and insignia on the streets of Goliad. They cut the buttons off his uniform, sending him home "greatly humiliated and with a revengeful heart," as he put it in his recollections.

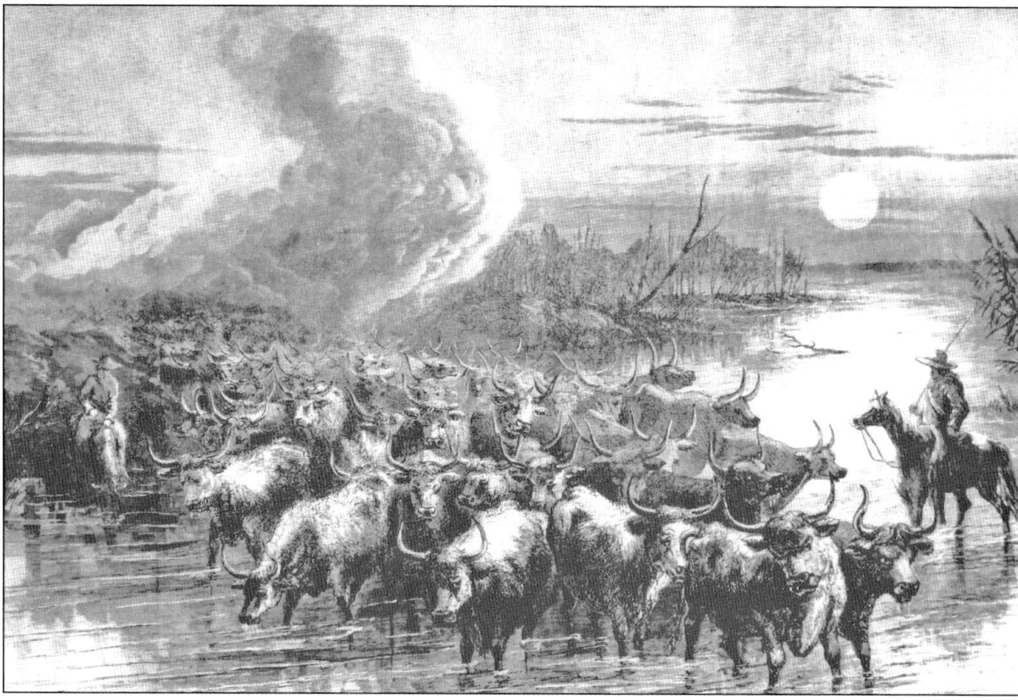

This illustration of a cattle drive from *Harper's Weekly* illustrates a major feature of post–Civil War life in Goliad. The area was the starting point for many of the cattle drives north in the 1870s, in which many locals participated. Many prominent Goliad names were associated with the drives, none more so than Dillard Rucker Fant, who drove as many as 200,000 cattle up the trail in 15 years. (Courtesy of UTSA Institute of Texan Culture.)

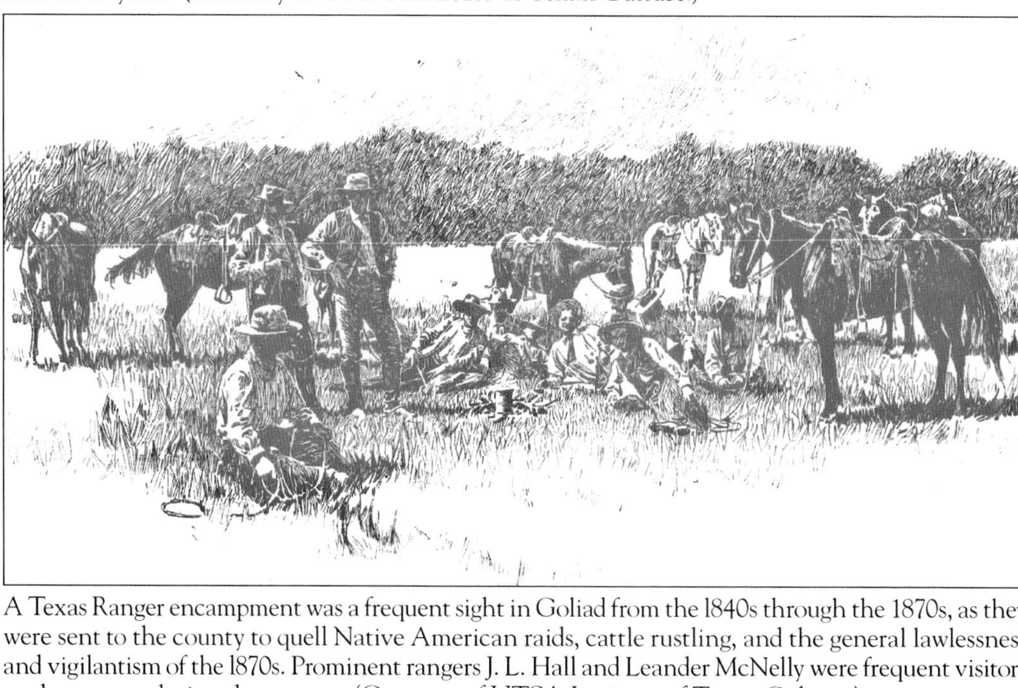

A Texas Ranger encampment was a frequent sight in Goliad from the 1840s through the 1870s, as they were sent to the county to quell Native American raids, cattle rustling, and the general lawlessness and vigilantism of the 1870s. Prominent rangers J. L. Hall and Leander McNelly were frequent visitors to the county during those years. (Courtesy of UTSA Institute of Texan Culture.)

Three

Years of Growth and Development 1880–1929

By 1880, the lawlessness and turmoil of Goliad's "frontier" era subsided, and in the peaceful environment that followed, the town took off, creating what might be called the golden age of Goliad. In the generation between 1880 and the Great Depression, the county's population increased from 5,832 to 10,093 (its highest ever), and the modern town emerged.

The foundation was ranching (cattle, sheep, and turkey) and agriculture, with crops such as cane, cotton, corn, feed, grain, and fruit. It was all stimulated by the arrival of the railroad in 1889, connecting all those products with outside markets. Based on that economic growth, a sizeable town grew up to meet the needs of the county.

The town of Goliad grew up mostly around the courthouse square (graced after 1894 by a magnificent new courthouse building), where a wide array of commercial and service structures were built (and sometimes rebuilt, since there were frequent fires). Beyond the courthouse square, residences notable and ordinary were built to house the growing population. The community built churches and schools. Many of the structures built in this period are still in existence today, giving Goliad a historical look.

While businesses and homes were being built, the accoutrements of a town were being established. There was a water system including a pipestem, a poor farm, telephones, radios, electricity, a movie house, and a gas-distribution system. The automobile arrived, and in due time roads were paved and bridges built across the San Antonio River.

There were some unfortunate events as well. There was an 1882 yellow fever epidemic, several major fires around the courthouse square, and the tornado of 1902. The death toll of the tornado still ranks as the second most deadly natural disaster in Texas behind the Galveston hurricane of 1900. The town also participated in World War I, which killed 18 local men. But all in all, the era from 1880 to 1930 was one of Goliad's best.

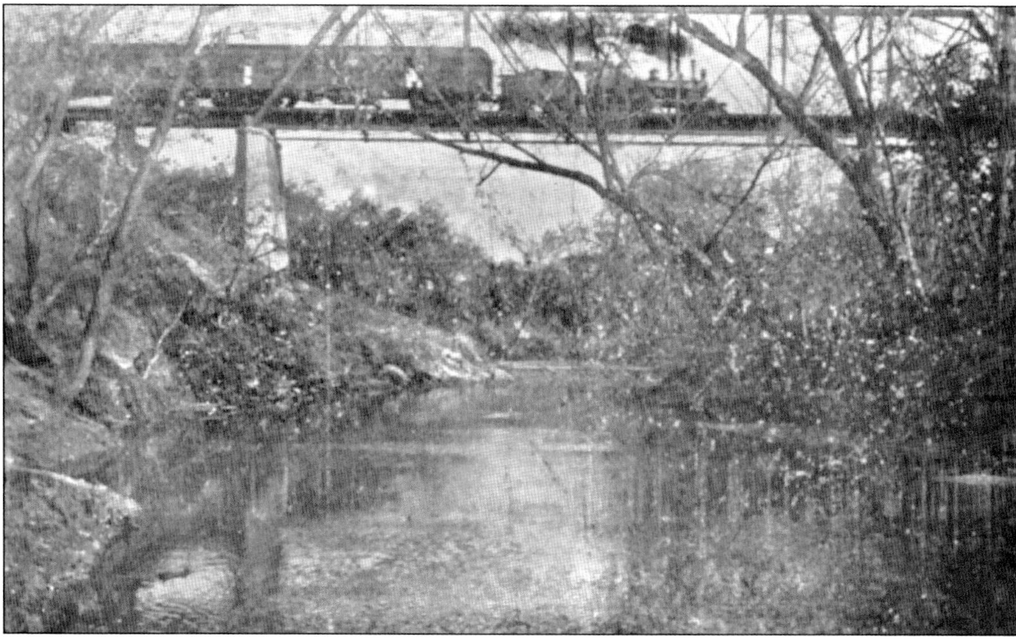

One of the key events of the period and a major stimulus to the community's growth was the arrival of the railroad in 1889. The train is shown above on the bridge over the river; the accompanying depot (now used as a community meeting place) is shown below. The community provided many incentives to entice the railroad to come to Goliad—permission to cross its streets, grants of land, and $60,000. The opening of the railroad was celebrated on June 28, 1889, with what the program called a "Goliad Barbeque and Railroad Jollification" with food, music, dancing, and speeches. There were two trains a day to Goliad with three passenger cars on each train. So many curious spectators congregated around the trains that the city had to pass an ordinance prohibiting people from gathering at the depot.

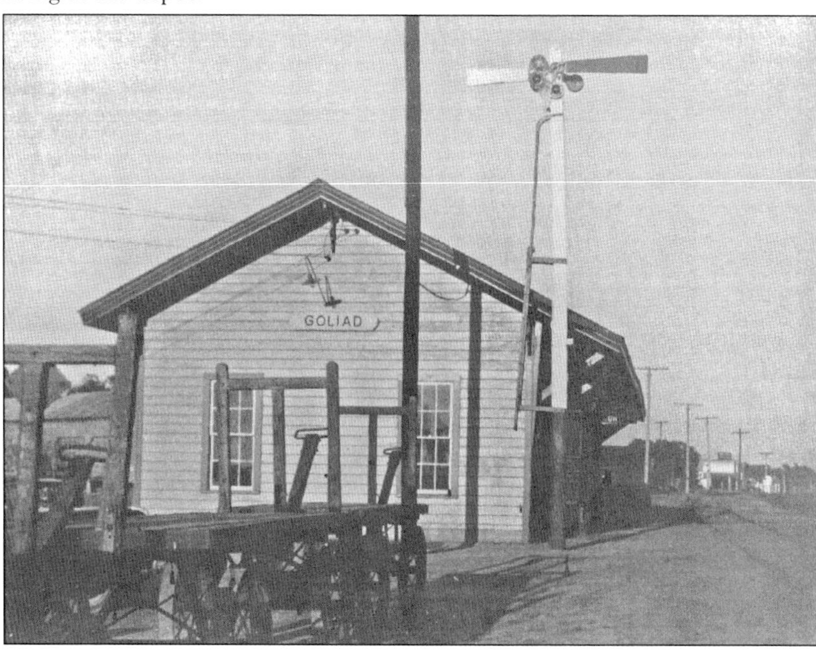

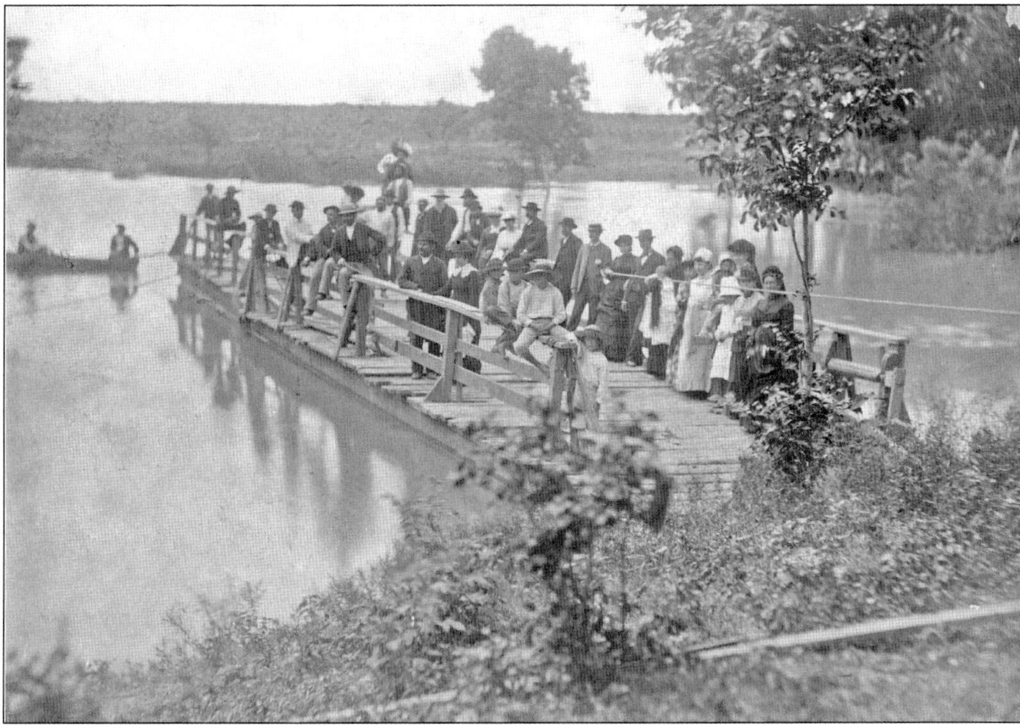

Even though the train had come to town, crossing the San Antonio River was still a problem. There had been a ferry since 1853; this is the Turner Toll Ferry, which was still operating in the late 19th century. In 1889, the town opened the first steel bridge over the river (at San Patricio Street), which lasted until the tornado of 1902.

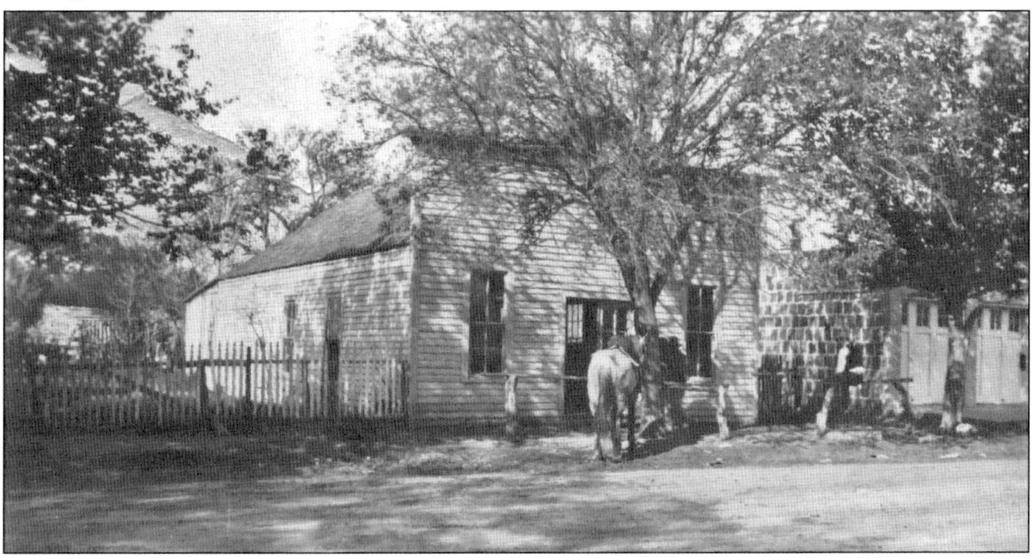

From early on, Goliad had newspapers: the *True American* and the *Goliad Express*, which became the *Goliad Messenger* and was at some point renamed *Southern Constellation*. After the Civil War, there was the *Goliad Guard* (with a variety of owners). In 1905, James A. White began publishing the *Goliad Advance* (whose post-1905 offices are shown here). The *Advance* energetically promoted the county, and James White became one of Goliad's most distinguished citizens.

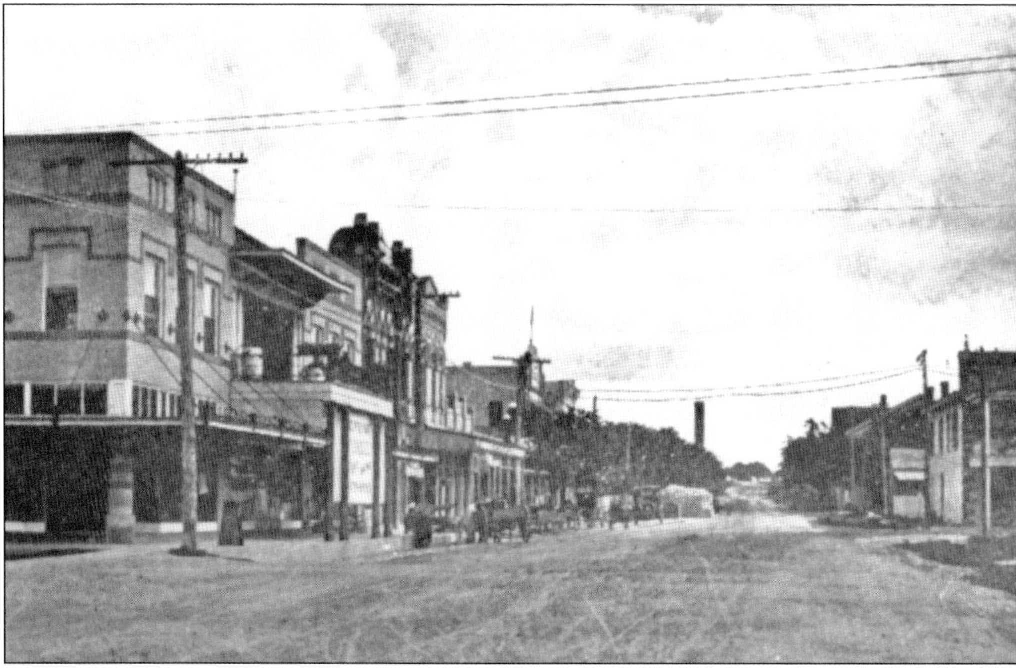

The photographs on this and the adjacent page show the downtown that emerged around the square between 1890 and 1915. Even before the impact of the railroad, the local newspaper reported the following in 1889: five law firms, three doctors, three drug stores, two hotels, four livery stables, five dry goods stores, three grocery stores, two saloons, one milliner, one photographer, one hardware store, two blacksmith shops, one meat market, two steam mills, one barber shop, one bakery, one shoemaker, two saddle and harness makers, and three real estate agents.

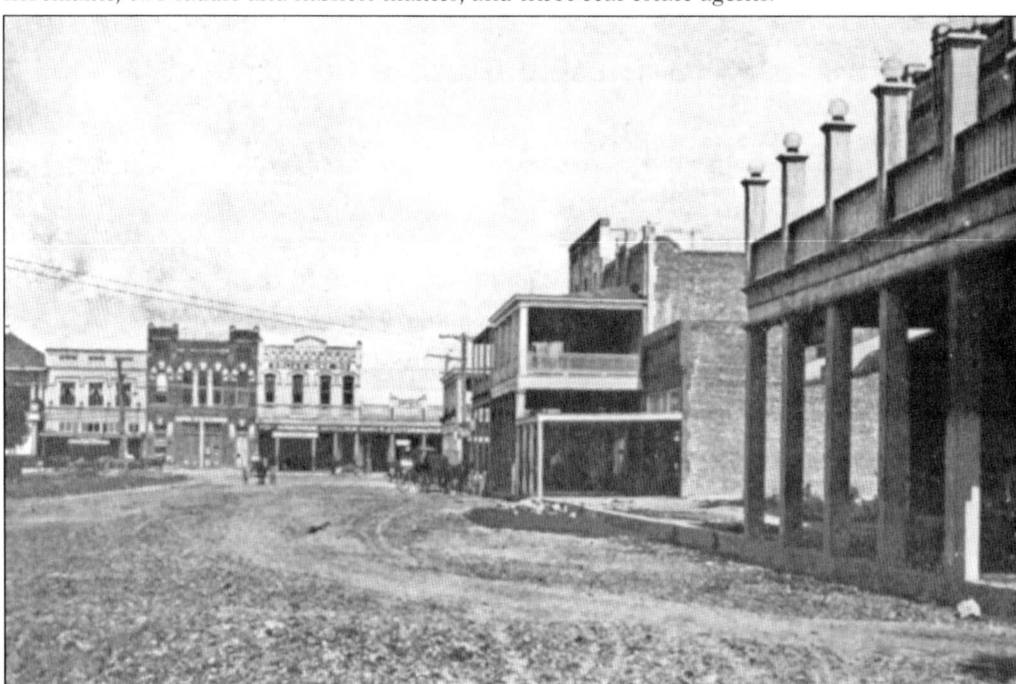

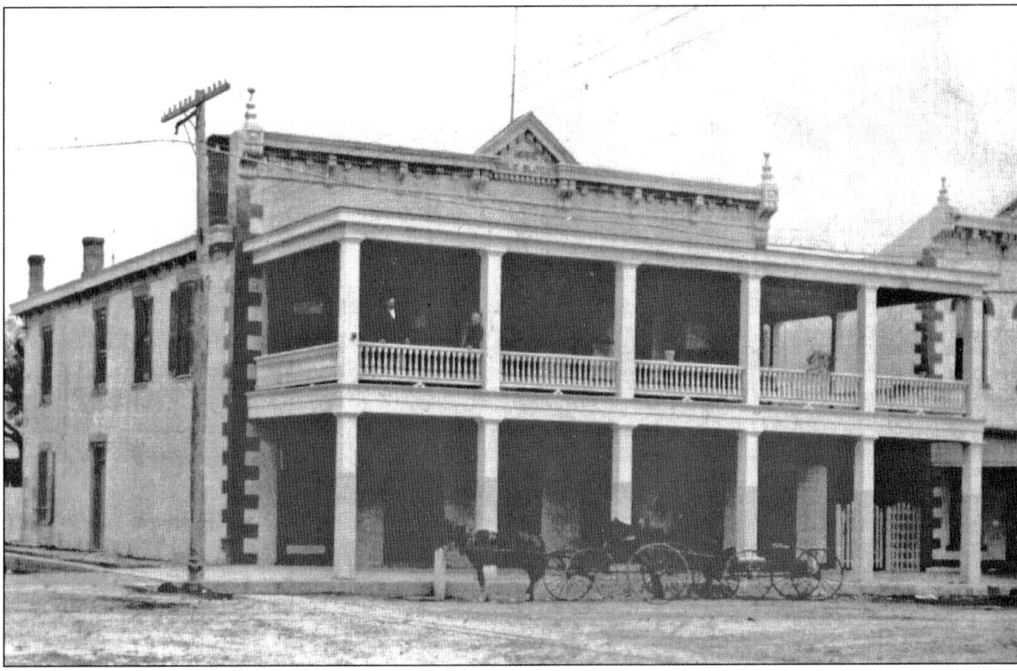

Note that most of the buildings around the square were made of brick (replacing an early pattern of stone buildings). Those bricks were made in Goliad in a brick factory operating southwest of the town square. It was destroyed by the tornado of 1902 but rebuilt, and newspaper stories in 1906 and 1909 indicated that bricks were ready to meet construction needs. In addition to a brick factory, Goliad also boasted a broom factory, a leather shop, and several inventors.

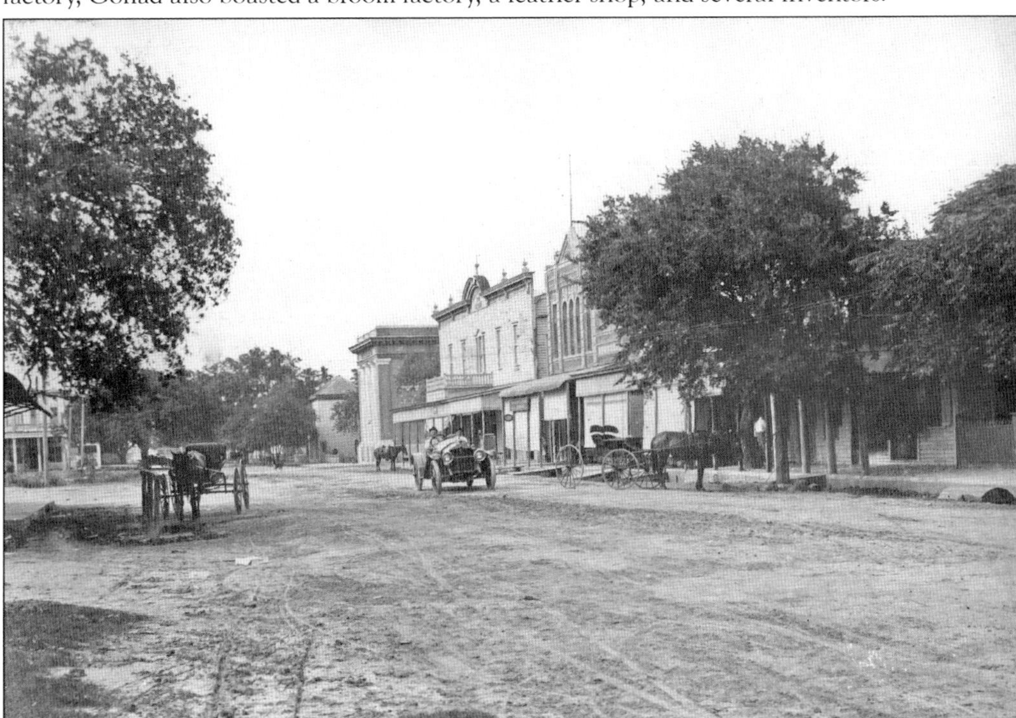

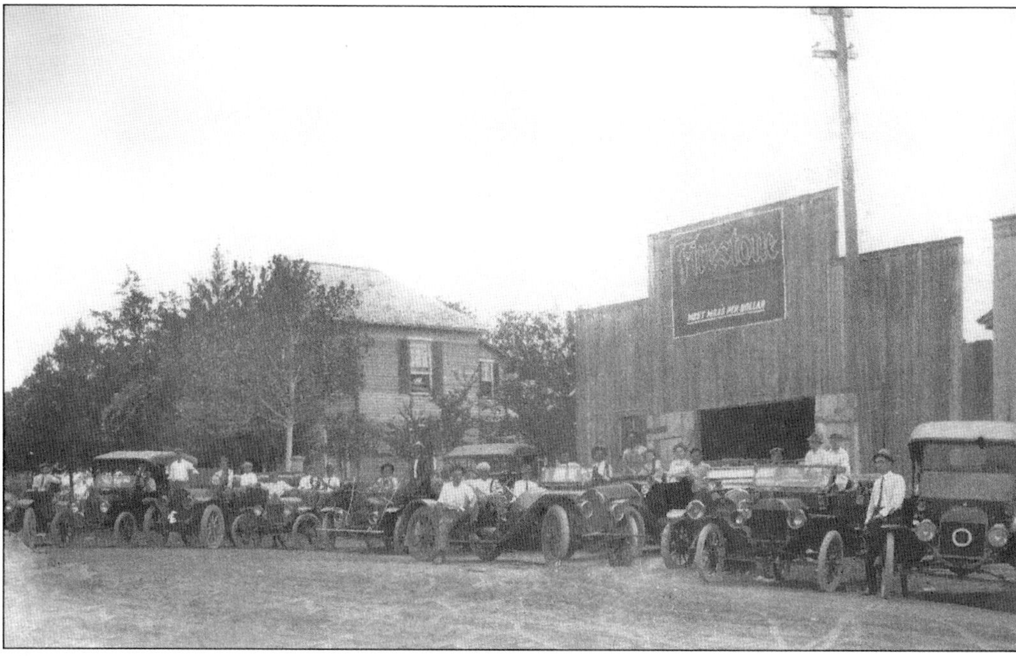

The first automobile in Goliad was Dr. Louis W. Chilton's "Red Devil," which he acquired in 1907. By 1911, there were 32 automobiles, and the ladies' millinery shop was advertising hoods and caps to be worn in the vehicle. This picture shows the Firestone store owned by Warner Lewis, an indication of how quickly the car began to make its mark on Goliad.

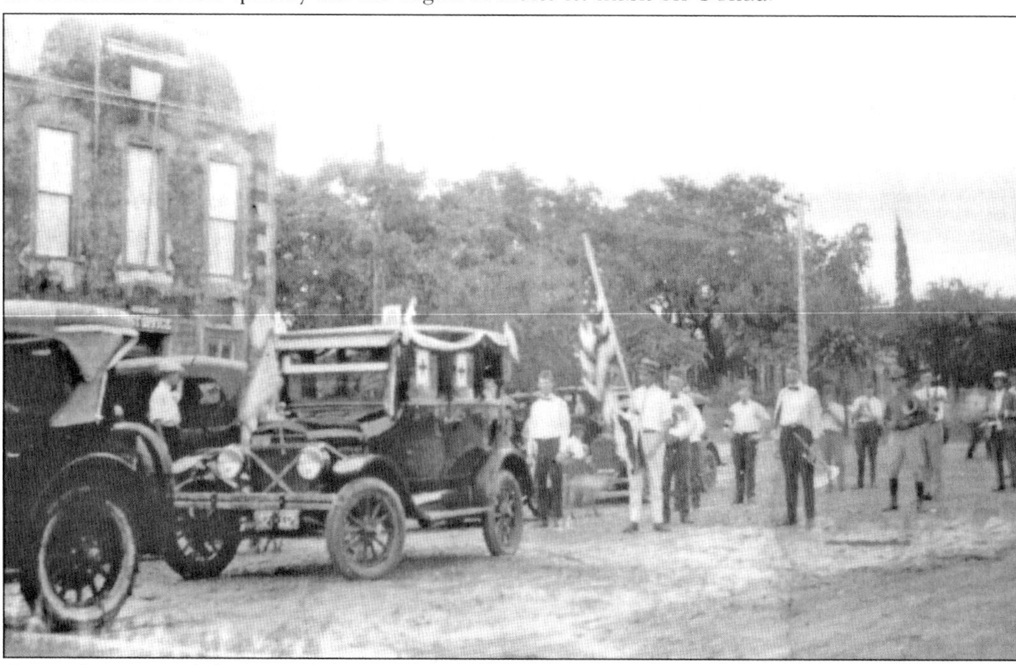

Once the automobile arrived, Goliad began a love affair with parades. This photograph shows decorated cars in front of the Masonic Lodge building on Commercial Street with the water standpipe in the background. Starting with this photograph, there are probably more pictures of parades in the Market House Museum picture collection than of any other activity.

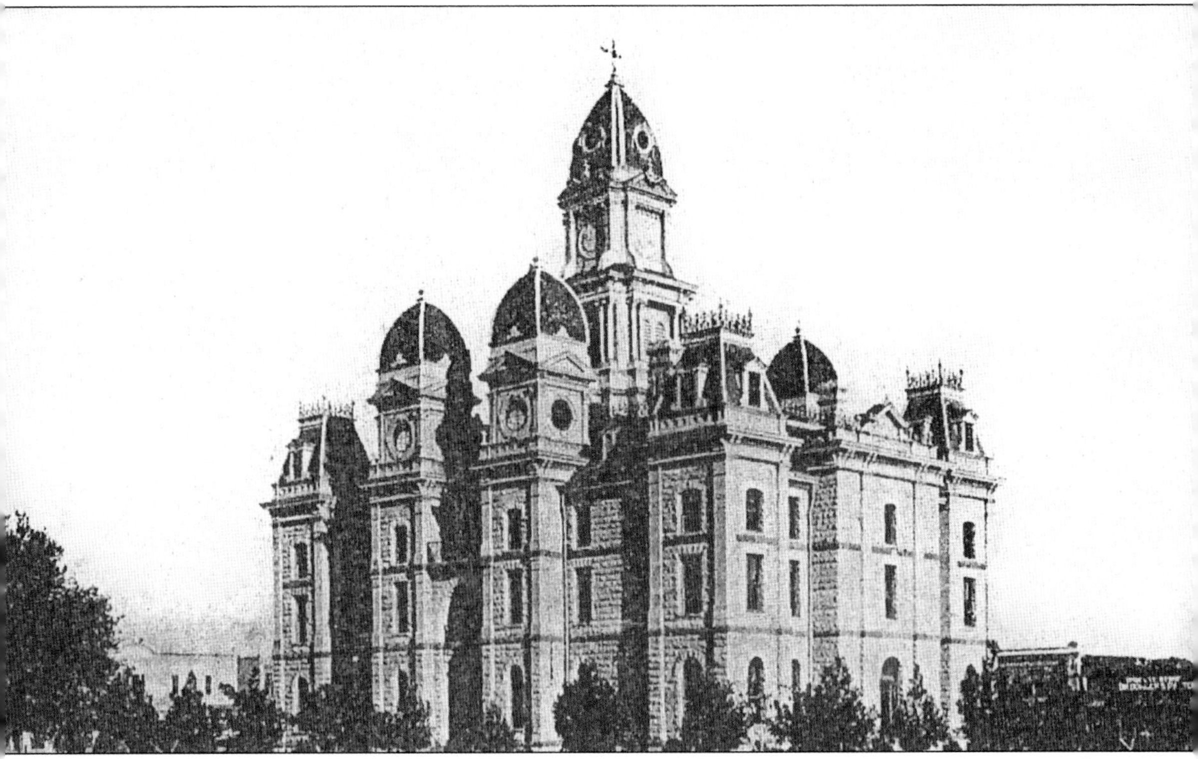

The most stunning addition to the city in this era was the courthouse. It was the third on site and was built for $75,000. Designed by the famous architect Alfred Giles, it was in the Second Empire style, with many towers and turrets. Its dedication on March 2, 1894, was a huge event with a crowd of 6,000 including many attendees arriving on special trains from Beeville and Victoria. Yorktown and Yoakum sent their brass bands. It took three hours to feed everyone barbeque, and at 3 p.m. the cornerstone was laid under the direction of local masons. This was followed by processions, an oyster bake, banquets, and public balls. As a newspaper reporter noted, "Not a single thing occurred to mar the pleasure of the day. There was no drunkenness and our guests praised the manner in which the entire affair was conducted."

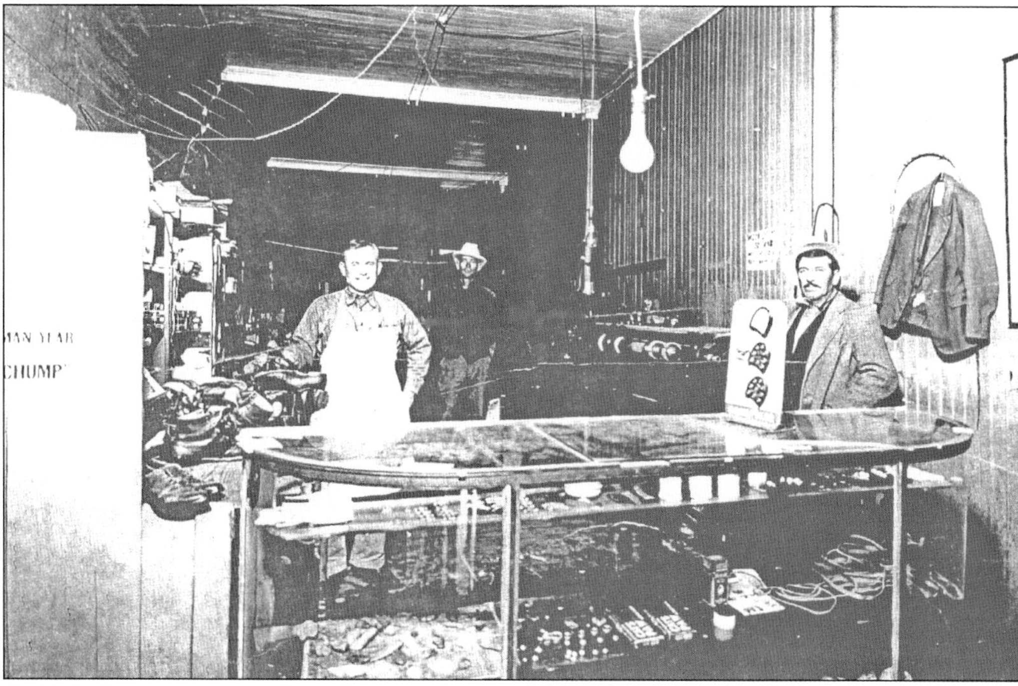

As Goliad grew, it attracted a wide array of enterprises, including small manufacturing and service industries, such as the Carbajal Leather and Shoe shop, shown here. It operated into the 1930s.

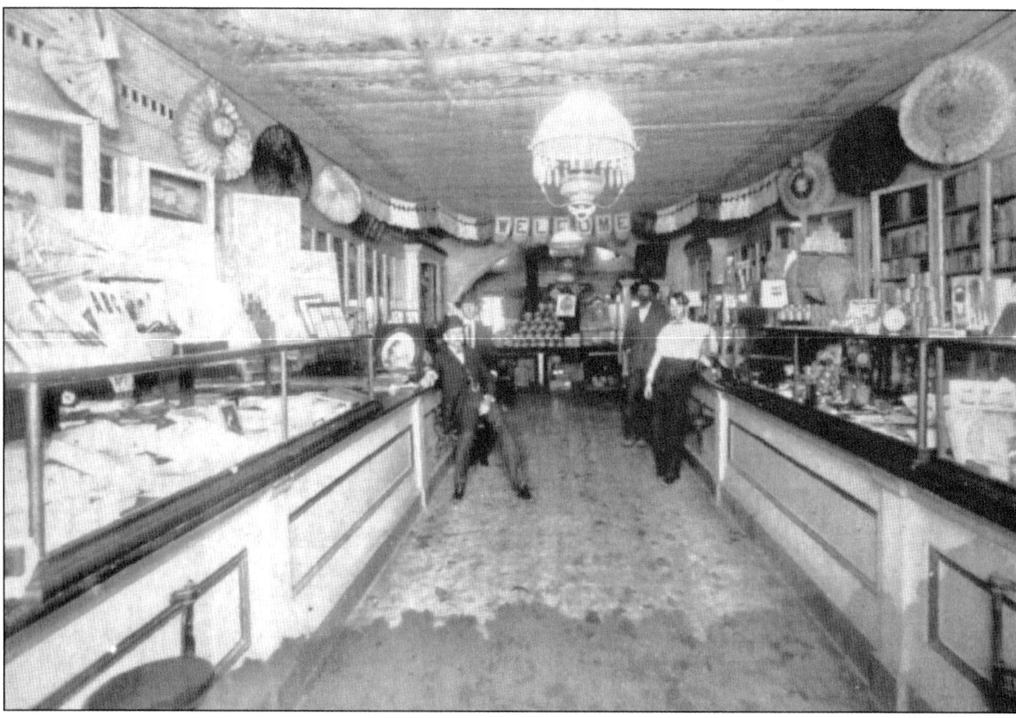

Among the kinds of stores that began to appear in Goliad were dry goods or general stores. One example was the Dillard Fant General Store on Market Street. Fant was also involved in the cattle business, having been one of the major cattlemen driving cattle up the trails in the 1870s.

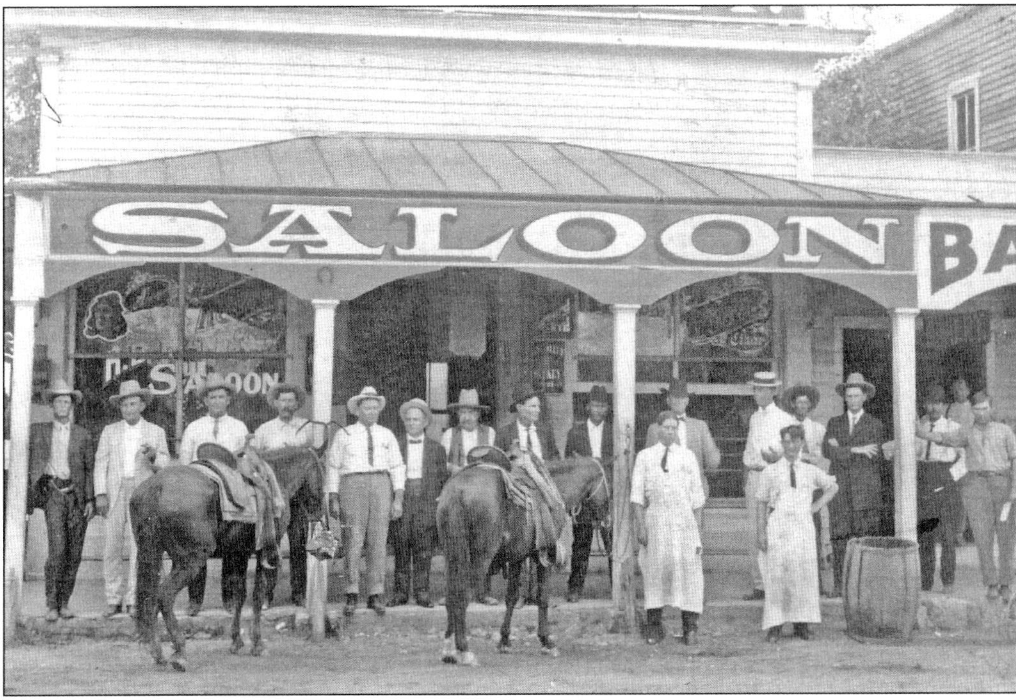

Not all businesses around the square were wholesome. The saloon, shown in the 1890s, had a very prominent spot on the south side of the square. It was one of two at the time. According to the reminiscences of elderly residents, there were saloons or bars around the square up until very recently. (Courtesy of Goliad County Library.)

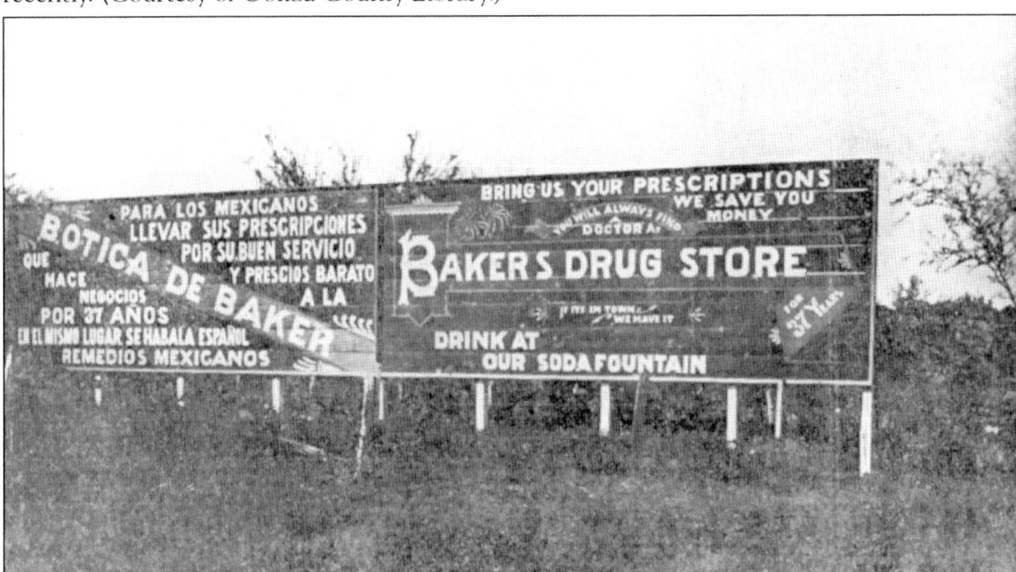

One of the major businesses in town was the Baker Drug Store, which came to Goliad in the 1870s and evolved into the Von Dohlen Pharmacy and then the Goliad Pharmacy, which is now the second oldest independent drug store still operating in Texas. This photograph of their bilingual billboard in 1910 shows the importance of the Spanish-speaking population in Goliad at the time.

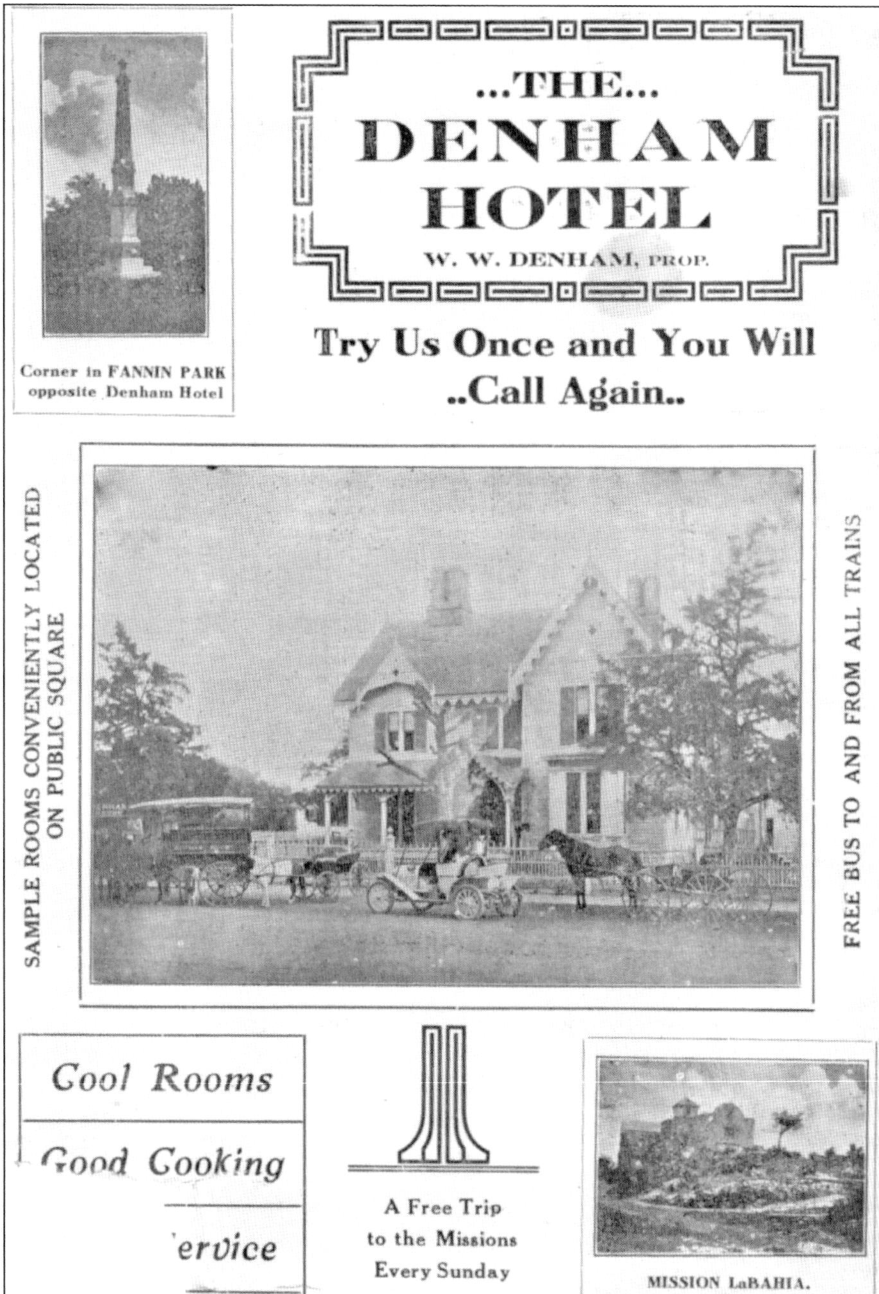

This 1910 full-page advertisement reminds us of a hotel's importance to a town in this era of train travel. The advertisement is interesting in that it shows the Fannin monument in the upper left corner and the presidio chapel (mislabeled "Mission" LaBahia) in the lower right-hand corner. This shows that even in that era Goliad was using its historical past to attract visitors. The Denham Hotel was unique because it originated as the residence of prominent cattle driver Dillard Fant. Mary Denham converted it to a hotel in 1908, with a new wing designed by prominent regional architect Jules Leffland. The hotel was noted by locals for its excellent food. Unfortunately, the building burned in 1980.

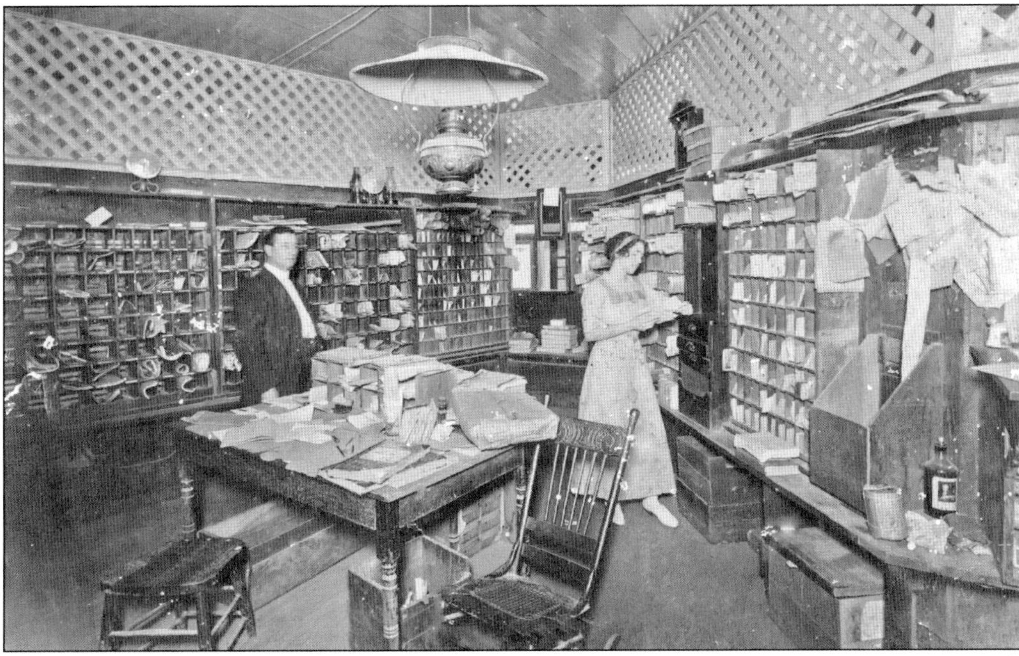

The U.S. Post Office has been located in a number of buildings, including the Masonic Hall. Here postmaster Thomas H. Danforth and Viola Franke are tending to business. In the 1930s, the post office moved down Commercial Street to the site of the Goliad Bank and Trust, which had failed in the Depression. It remained there until the current building was constructed.

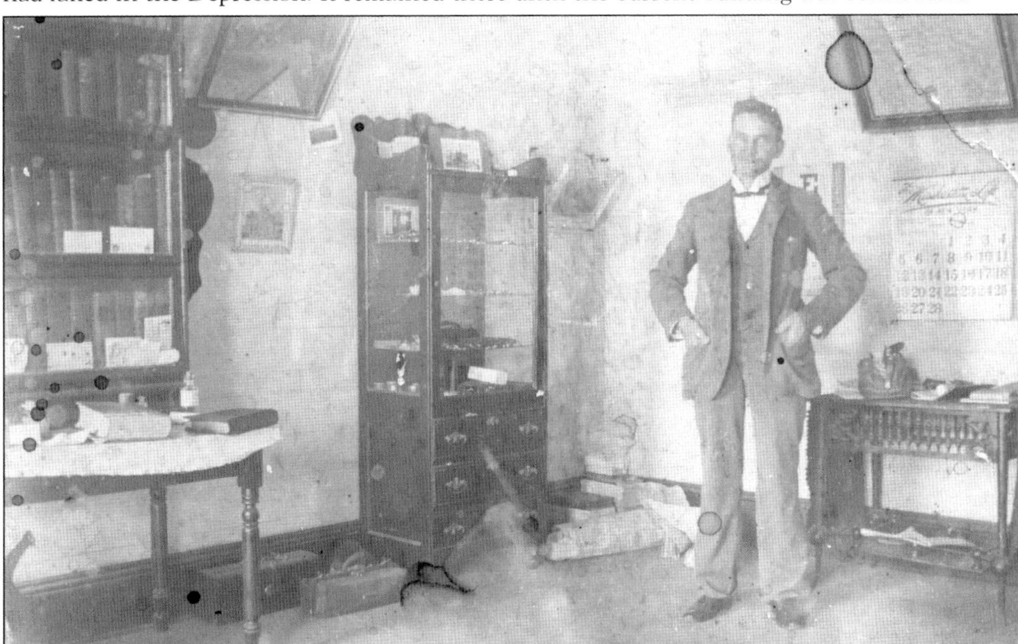

Dr. Louis Chilton was the town's premier doctor around the turn of the century. In addition to being a much-loved physician, he was also an important town builder. When he acquired the first x-ray machine in town, there was no electricity, so he constructed Goliad's first electric power plant. He also built a major building on the square, which still stands.

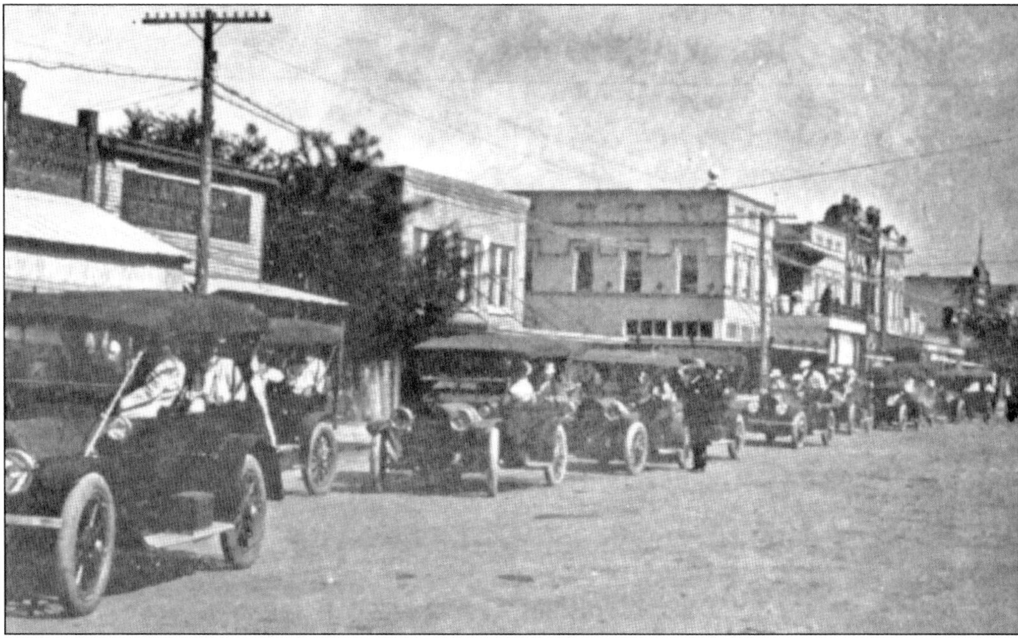

Between 1880 and 1930, the Goliad County population grew from 5,832 to 10,093. This was not by accident; community leaders worked hard to make it happen. Some of them founded the Young Men's Business Club to promote the community in 1905. This convoy of boosters leaving for a trade excursion in 1910 is an example of their activities.

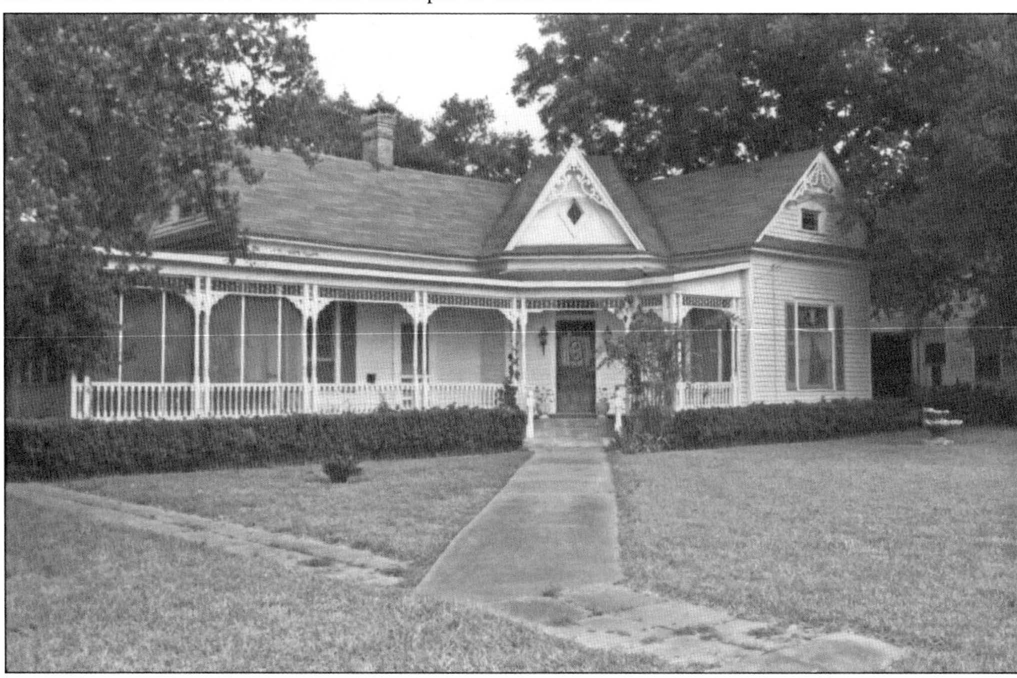

As the town grew and prospered, many impressive homes were built. The Appleby House on Commercial and Franklin streets near the square is an example that still stands. For a few years it was operated as the Little Moore Hotel; after 1910, its various owners included Mame Appleby, known as Miss Mame, who lived there for half a century.

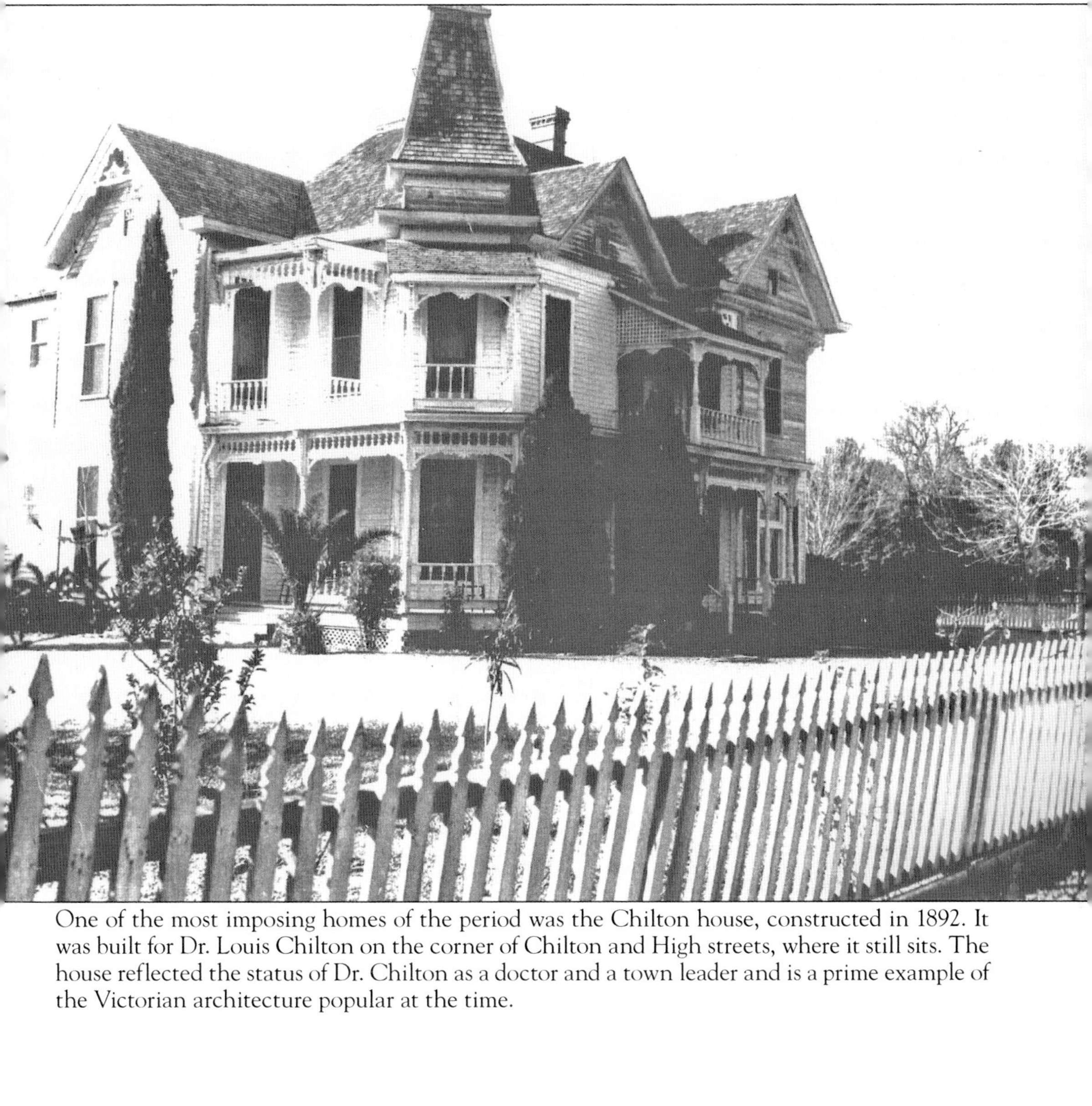

One of the most imposing homes of the period was the Chilton house, constructed in 1892. It was built for Dr. Louis Chilton on the corner of Chilton and High streets, where it still sits. The house reflected the status of Dr. Chilton as a doctor and a town leader and is a prime example of the Victorian architecture popular at the time.

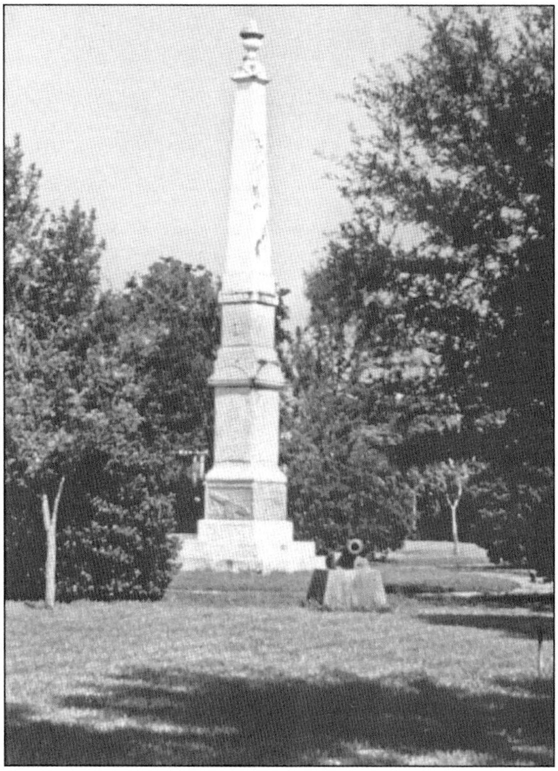

In 1885, Goliad took one of its first steps toward memorializing its past when it dedicated a monument "Erected in Memory of J. W. Fannin and His Comrades in Arms." Originally planned for the grave site of Fannin and his men south of the San Antonio River, the city decided that location was too isolated, so it created City Park (sometimes called Fannin Plaza) across the street from the Market House as a site for the monument.

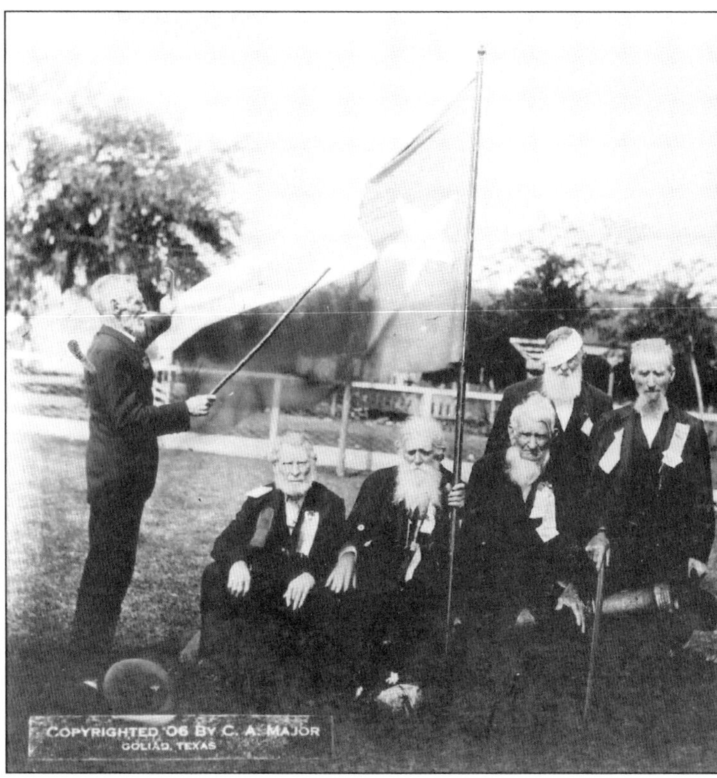

In another celebration of its past, in 1906 Goliad hosted the state meeting of the Daughters of the Texas Revolution (DRT), which included a reunion of the surviving veterans of the Texas Revolution, shown here (see also cover photograph). During the convention, there was a memorial service for deceased veterans, and the five survivors who attended were honored. The DRT met in the courtroom of the courthouse, and the community provided entertainment, music, and a visit to Presidio La Bahia.

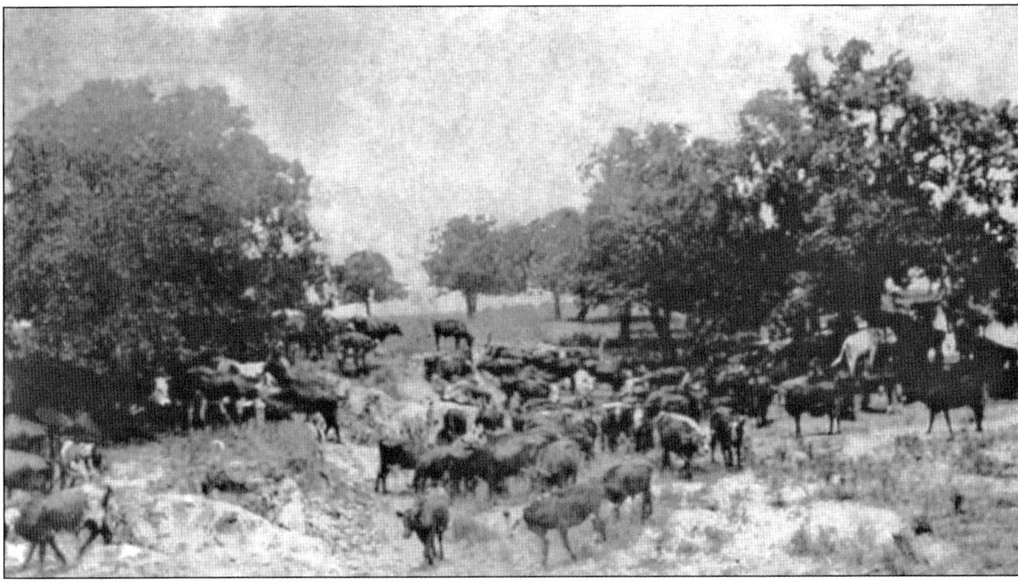

As Goliad developed during its golden age, ranching was the foundation upon which it was built. In the beginning, ranchers drew upon the longhorn herds originating at the missions, but as time went by Goliad ranchers began to improve their herds by introducing a variety of other breeds of cattle. They also utilized barbed wire to enclose their pastures, eliminating the open ranges of the past, and shipped their cattle on the railroad instead of driving them to the market. The photograph above shows a cattle roundup on the Parks Ranch in 1914; the one below shows W. W. Albrecht and men working cattle on his ranch.

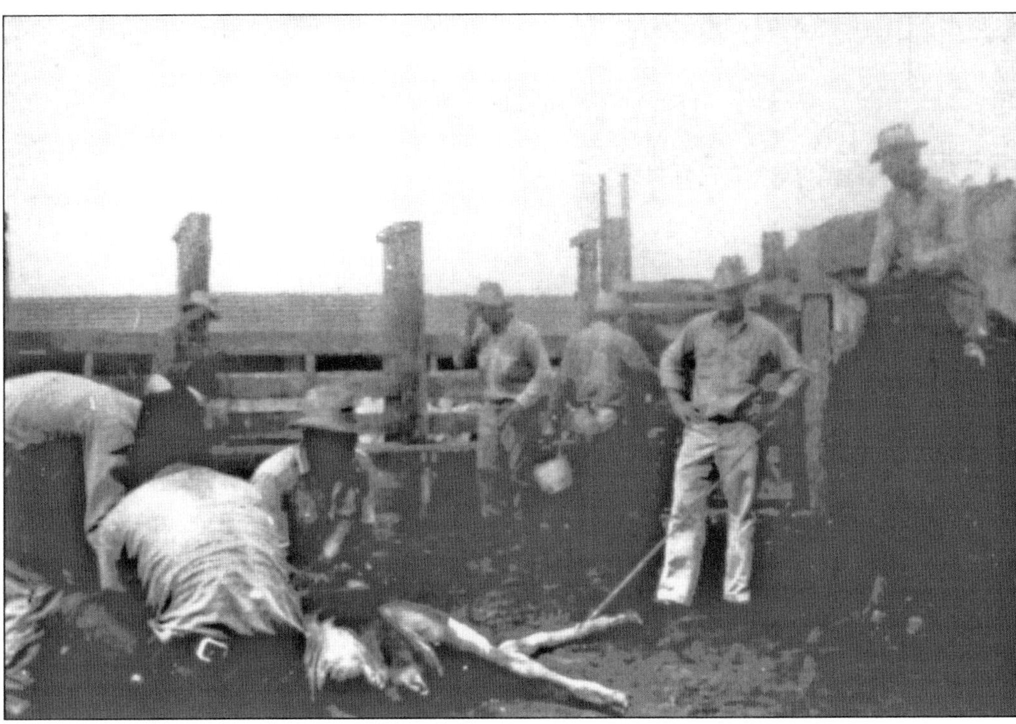

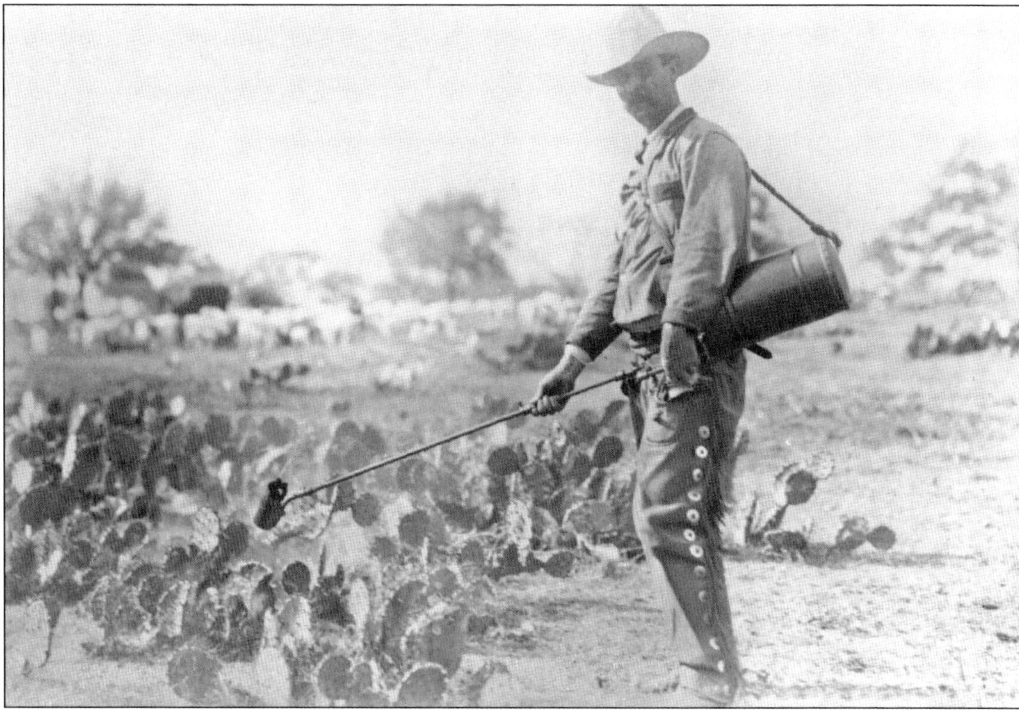

Ranching in south Texas was always a chancy occupation because of the limited and erratic distribution of rain. In dry times, native prickly pear cacti (along with mesquite tree beans) often saved ranchers' herds from disaster. Ranchers burned the thorns off the cactus pear so the cattle could safely eat them. This ranch hand is doing just that on the J. E. Pettus Ranch in 1910.

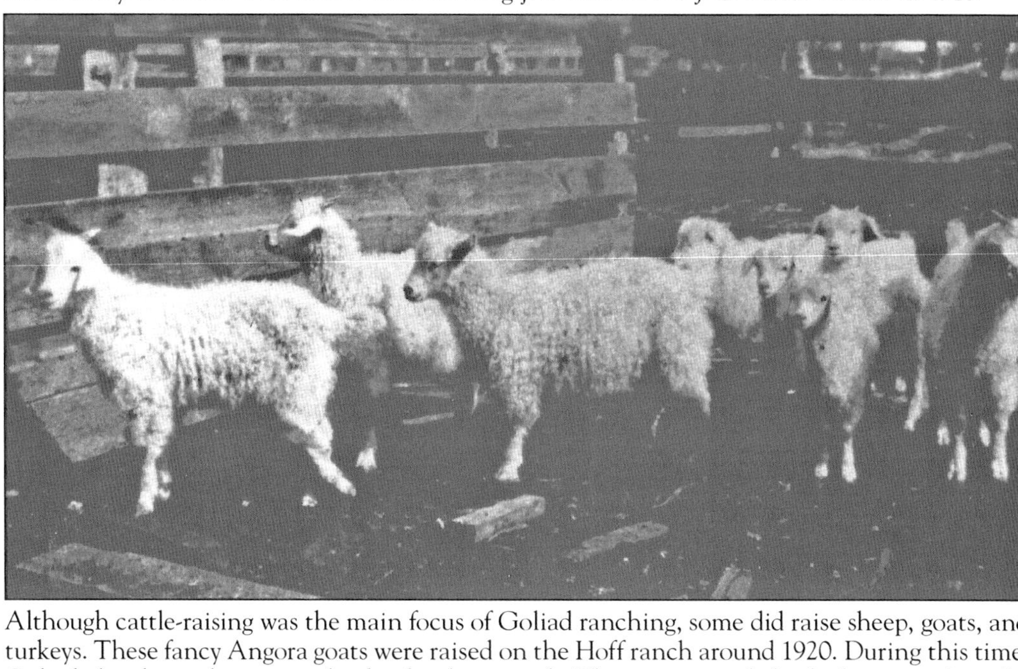

Although cattle-raising was the main focus of Goliad ranching, some did raise sheep, goats, and turkeys. These fancy Angora goats were raised on the Hoff ranch around 1920. During this time, Goliad also shipped train car–loads of turkeys north. They were mostly birds that grazed on the pastures, eating nuts, bugs, and anything else they could find.

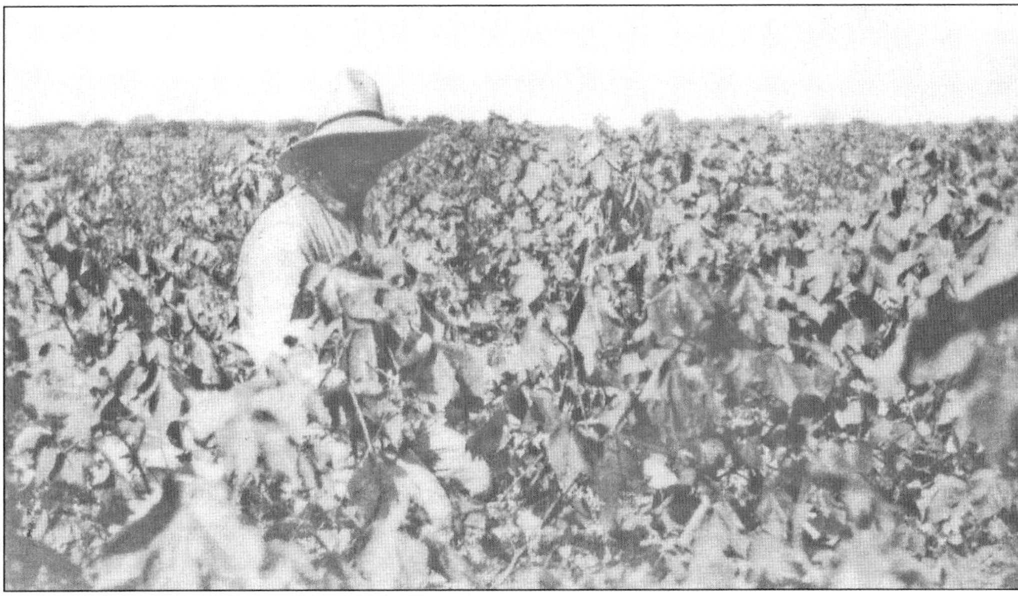

One of the main crops in the county was cotton, much of it grown by tenant farmers. Along with cotton production came cotton picking. Although itinerants and poor people picked much of the cotton, in peak season many prominent farmers and their families also pitched in.

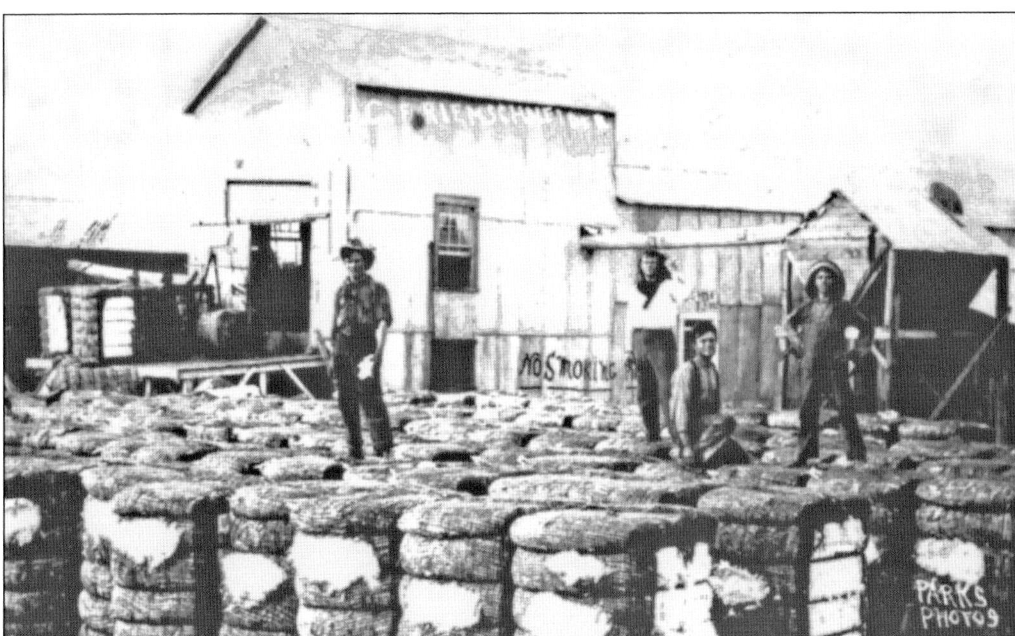

As cotton production grew, so did the number of cotton gins, which became ubiquitous around the county. This one was the Riemenschneider Gin, shown in 1912. At the peak of cotton production, there were 12 gins in the county; as cotton production declined after World War II, cotton gins disappeared entirely from the Goliad County scene.

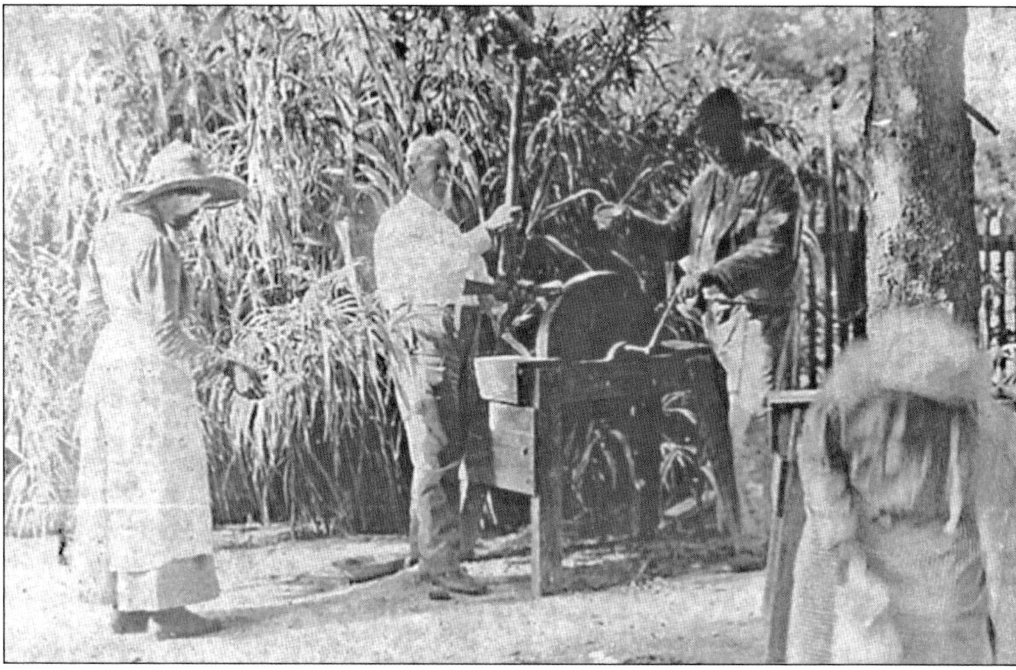

There were other crops, including cane. Solomon Parks is shown sharpening tools used in harvesting the cane on a grub wheel in 1914. The cane was used to feed cattle, and some was processed as foodstuffs. In addition to cotton and cane, local farmers also grew corn and grains.

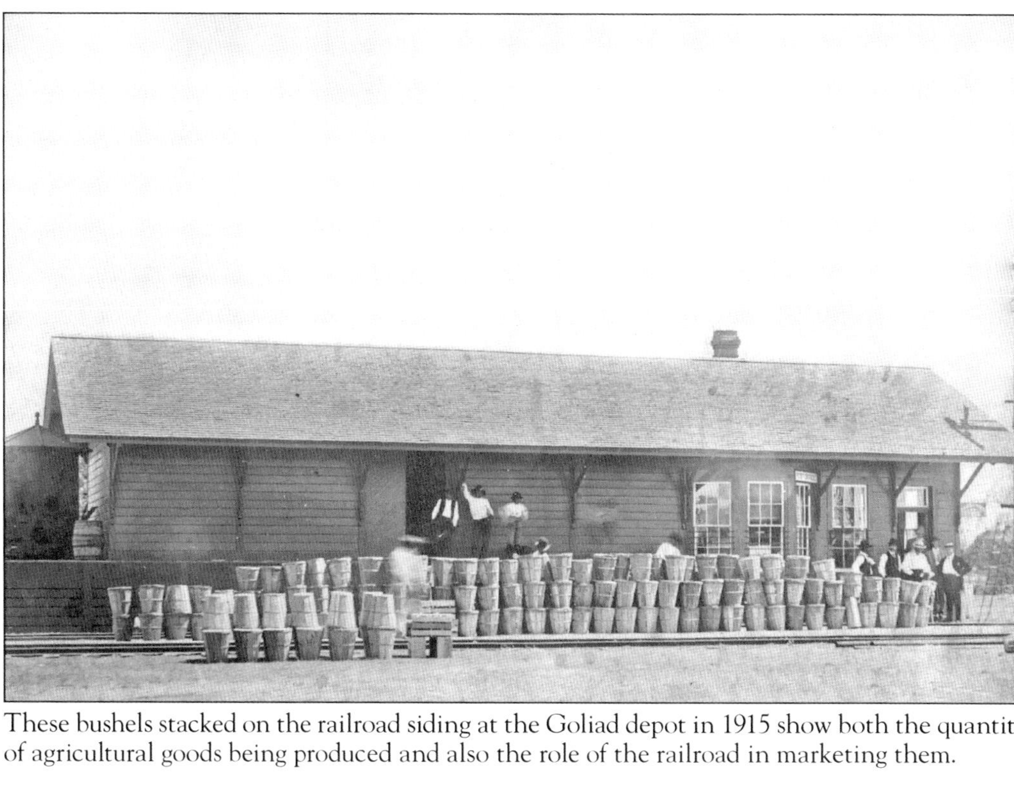

These bushels stacked on the railroad siding at the Goliad depot in 1915 show both the quantity of agricultural goods being produced and also the role of the railroad in marketing them.

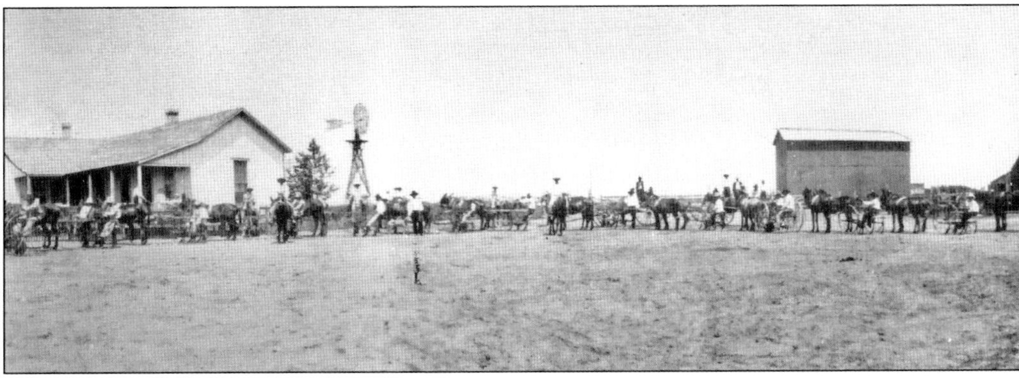

This photograph shows a large number of horses pulling cultivators, illustrating the major mode of power used by farmers during this period. By the 1930s, many farmers were replacing their horses and mules with steam- or gasoline-powered tractors. (Courtesy of Goliad County Library.)

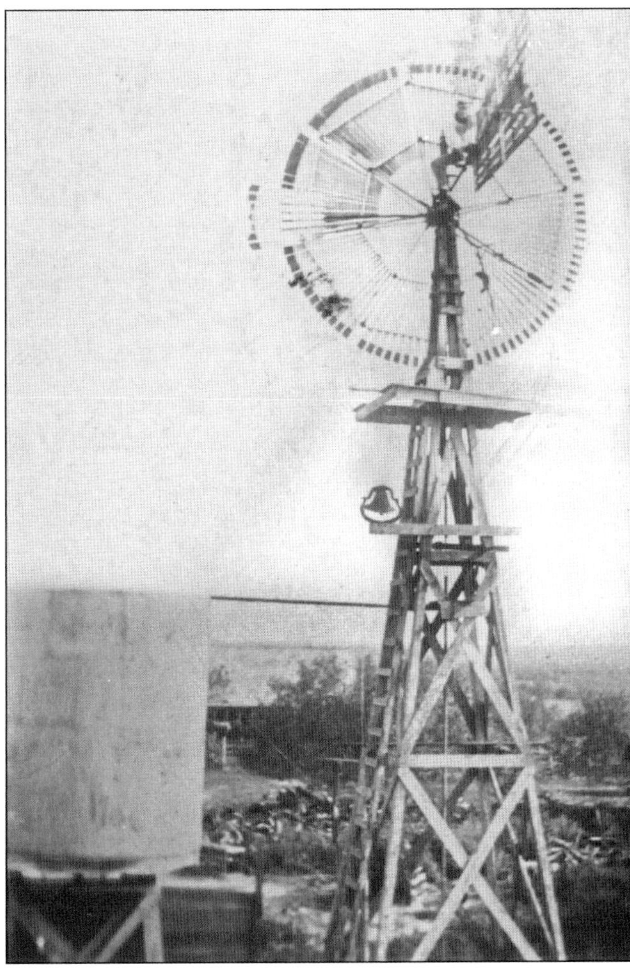

There were few things as ubiquitous in Goliad County at the dawn of the 20th century as the windmill. It appears in many of the photographs of the time (see above, for example) and can still occasionally be found in rural areas. The windmills pumped water for household and domestic use and for ranch animals and agriculture. For many, the windmill is a romantic manifestation of rural life in Texas.

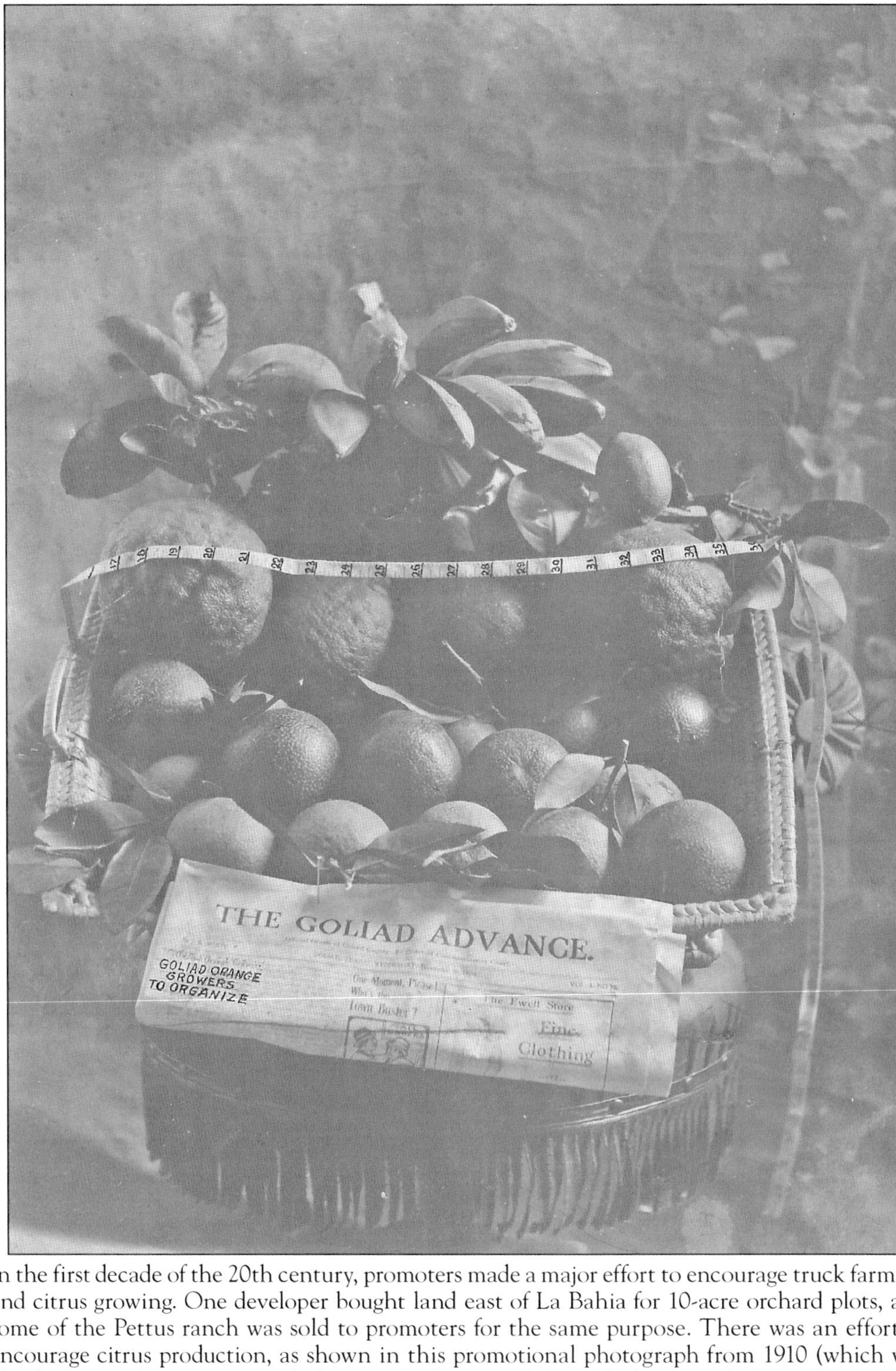

In the first decade of the 20th century, promoters made a major effort to encourage truck farming and citrus growing. One developer bought land east of La Bahia for 10-acre orchard plots, and some of the Pettus ranch was sold to promoters for the same purpose. There was an effort to encourage citrus production, as shown in this promotional photograph from 1910 (which was clearly designed to promote both the citrus industry and the *Goliad Advance*). Citrus farming did not, however, become an important part of Goliad agriculture.

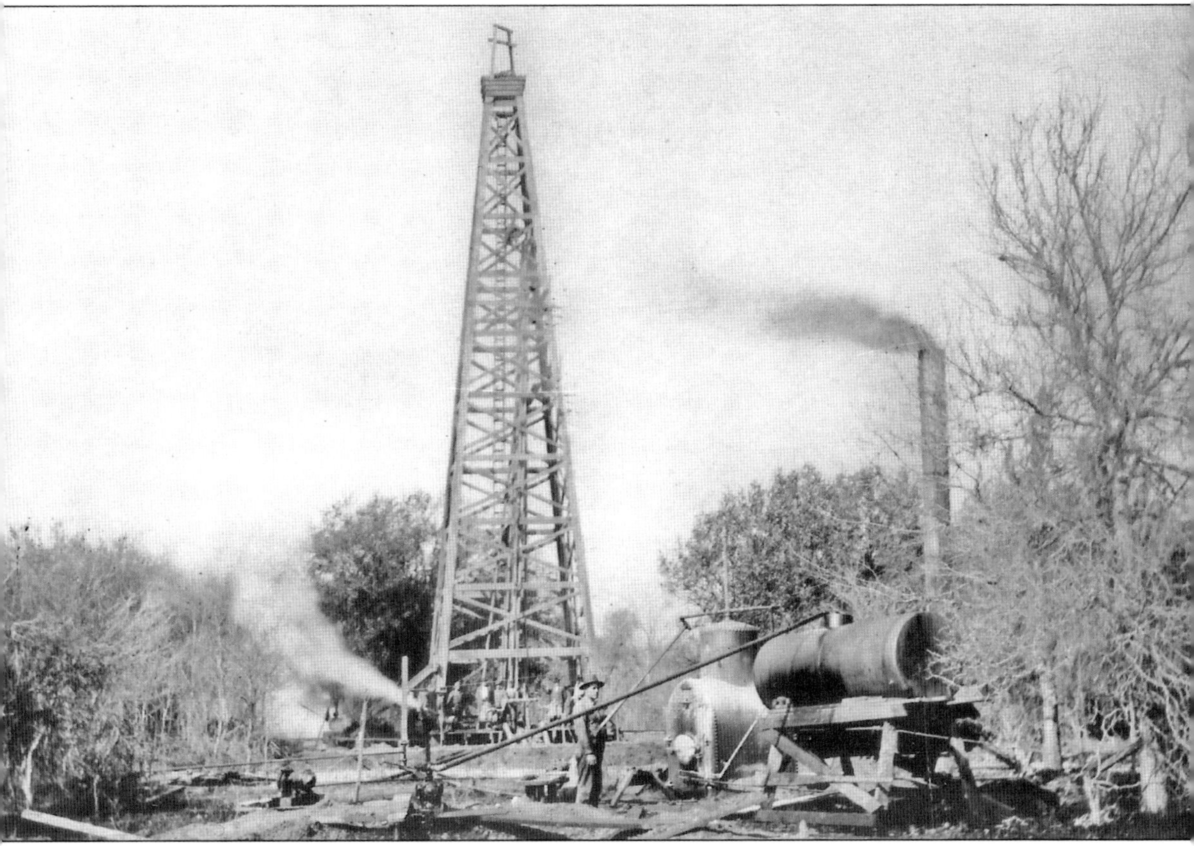

Although ranching and agriculture had dominated the Goliad scene since the start of European settlements, competition entered the economic picture in 1925 with the first oil rig, shown here on the Louise Parks Donoghue property. Oil and gas production have continued ever since, with a major boom in the 1950s; it is still a main feature of the Goliad economy and has produced considerable wealth for many citizens.

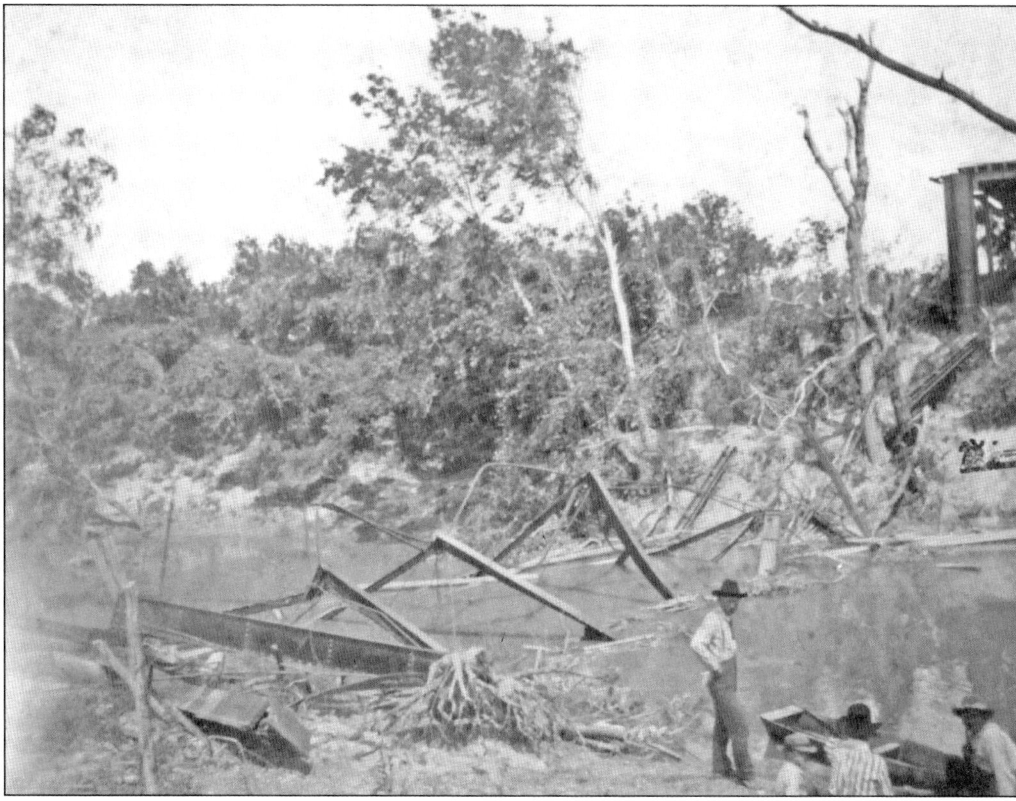

Around 3:30 p.m. on May 18, 1902, a tornado cut a mile-long, half-mile-wide swath through the northwestern part of Goliad. The cyclone killed at least 115 and wounded 230 (official death record–keeping was primitive at that time, and there were probably casualties undocumented). The worst tragedy was at the Fannin Street Methodist Church, where over 50 people attending services were killed. Goliad locals rushed to aid the wounded, converting the undamaged courthouse into an emergency hospital. Trains from neighboring towns brought doctors, nurses, and supplies to help the wounded, and the National Guard maintained order. Many of the injured did not die in the storm but died later from lockjaw. The photograph above shows the destruction of the steel bridge and the one below shows the remains of a house.

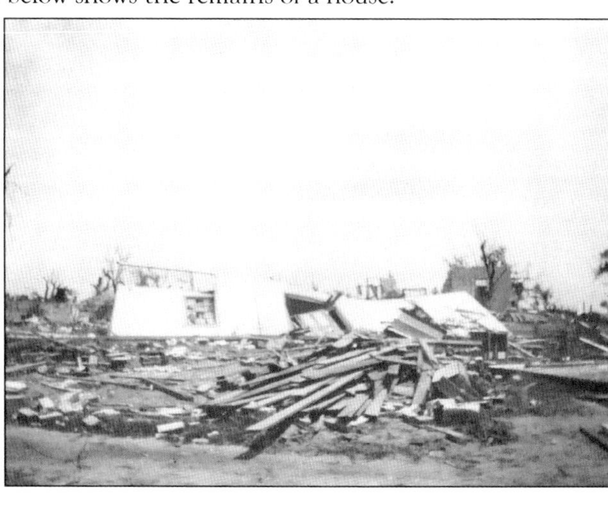

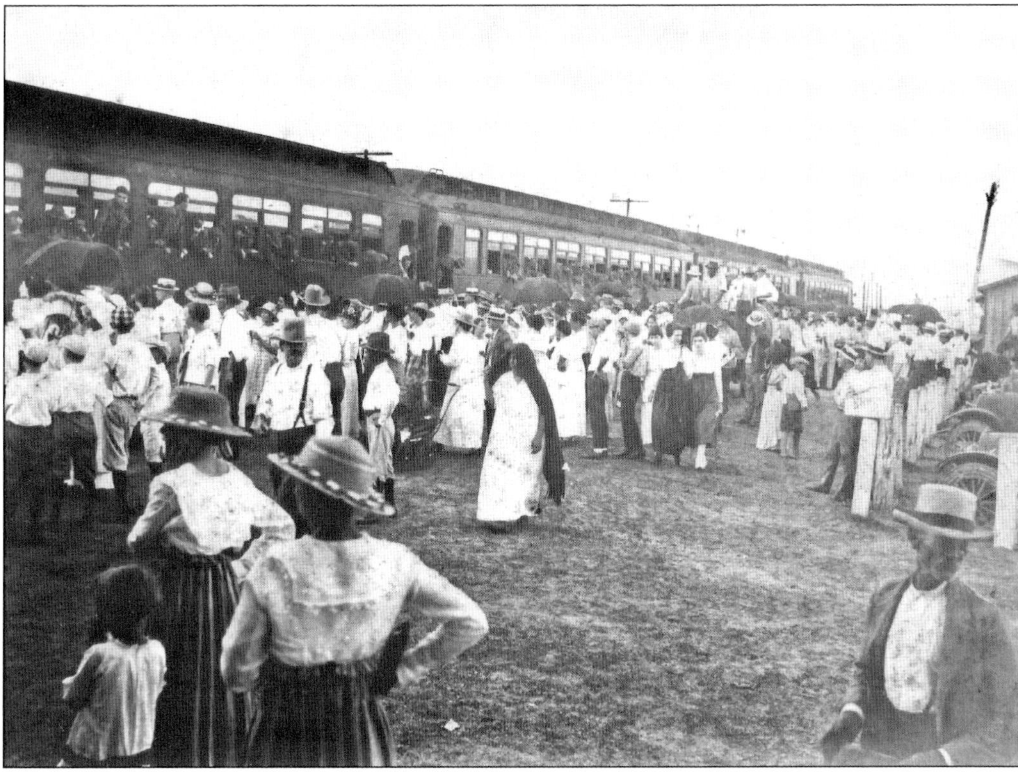

World War I had a considerable impact on Goliad. Many men from the area joined a company of the 36th Division, which had its own Goliad County officers. The division saw service and suffered heavy casualties in France. This photograph shows local citizens at the train station to see the troops off to Camp Bowie for training followed by shipment overseas. (Courtesy of UTSA Institute of Texan Culture.)

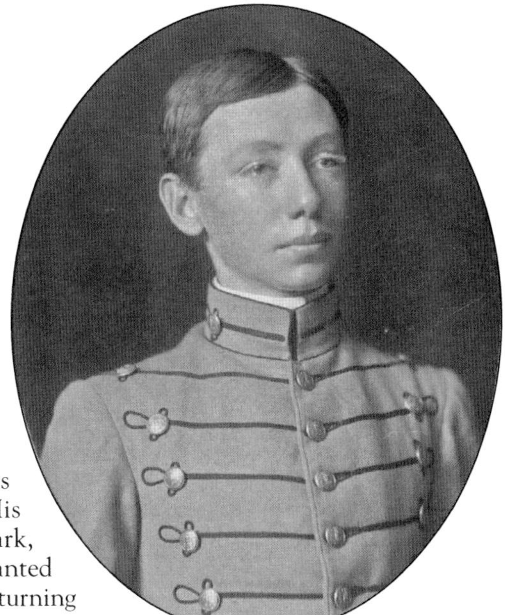

One of the 18 local men who died in the war was Heath Ewell, the son of a prominent family. His mother planted a tree in his honor in City Park, which still stands. The text reads, "This Tree Planted in Memory of Lieut. James Heath Ewell, Jr. Died Returning to France. 1899–1918."

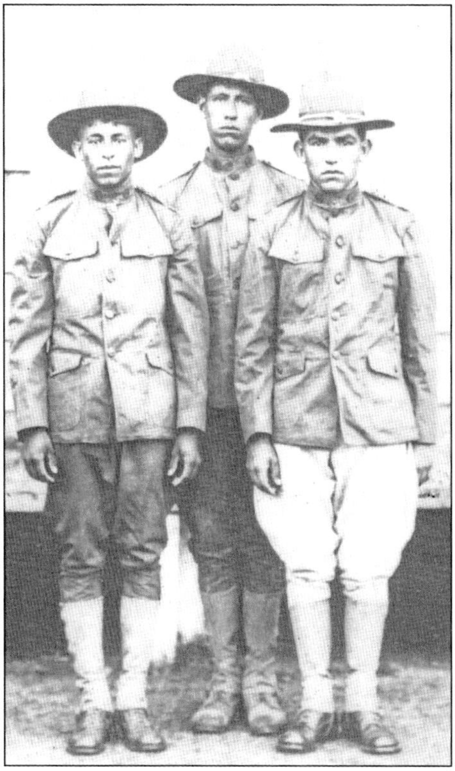

Three Goliad men who served in World War I were cousins Estevan Rubio (left), Placido Martinez (center), and Gumecindo Salazar. They were all from La Bahia and exemplify the large number of local Tejanos who have served in the U.S. armed services. (Courtesy of Estella Zermeno.)

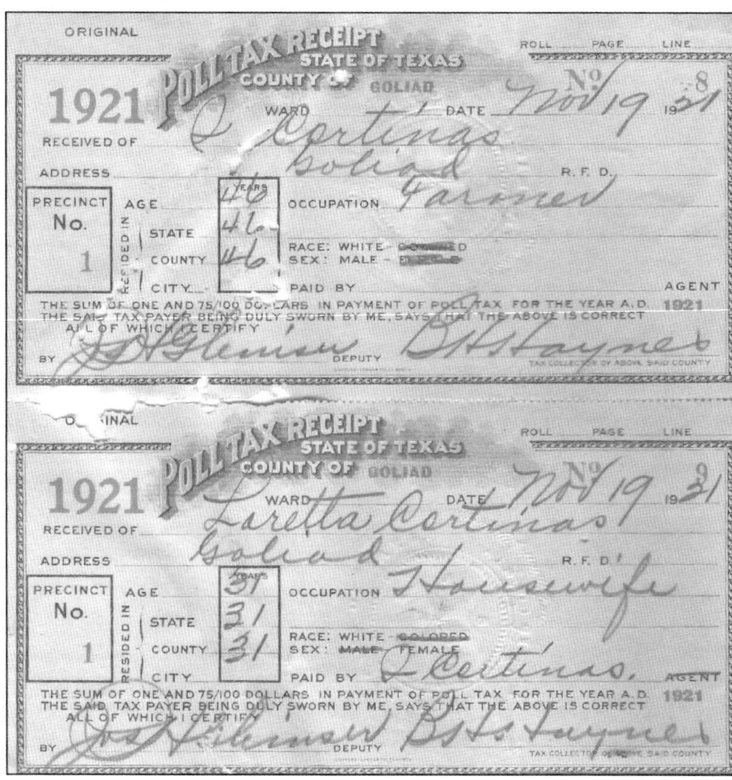

ORIGINAL — ROLL — PAGE — LINE

POLL TAX RECEIPT — STATE OF TEXAS — COUNTY OF GOLIAD

1921 — No. 8 — WARD 1 — DATE Nov 19 1921

RECEIVED OF Q Cortinas

ADDRESS Goliad — R. F. D.

PRECINCT No. 1 — AGE 46 YEARS — OCCUPATION Farmer

RESIDED IN STATE 46 — COUNTY 46 — CITY

RACE: WHITE - COLORED — SEX: MALE - FEMALE

PAID BY — AGENT

THE SUM OF ONE AND 75/100 DOLLARS IN PAYMENT OF POLL TAX FOR THE YEAR A.D. 1921 THE SAID TAX PAYER BEING DULY SWORN BY ME, SAYS THAT THE ABOVE IS CORRECT ALL OF WHICH I CERTIFY

BY — DEPUTY — TAX COLLECTOR OF ABOVE SAID COUNTY

ORIGINAL — ROLL — PAGE — LINE

POLL TAX RECEIPT — STATE OF TEXAS — COUNTY OF GOLIAD

1921 — No. 9 — WARD — DATE Nov 19 1921

RECEIVED OF Loretta Cortinas

ADDRESS Goliad — R. F. D.

PRECINCT No. 1 — AGE 31 YEARS — OCCUPATION Housewife

RESIDED IN STATE 31 — COUNTY 31 — CITY

RACE: WHITE - COLORED — SEX: MALE - FEMALE

PAID BY Q Cortinas — AGENT

THE SUM OF ONE AND 75/100 DOLLARS IN PAYMENT OF POLL TAX FOR THE YEAR A.D. 1921 THE SAID TAX PAYER BEING DULY SWORN BY ME, SAYS THAT THE ABOVE IS CORRECT ALL OF WHICH I CERTIFY

BY — DEPUTY — TAX COLLECTOR OF ABOVE SAID COUNTY

These two poll tax receipts tell an important story. For years, Quirino Cortinas paid his poll tax so he could vote; in 1921, for the first time, he paid the tax for himself and his wife, Loretta Cortinas. It was the first time women could vote. Loretta's poll tax marks a step forward in the development of American democracy. (Courtesy of Estella Zermeno.)

Four
Life in Goliad County 1880–1929

History is, after all, the story of people and what they do. This chapter draws upon the rich photograph collection of the Market House Museum to show some of the people of Goliad in the generation between Reconstruction and World War II. It gives you an idea of the kind of people who lived in Goliad, who they were, what they valued, how they looked, and what they did.

From these pictures several things become clear. Many local residents today are descendants of the people shown in these photographs. The continuity between the past and the present in Goliad is one of its strongest characteristics. Most of the pictures are of Anglos, but Tejanos and African Americans, who have always been part of Goliad's population, are also represented.

These pictures show Goliadians engaged in a wide range of activities. Community historians tell us that the organizations people belong to and the activities they participate in tell us much about the values and beliefs of a community. In Goliad, we find people active in schools, churches, sports, and cultural activities, indicating a value system in the mainstream of Texas culture. That the people took and kept so many photographs of children, churches, and schools reinforces the assumption that Goliad valued these things.

The pictures of people during Goliad's golden age also show many images that reflect the life of a rural community, one with a heavy emphasis on ranching. That was true of the county then and is still true to a certain extent.

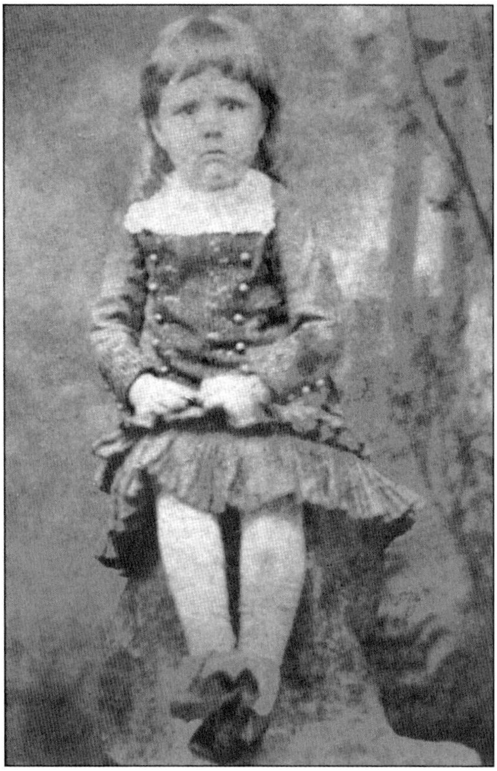

Children were favorite subjects of late-19th-century photographers. These Goliad samples feature (at left) Sallie Pettus Lott Baker, who clearly was not too happy to be having her picture taken and John Freeman Pettus (below) at age three, taken in 1891. He was a descendant of William Albert and Elizabeth Pettus, who came to Texas as members of Stephen Austin's original colony. Notice how the families intertwine.

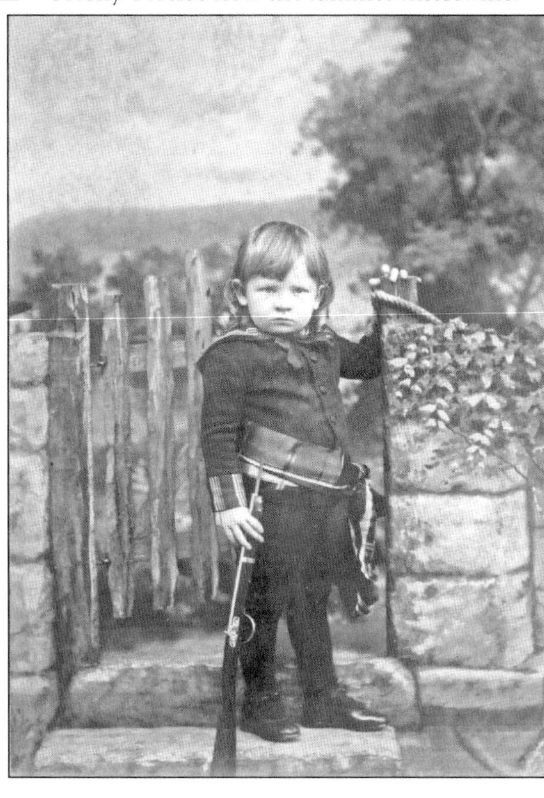

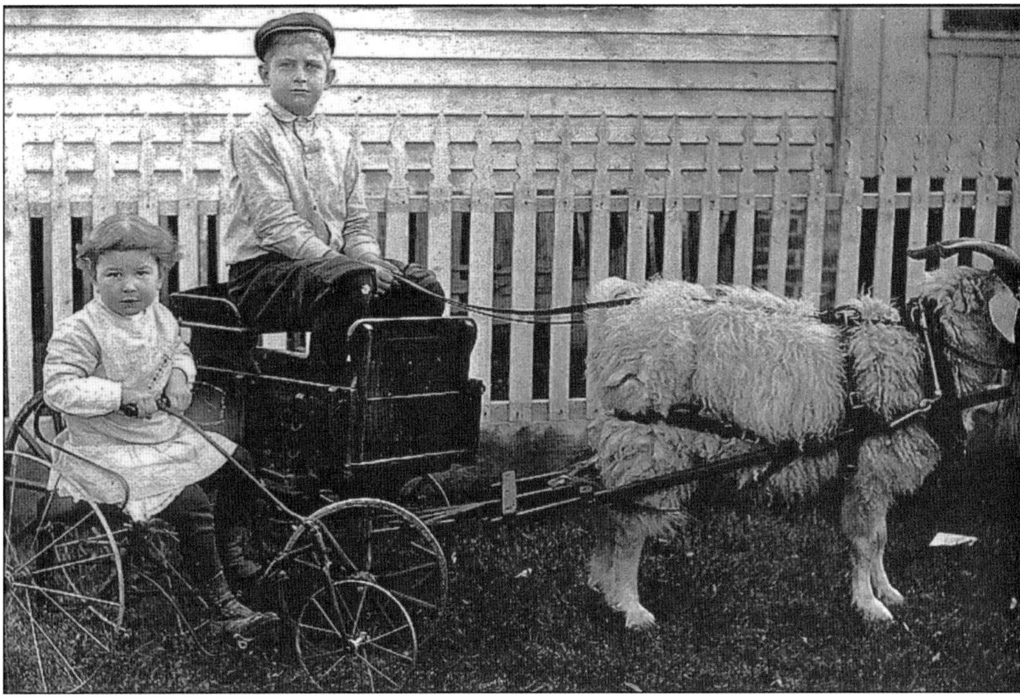

Group photographs with farm animals were also very popular. The picture above was taken in 1912 on the Parks Ranch and features cousins Louise Huggins (Donoghue) and Sol Minchen Parks in a cart drawn by a goat. The picture below shows a group of children and a horse under the windmill on the Ramsey Farm. The children on the horse are Cecil, Ralph, and Walton Ramsey; the other people are unidentified, which might say something about social stratification at the time.

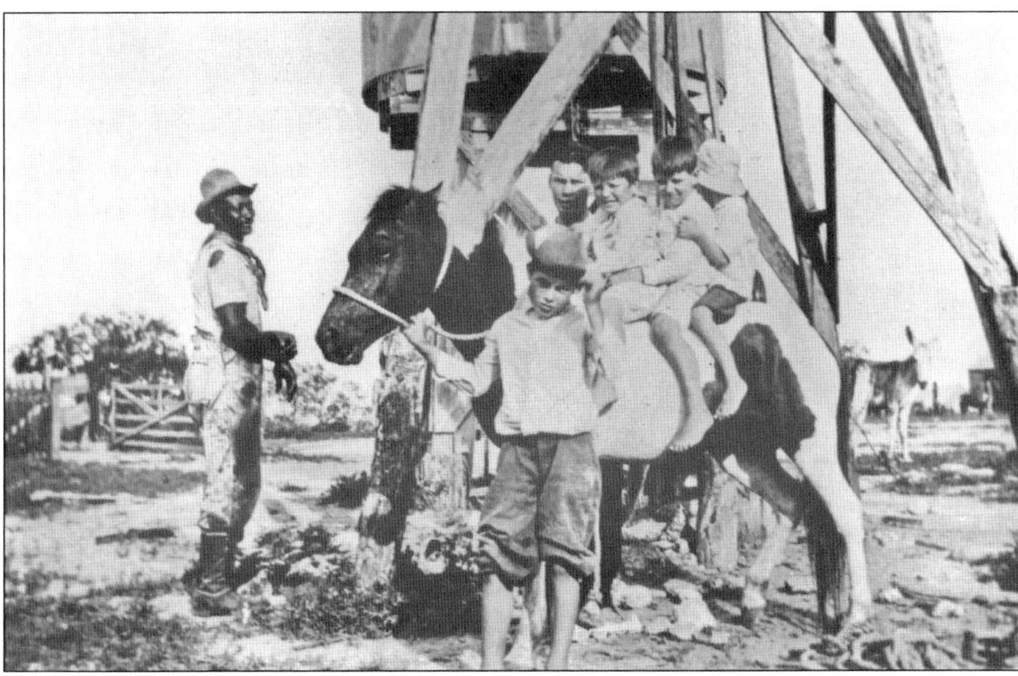

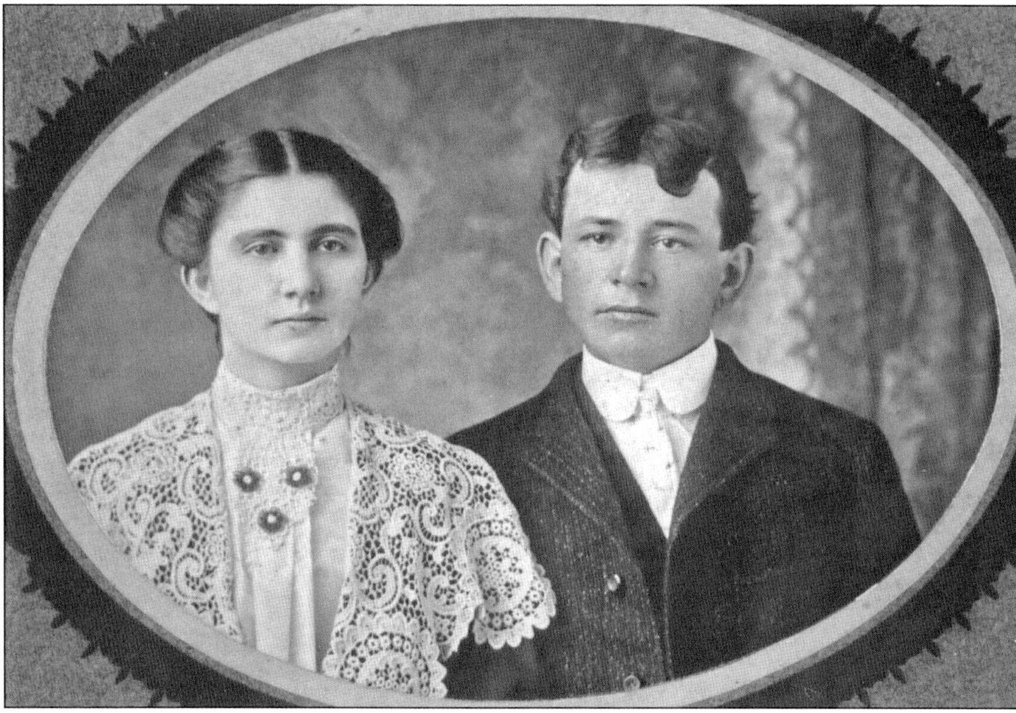

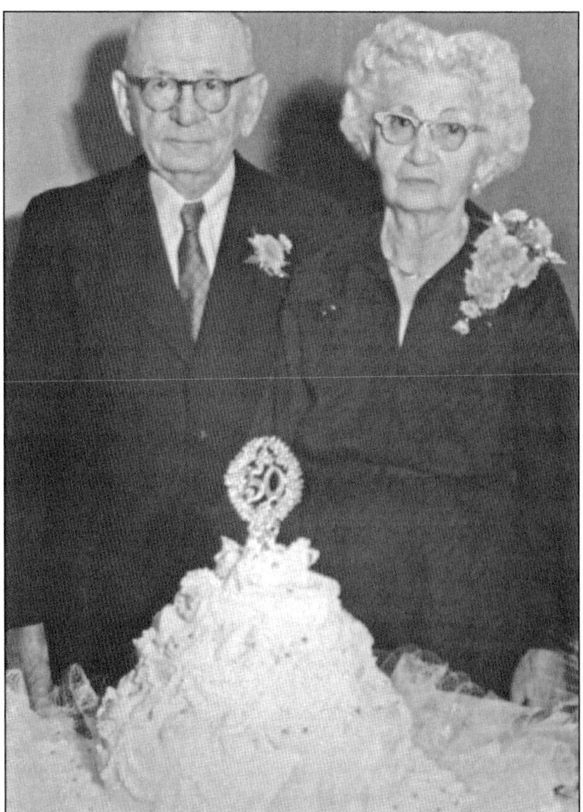

Family and continuity have long been features of Goliad County life, as illustrated by the 1906 engagement picture of Arthur F. Jacobs and Martha Wilhelm and the golden wedding anniversary photograph of the same couple in 1956.

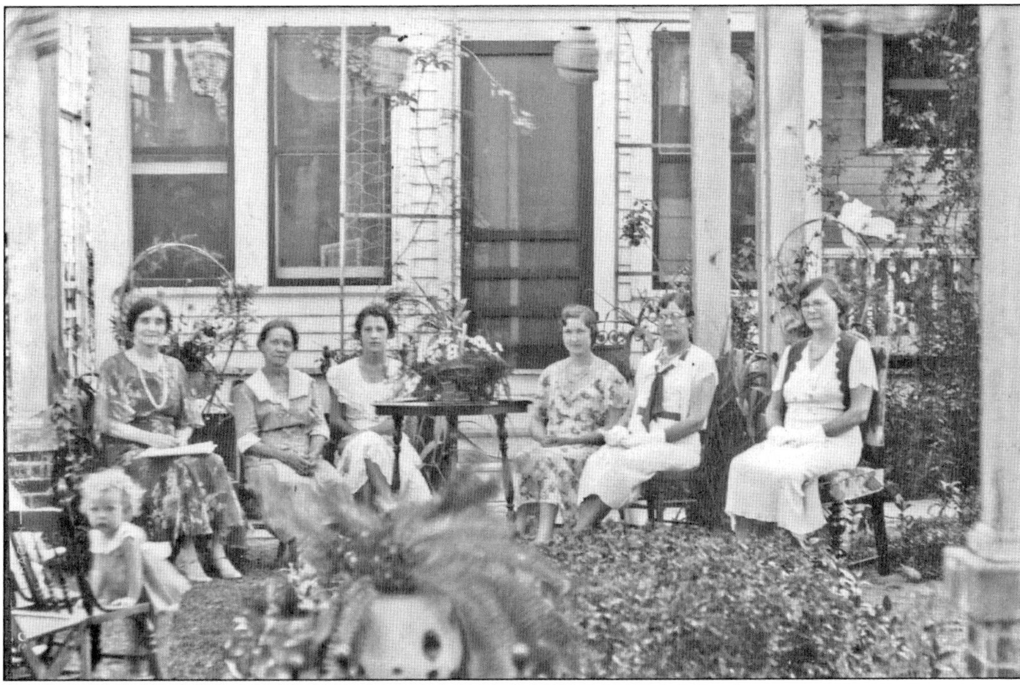

Church-related activities took up much of the time of early Goliad residents. This is a 1931 meeting of the Methodist Women's Christian Missionary Society officers held at the home of Ida LeMaster.

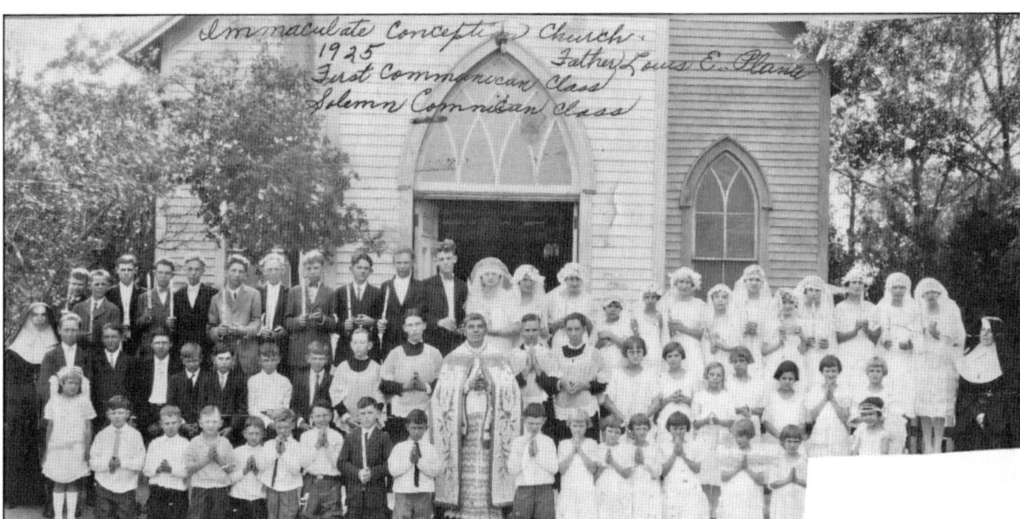

This 1925 photograph of the "First" and "Solemn" communion classes at the Immaculate Conception Catholic Church demonstrates the role of churches in the community. The chapel at Presidio La Bahia served as the first Roman Catholic Church in Goliad. An Immaculate Conception congregation existed at least by 1854 and held services in several locations (including the one pictured above) before a new church was built in 1962.

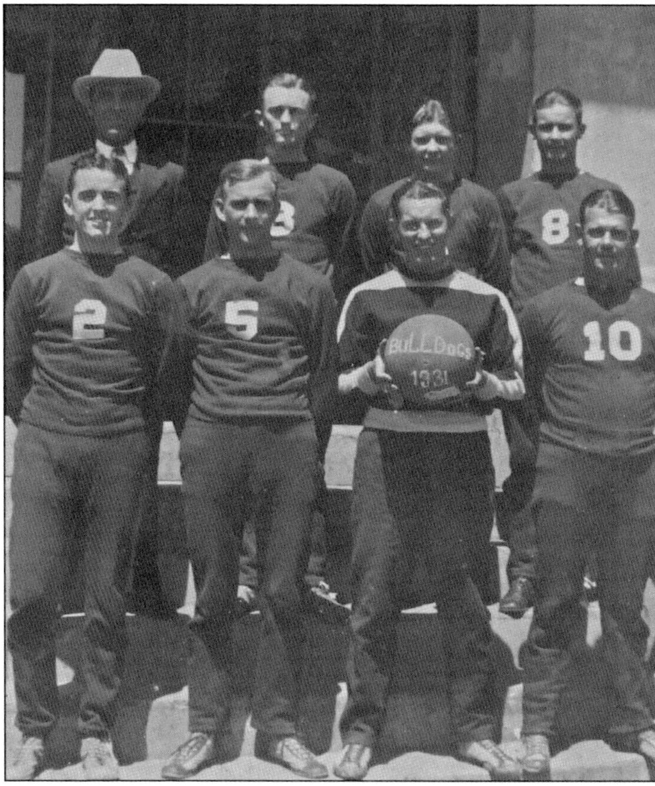

Sports played a large role in the community's recreational life in the years before World War II. This example is the "independent basketball team" of 1931, from left to right, featuring (first row) John R. Eckhart, Edward Angerstein, Robert McFarland, and Lee Angerstein; (second row) Edgar Albrecht, Charlie Bauch, Jack Leggett, and Babe Angerstein.

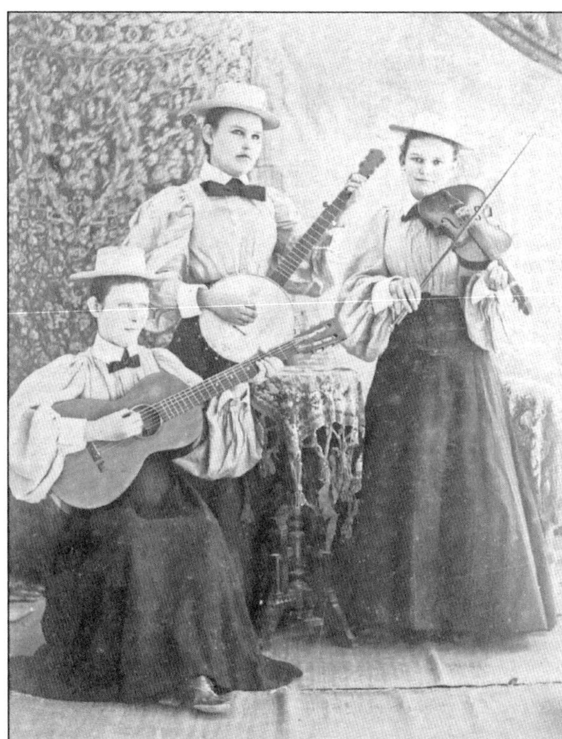

Music, likewise, was important during Goliad's golden age. There were community and school bands, professional musical groups, and music performances in the home. These musicians at home are, from left to right, Mamie Albrecht, Sophia Albrecht Schumacher, and Matilde Albrecht.

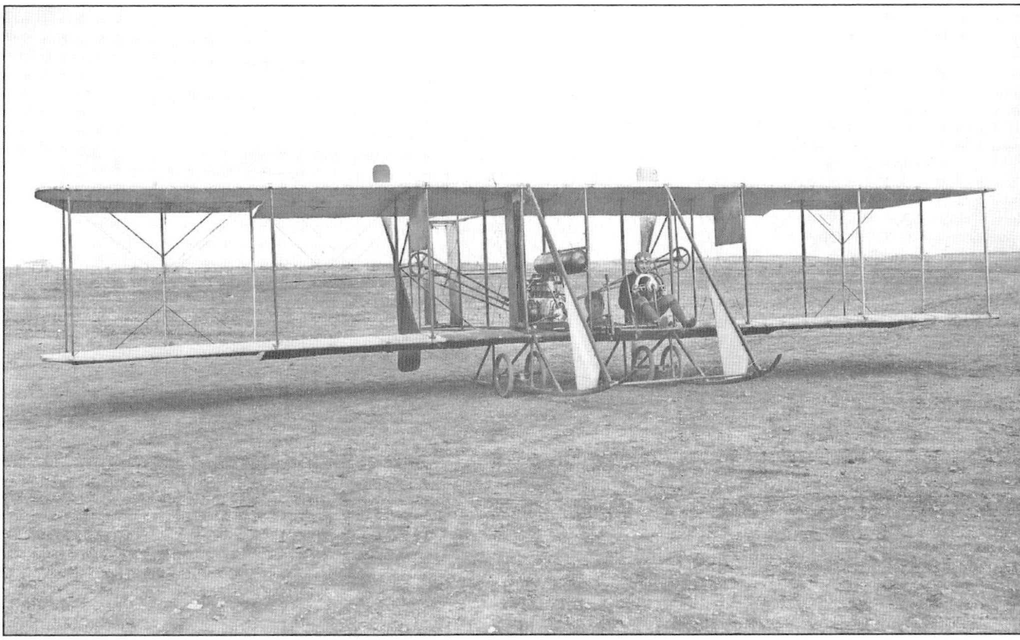

Katherine Stinson of San Antonio provided some brief recreation for Goliad citizens in 1916 when she brought her airplane to the Goliad County Fair. The County fair was always a major annual event in the rural community and featured many such entertainments. (Courtesy of Goliad County Library.)

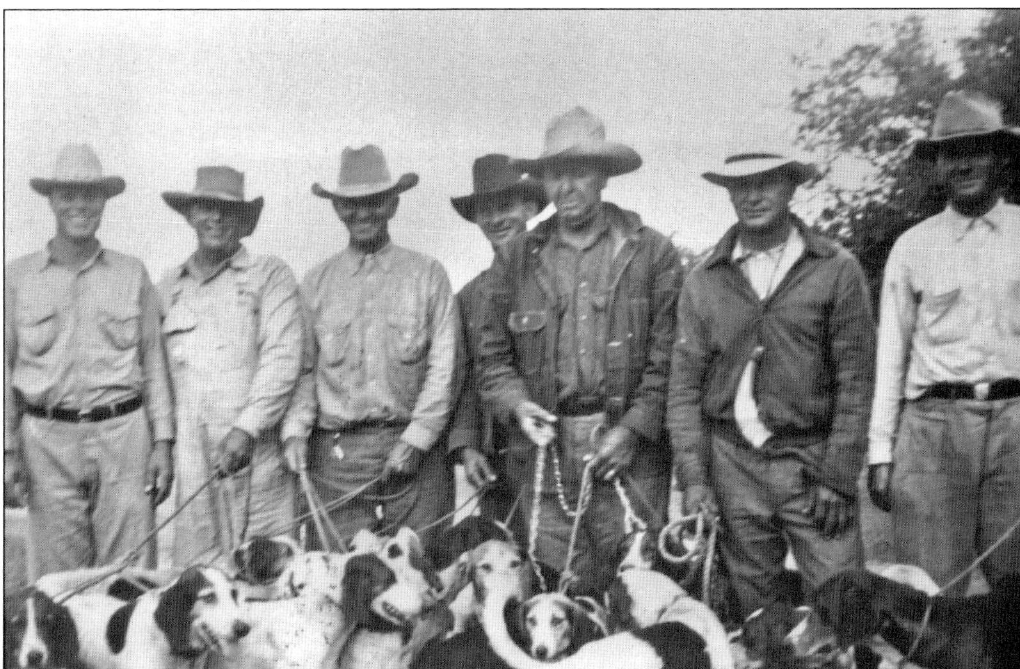

Another recreation of the time was hunting—although it was also a necessary means to rid the ranch country of predators. As far back as 1892, the city paid $5 for each lobo wolf scalp; they only paid $1 for wild cat scalps and $2 for ordinary wolf and coyote scalps.

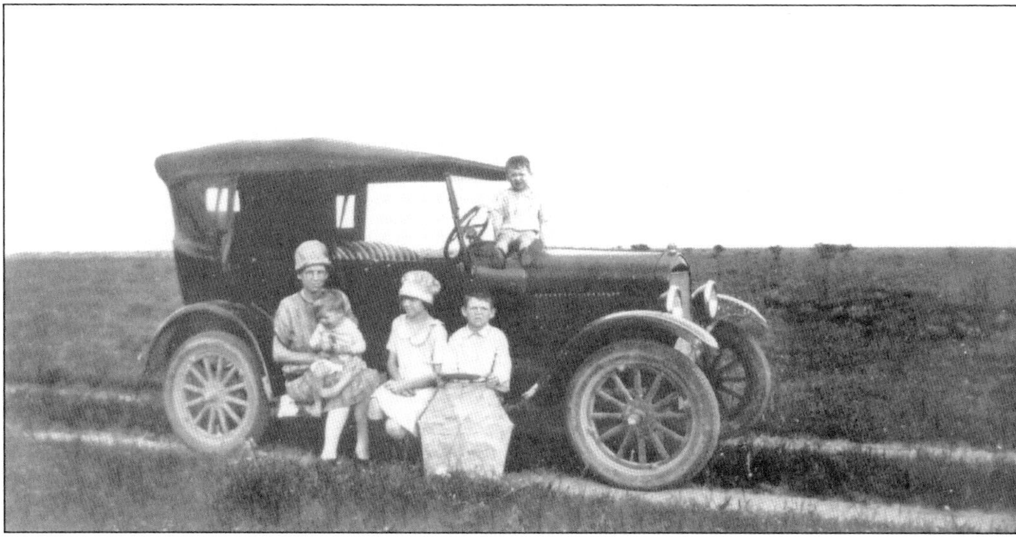

The arrival of the automobile transformed life in many ways. Owners were so proud of their vehicles that they were often photographed with them, like the Bolding family shown here on Refugio Road in 1926. Pictured from left to right are Grace, Joe, Helen, Pete, and John. Another proud automobile owner was Emil Weber, shown with his 1932 Buick in front of the restored granary at Mission Espiritu Santo.

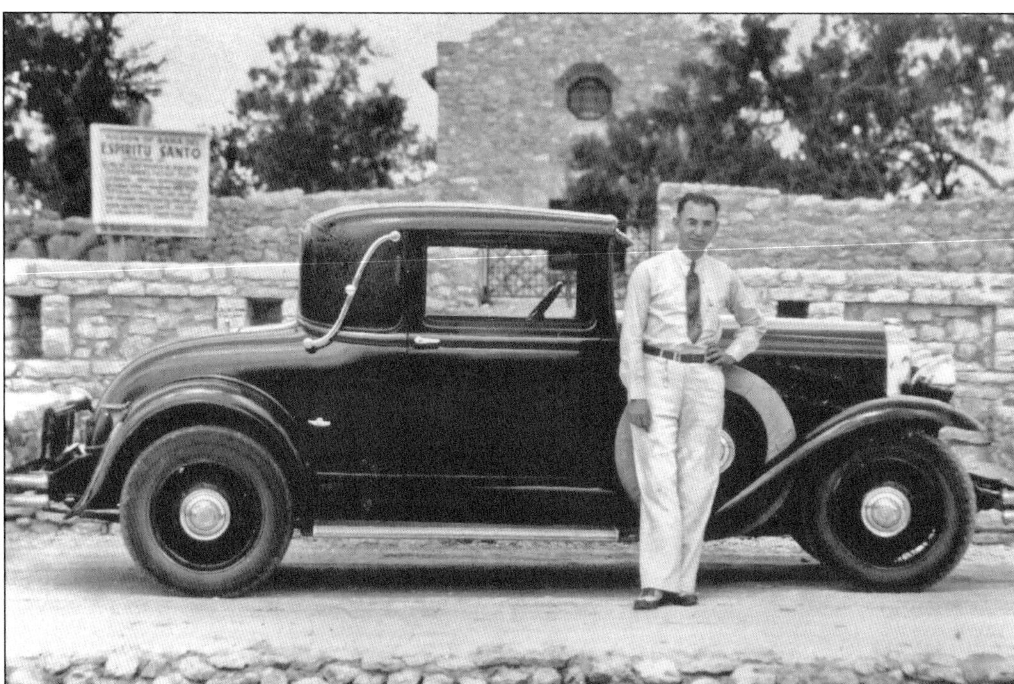

This photograph of Hattie Klump Fults and Hugh Fults, taken in the 1920s, shows that Goliad was very up-to-date with period clothing styles. Hattie Fults could have been a poster girl for a 1920s flapper with her long-waisted dress and her go-to-hell hat.

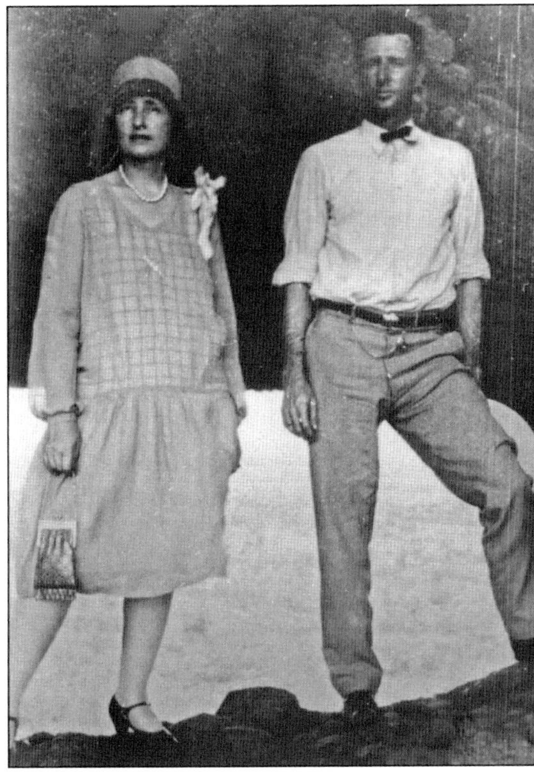

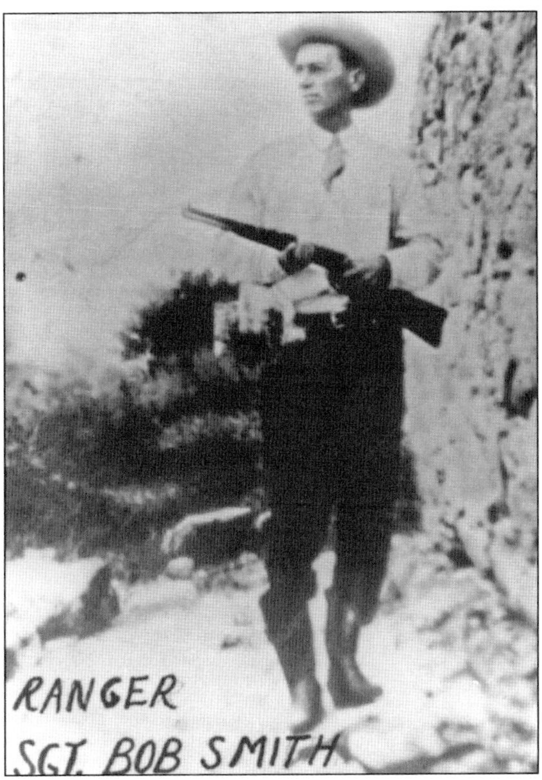

Bob Smith was a Goliad man of a different sort. He was a sergeant in the Texas Rangers Company D who helped protect Goliad from outlaws and drug smugglers. He was photographed at the mission ruins in 1928.

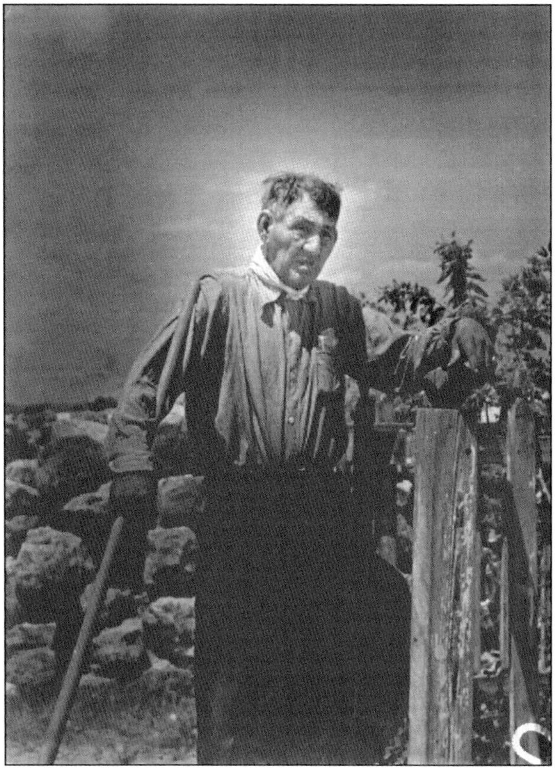

One of the most artistic photographs in the Market House Museum Collection is of Juan Nepomuceno Cortinas. The brother of Quirino Cortines (see page 54), Nepomuceno was the caretaker for Presidio La Bahia in the 1930s. He rang the bell to call people to services at the Loreto Chapel.

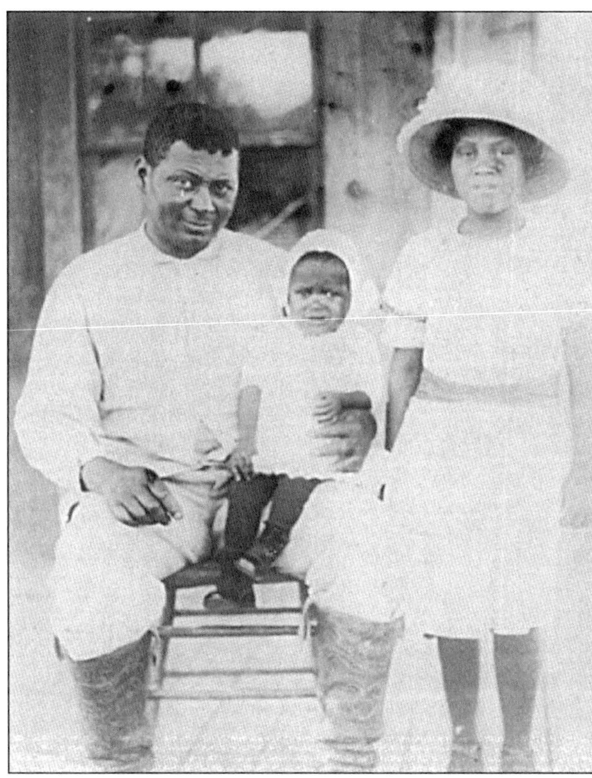

This Goliad resident, identified only as "Clarke," worked on the Parks Ranch in 1914. As Louise O'Connor has shown in *Cryin' for Daylight: A Ranching Culture in the Texas Coastal Bend* (1989), many of the workers on ranches in the San Antonio River valley were African American.

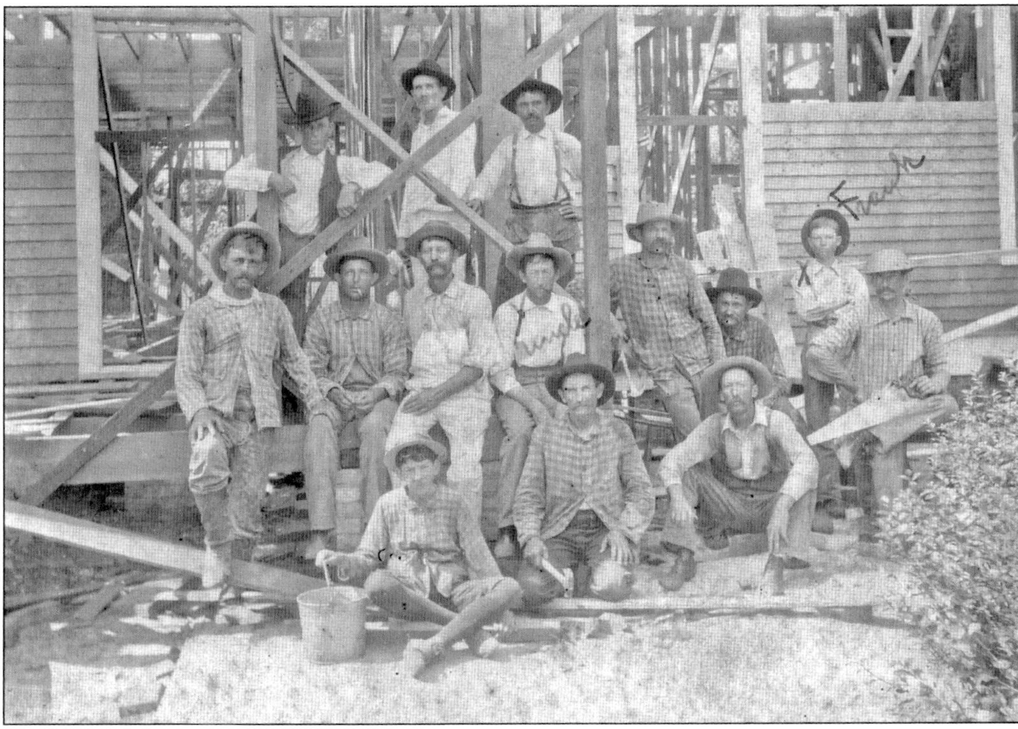

Between 1880 and 1930, Goliad locals worked. They worked on ranches and farms, in the stores in town, and provided services to the residents and visitors. They also worked on construction crews, such as this one run by Frank J. Wallace Sr.

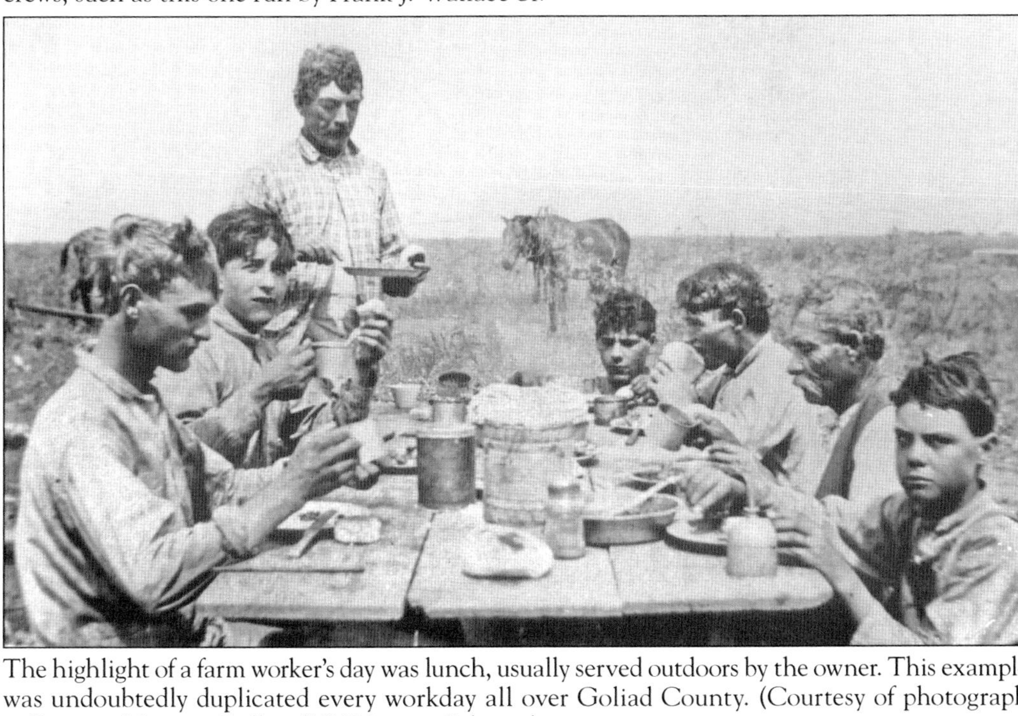

The highlight of a farm worker's day was lunch, usually served outdoors by the owner. This example was undoubtedly duplicated every workday all over Goliad County. (Courtesy of photograph collection, Victoria College/UH-Victoria Library.)

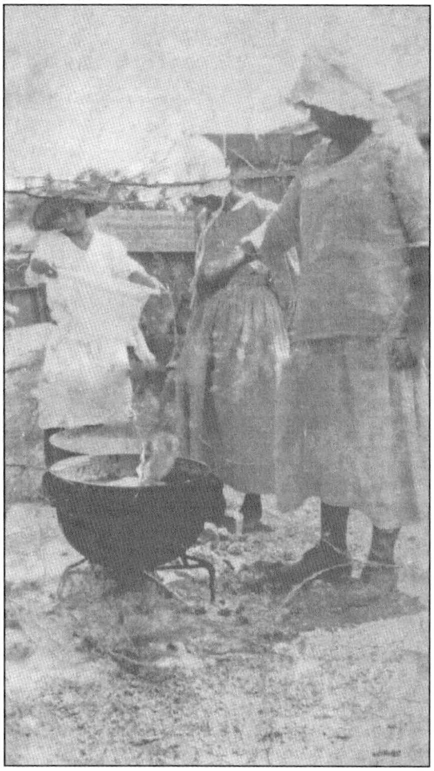

A woman's work is never done. Olivia Najar (left), Avelina Najar Perez (center), and Aveline Najar show how the laundry was done in 1927. It was a daylong process that involved boiling the laundry in cast-iron pots. This would have been the scene in every home until the gradual introduction of labor-saving devices in the years just before World War II.

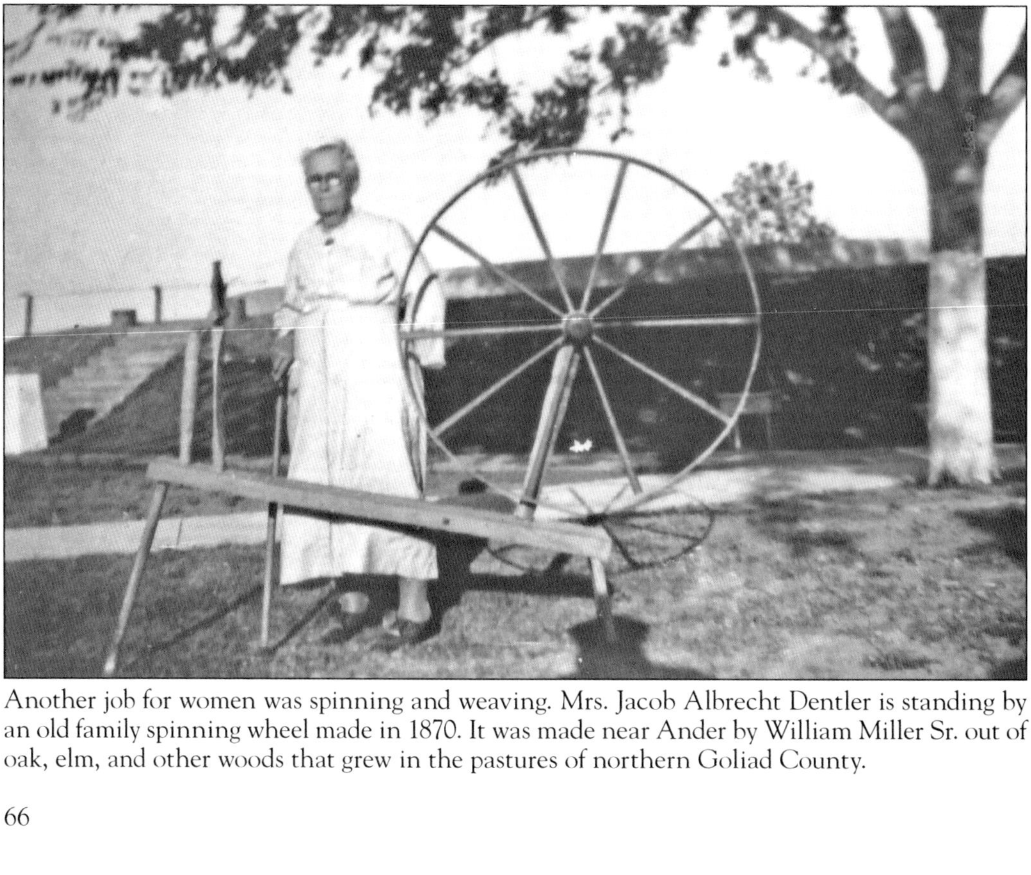

Another job for women was spinning and weaving. Mrs. Jacob Albrecht Dentler is standing by an old family spinning wheel made in 1870. It was made near Ander by William Miller Sr. out of oak, elm, and other woods that grew in the pastures of northern Goliad County.

Five

Goliad in the Thirties and Forties

The 1930s and 1940s were both good years and bad years for Goliad. There was the Great Depression, but there were also huge developments in preserving the town's heritage and in creating public facilities. Goliad was also touched by the Second World War.

The Depression hit Goliad as it did most of the area. There was economic distress as banks failed, and the city ran out of funds and had to issue warrants to pay its bills—as did many communities in the nation. Some local residents joined the Civilian Conservation Corps (CCC) as a means of helping alleviate their family's economic distress. Others found employment with various other governmental relief agencies.

While that was happening, the leadership of Judge James A. White brought wonderful things to the community. He got the state of Texas to establish Goliad State Park and to use some of the state's centennial funds to build an auditorium and other facilities to honor the important role of Goliad in the state's origins a hundred years earlier. First, the Works Progress Administration and then the CCC reconstructed many of the buildings of Mission Espiritu Santo within the State Park, making them historical showplaces for Goliad history and tourism. Finally, the state helped fund the construction of a large monument to Col. James Fannin and his men, who were killed in the Goliad Massacre of 1836. By the time World War II arrived, Goliad had experienced significant improvements.

During this period, the Tejano population continued to be centered in La Bahia. Their schoolchildren were segregated from the Anglos (as were African American students), but Mexican Americans began to become more politically active, especially through the League of United Latin American Citizens (LULAC). This activity accelerated when Tejano veterans returned from World War II and fought to break down barriers for Tejanos. Mexican Americans also began to play a larger role in the leadership of the community.

The other event that impacted this time period was World War II. As in previous wars, many Goliad citizens served in the war. At least 32 people died. The civilians pitched in to do their part in the war effort, as did Americans throughout the nation. When the soldiers returned home, they became the foundation for a new generation, one which carried Goliad through to the present.

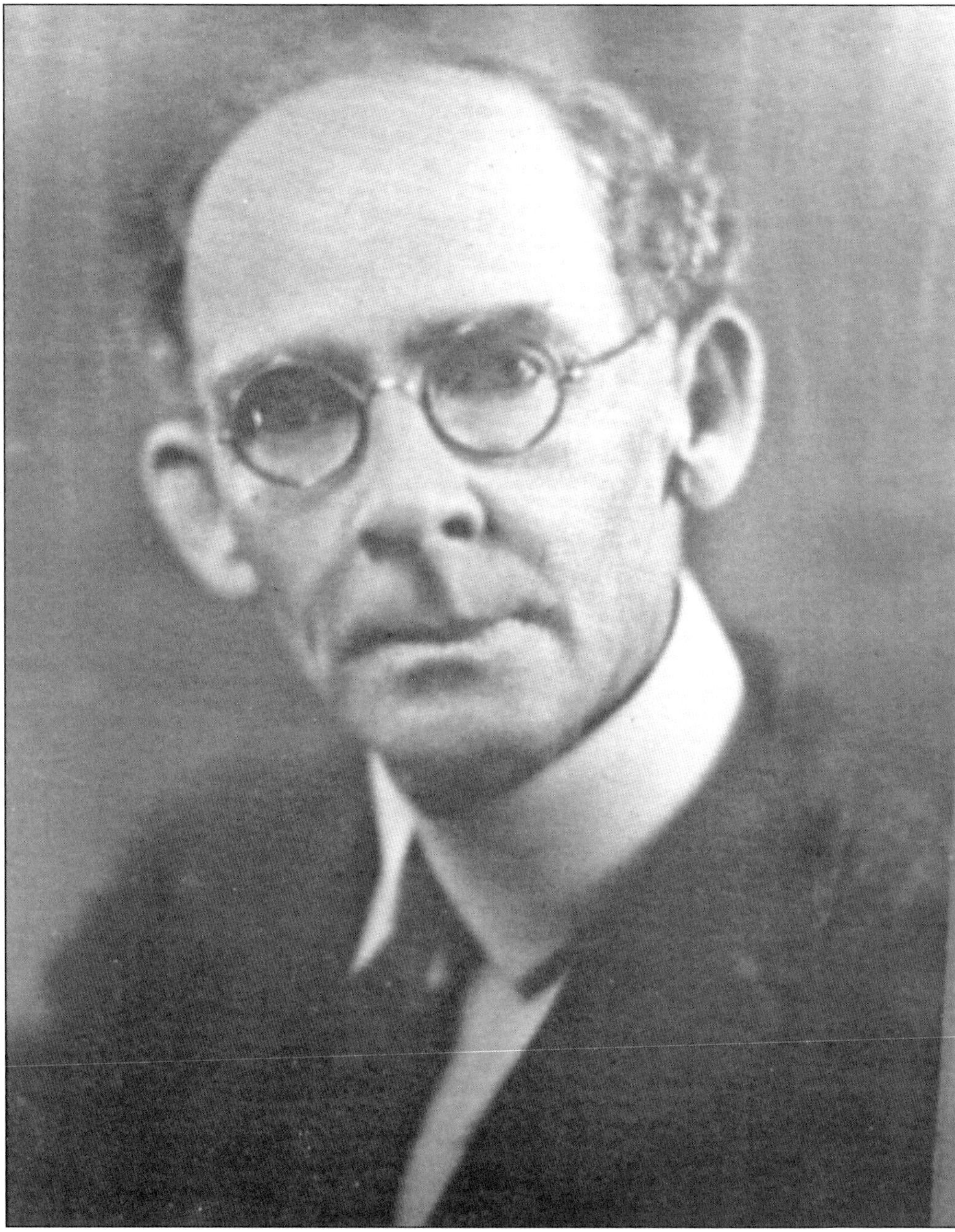

The most important leader in Goliad in the 1920s and 1930s was Judge James A. White, shown in 1924. He came to Goliad from Mississippi and, in 1905, began publishing a newspaper. He used the paper to aggressively promote Goliad. Elected county judge in 1924, he served in that position for 22 years. His most significant contributions came in the 1930s. In 1931, he secured legislation to create a state park and to build a bridge over the San Antonio River. During the depression, he secured federal and state funding (especially from the Civil Works Administration and the CCC) for a number of projects. The most significant was the restoration of Mission Espiritu Santo. He also got money from the state's centennial celebration program to build the Memorial Auditorium and the monument honoring Col. James Fannin and his men.

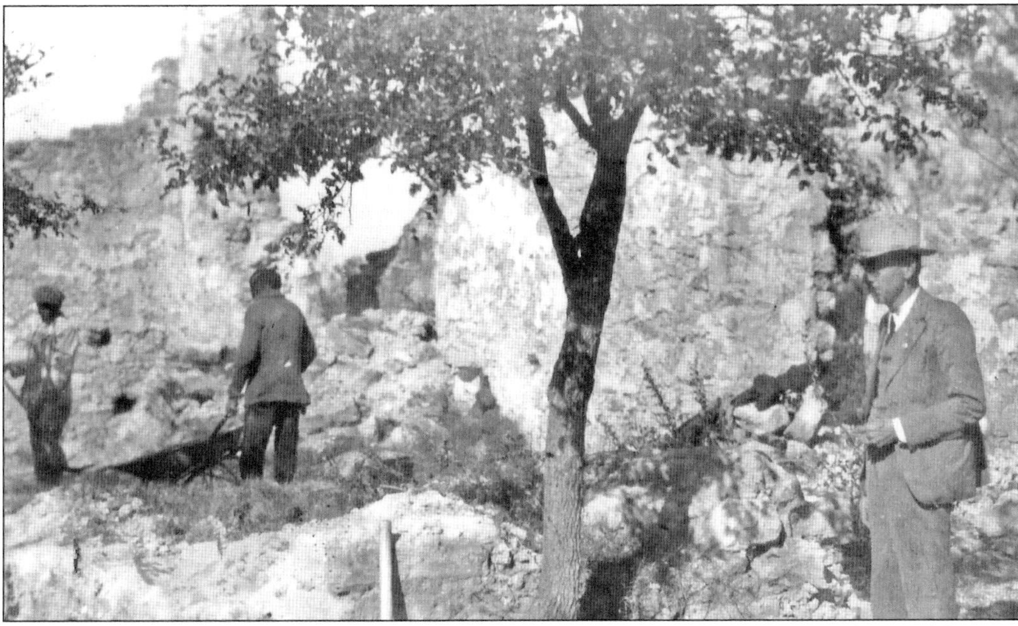

In the 1930s, the old Mission Espiritu Santo was in a terrible state of ruin, having been used for many purposes and then abandoned for many years. Townspeople had taken many of the stones for building materials for their structures in town. The first task in restoration was the clearing of the brush, undertaken here by Civil Works Administration (CWA) members with Judge White observing.

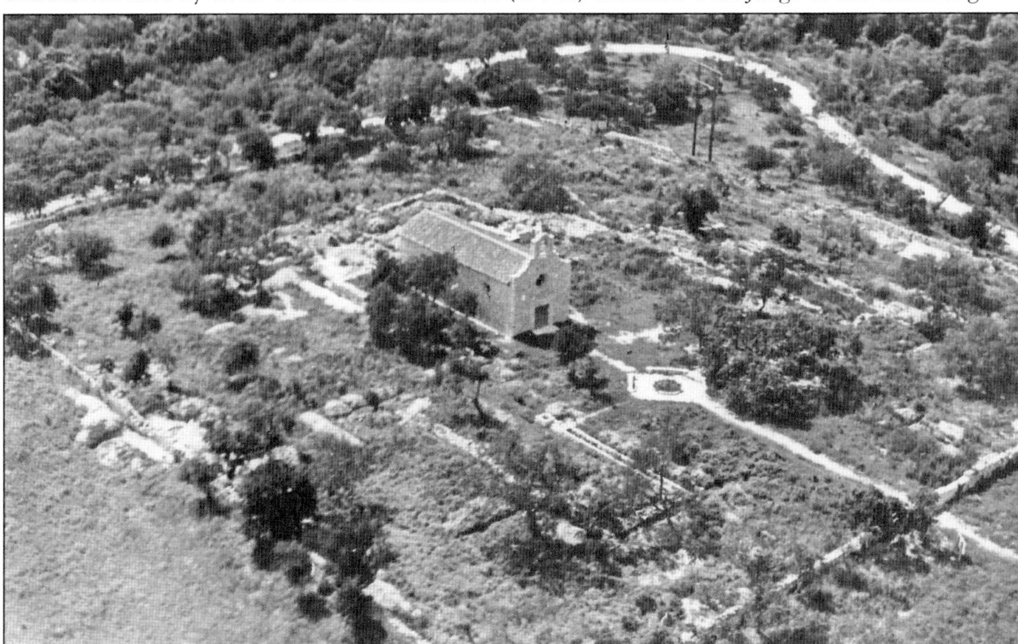

The work of the CWA was not altogether successful. Their major achievement was the reconstruction of what they thought was the chapel; it turned out to be the granary, and it was not restored in an entirely accurate manner. This aerial view shows the completed building with its walkway and entrance to the east of the building. The placement of the entrance to the mission was also incorrect. (Courtesy of Goliad County Library.)

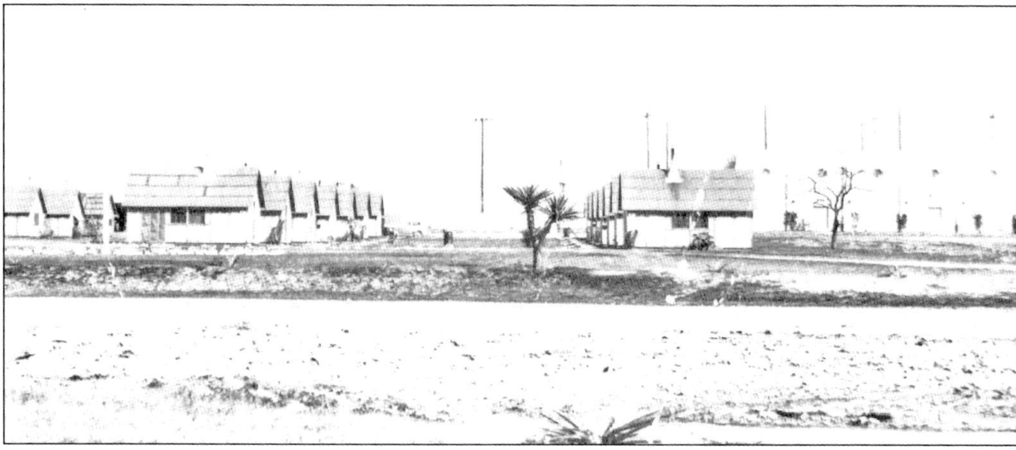

In 1935, the CCC took over the project. They built this camp, across the road from the ruins, and were active until 1941 and World War II. The CCC brought a new level of professionalism to the restoration. They brought in archaeologists from the University of Texas to research the site and hired experienced and highly qualified architects to direct the work.

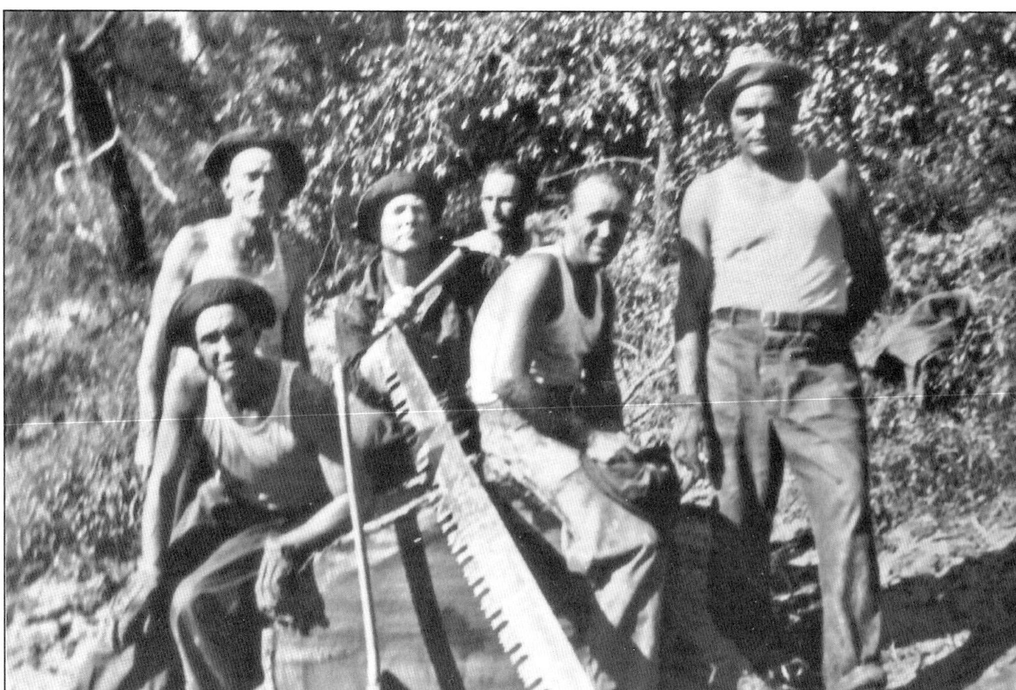

These CCC workers are taking a break. As can be seen, they are older than most CCC workers. The Goliad workers were veterans of the Spanish American War, Boxer Rebellion, and World War I. They established a full life in their camp, featuring classes, crafts, and entertainment. For their monthly dances (held Friday nights in the mess hall) they dispatched trucks to Goliad and Victoria to bring in local girls.

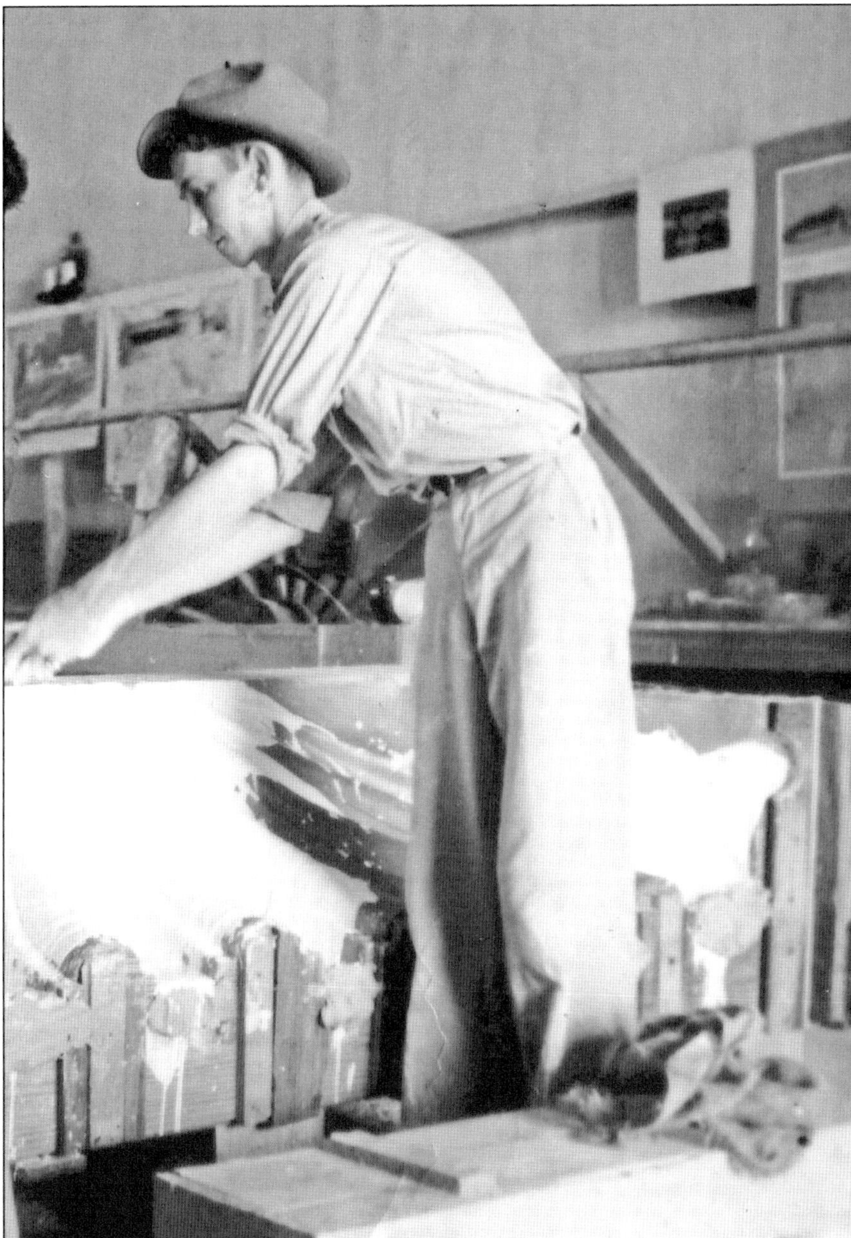

The person most responsible for shaping the restoration of the mission was architect Raiford Leak Stripling, who became a major figure in Goliad life. He had extensive training as an architect, and in the 1930s, assisted Samuel Vosper in designing a new Texas A&M campus. Because of their expertise in Spanish Revival architecture, the two of them were brought to Goliad to supervise the restoration of Espiritu Santo; Stripling eventually became head of the project. The CCC corrected errors to the granary, rebuilt the church and workshops, and also constructed other buildings for the state park. Stripling married a local woman, Roberta Ragland, and established residence in town for several years. In the 1960s, he came back to direct the restoration of the Presidio La Bahia and to design the Zaragoza house (see pages 108–110 and 117). (Courtesy of Goliad County Library.)

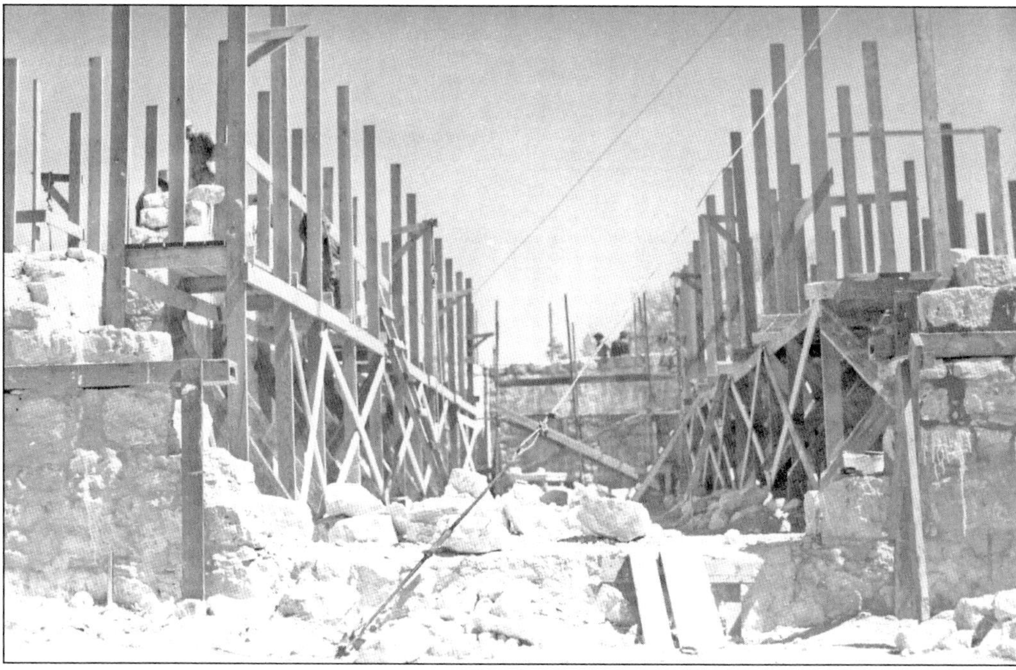

These photographs show the kind of work done during the restoration at the mission. The picture above of the church shows how the buildings were essentially rebuilt from the ground up, based on the research of the leadership team. The picture below shows work on the nearly completed chapel (with the granary to the left). (Courtesy of Texas Department of Parks and Wildlife.)

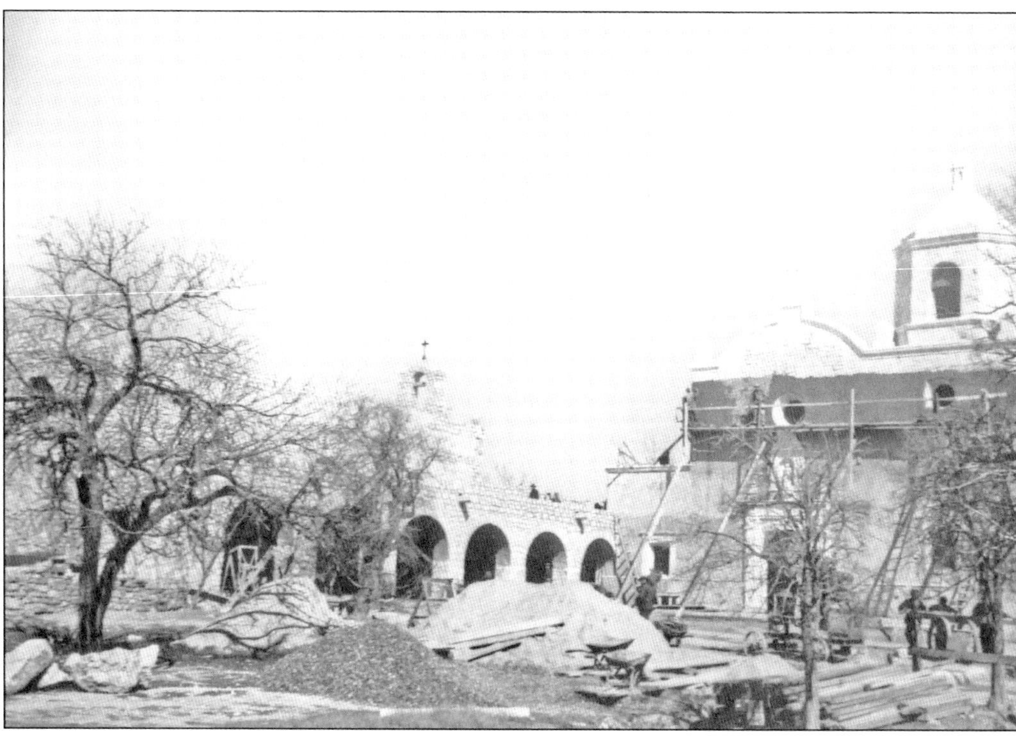

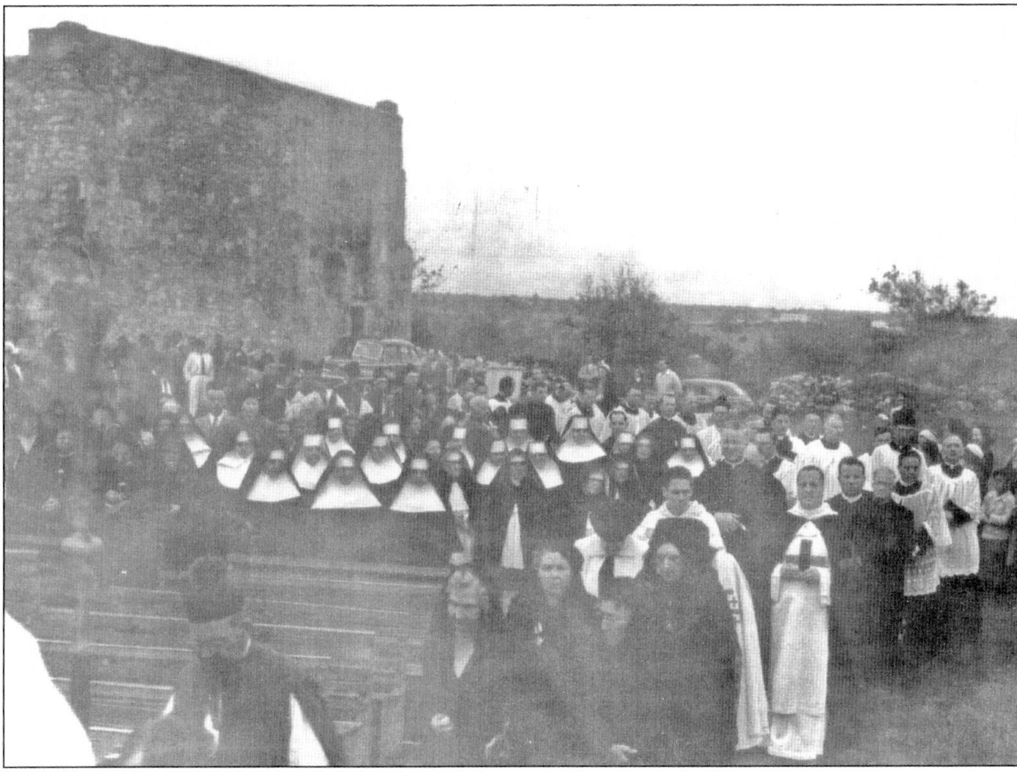

In 1936, there were many celebrations of Texas Independence, including this Pontifical Mass attended by 10,000 at the chapel of Presidio La Bahia. A big part of Goliad's celebration was a trip to San Antonio for a special presence at San Antonio's Fiesta Battle of Flowers. Over 400 people from Goliad took the trip, including the band and five floats.

As part of the Texas Centennial celebration, Goliad acquired an auditorium (with stadium seating on one side). It was referred to as a memorial auditorium, was dedicated in 1937, and has been a central feature of Goliad life ever since. Over the years, major bands have played there—Phil Harris, Count Basie, and Jimmy Dorsey for example—and it has hosted sports events, high school graduations, and banquets. In 1986, a Sesquicentennial Ball raised money to begin repairing and refurbishing the building. (Courtesy of Texas Department of Parks and Wildlife.)

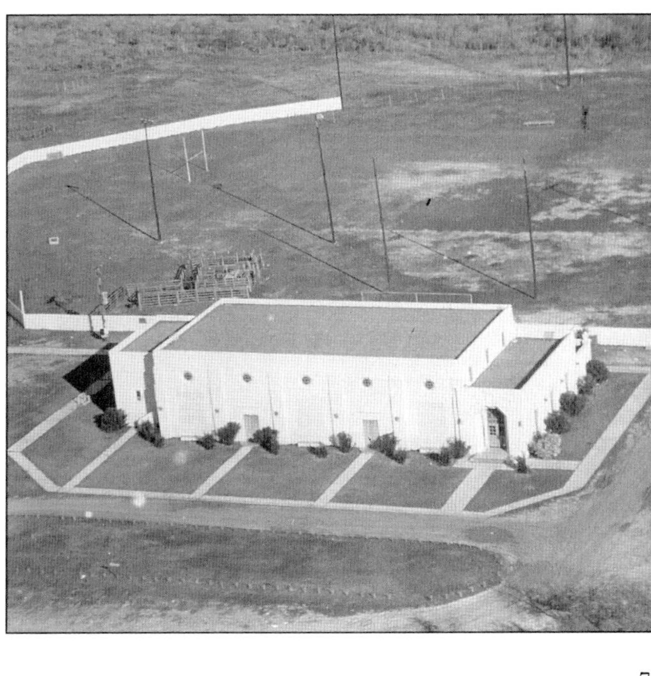

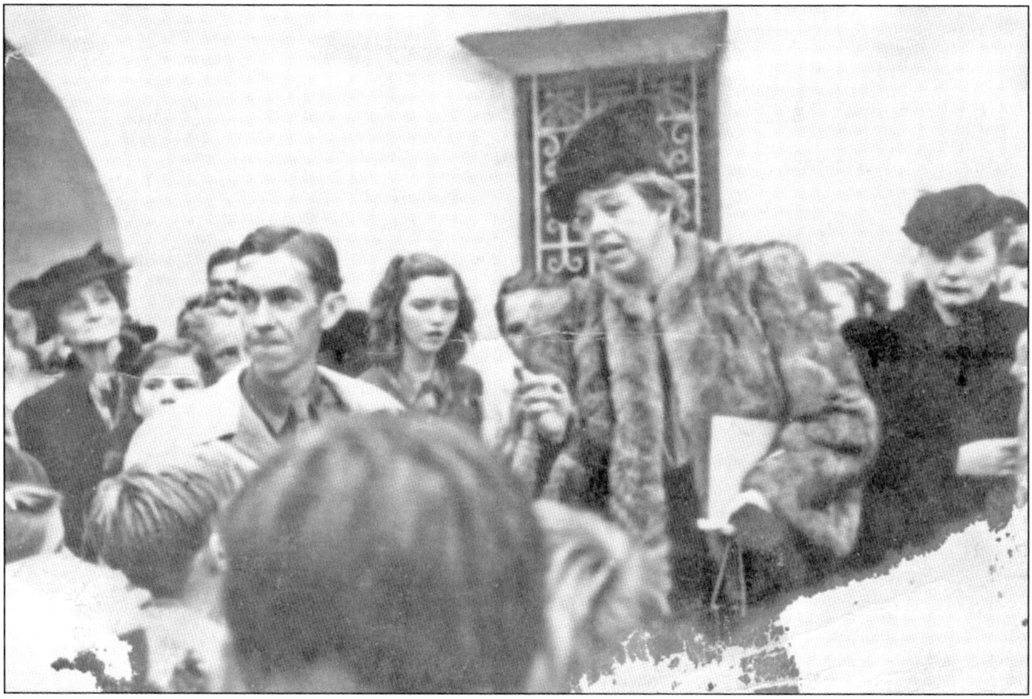

The president's wife, Eleanor Roosevelt, visited in 1940 to see the CCC's historical reconstruction work. Goliad was not originally on the First Lady's itinerary, but Judge White talked her into making a visit. She commented, "I think the work here is wonderful." Eleanor Roosevelt is in front of the restored mission; to her left is Raiford Stripling. (Courtesy of Texas Department of Parks and Wildlife.)

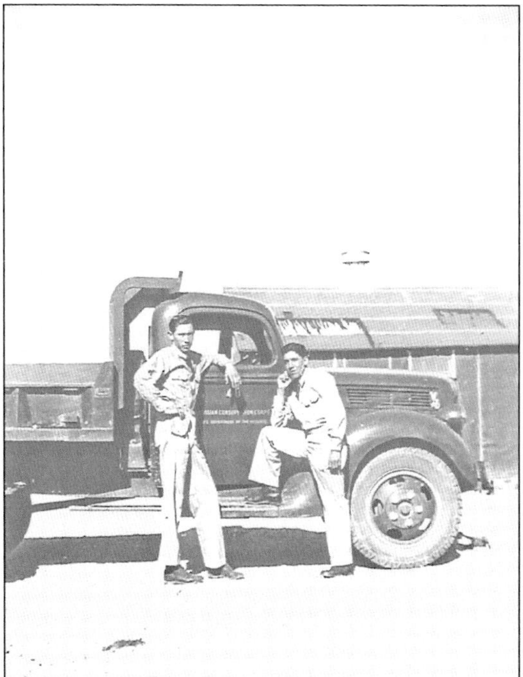

Most people in Goliad think of the CCC as the group that rebuilt the mission. In fact, it was also the organization young men joined to find work and to help their families during financial crisis. Two men from Goliad who joined were close friends Raul C. Martinez (left) and Julian Flores. They were sent to Kennedy and then to Carlsbad, New Mexico, before World War II ended the CCC. (Courtesy of Estella Zermeno.)

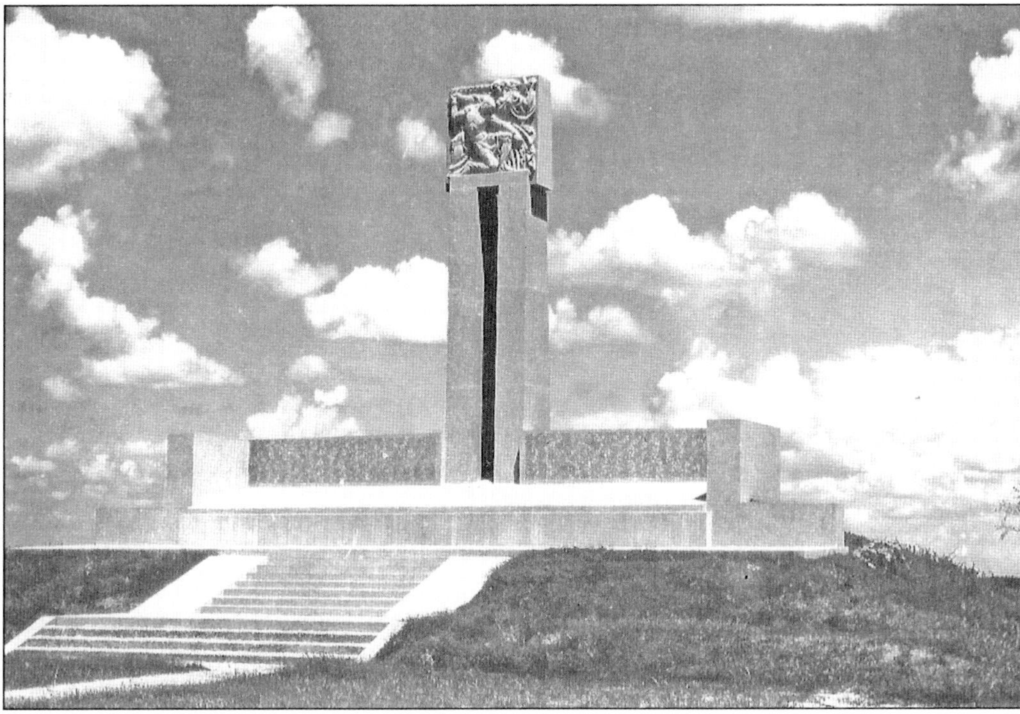

The absence of proper protection for the grave site of Fannin and his men's remains had long concerned Goliad. Over the years, efforts had been made to identify the exact location of the grave site and to protect it. As part of the Texas Centennial celebrations, plans were made for a suitable monument. It was designed by Austin architect Donald Nelson, and the sculpture was done by Raoul Jossett. The monument is of Texas granite, and it was the largest granite marker erected by the Centennial Commission. The dedication was held on June 4, 1939, the anniversary of Gen. Thomas Rusk's burial of the bodies in 1836. The speaker shown at the dedication ceremony is D. B. Hardeman, the great-grandson of Massacre survivor J. H. Barnard.

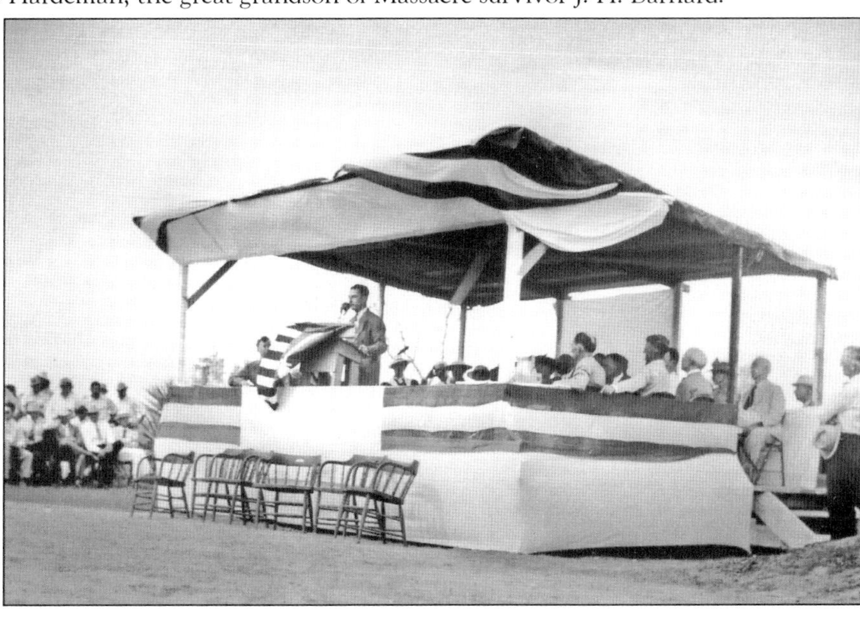

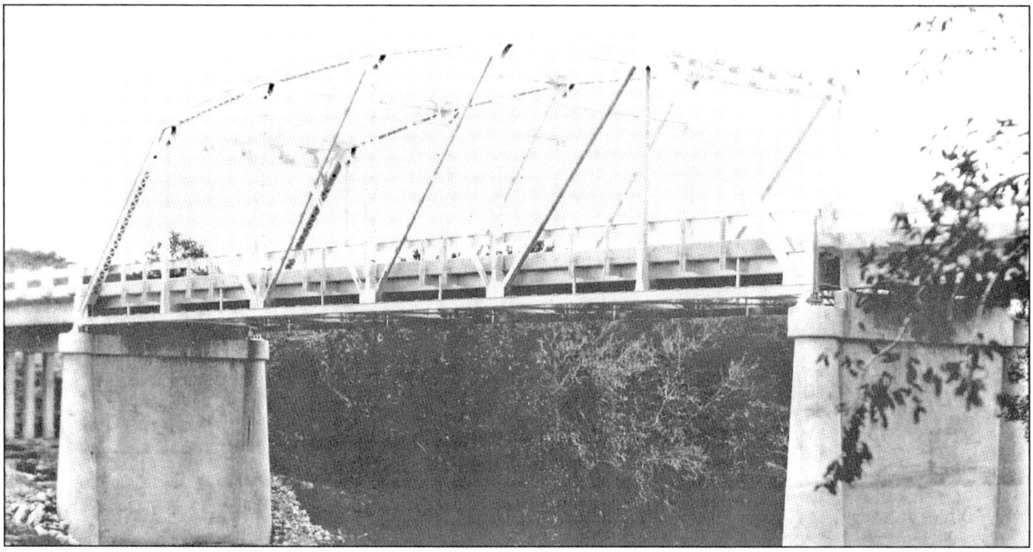

This major concrete bridge with a span of 120 feet over the San Antonio River was named after Judge White for all his contributions to the area. He said the dedication "will be treasured . . . as one of the most pleasing incidents of my life." The bridge was part of the first system of paved roads in Goliad County, which began in 1930.

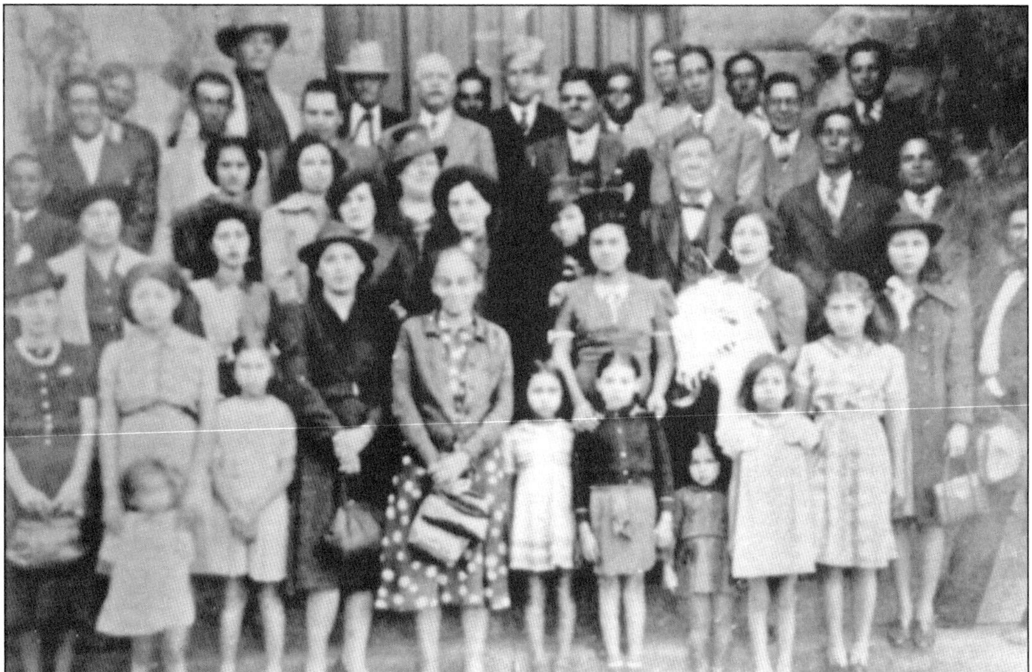

In 1929, Latin Americans formed LULAC to improve the Tejanos' circumstances. Under the leadership of Placido Martinez, Goliad established a chapter in 1932 and in 1937 hosted this convention. LULAC, nationally and in Goliad, fought to end widespread segregation against Hispanics (in restaurants and theatres, for example), to secure their constitutional right to vote, and most importantly, to end segregation in schools and improve the quality of education available to Mexican American children.

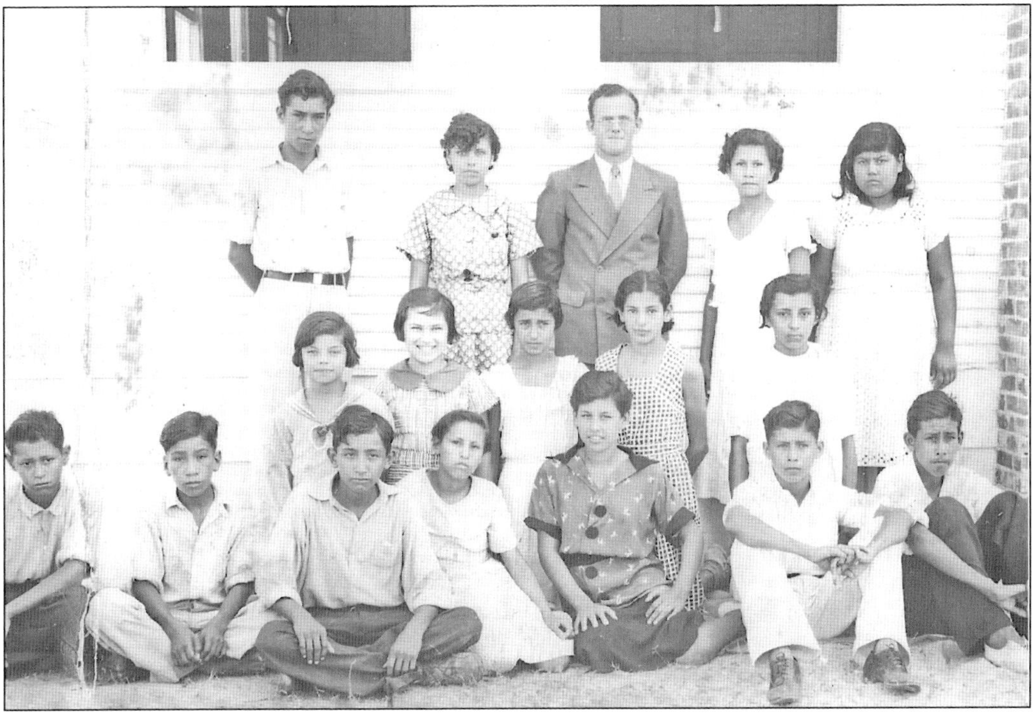

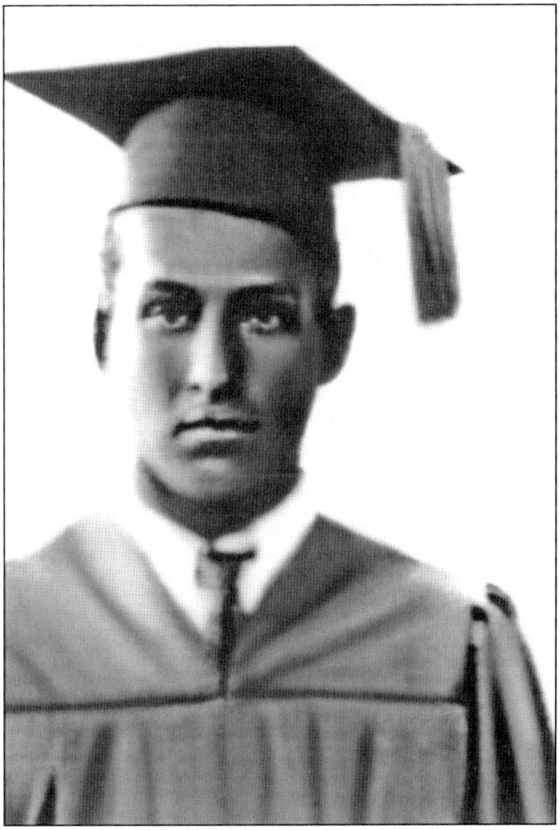

These students are the fourth- through seventh-grade classes of Goliad's Mexican School in 1935. At that time, Mexican children were segregated into this school; African American children attended a separate school nearby. These schools ended with the seventh grade, and it was assumed the students would not be educated beyond that point. One bright student, William Carbajal, fought the system and in 1935 became the first Hispanic student to graduate from the Goliad high school. It took efforts locally and in Austin to break the segregation. Even then, when William reported to the high school, he was forced to sit on the school steps for three days before he was finally admitted to classes. The segregation of public schools did not end until 1948. (Courtesy of Estella Zermeno.)

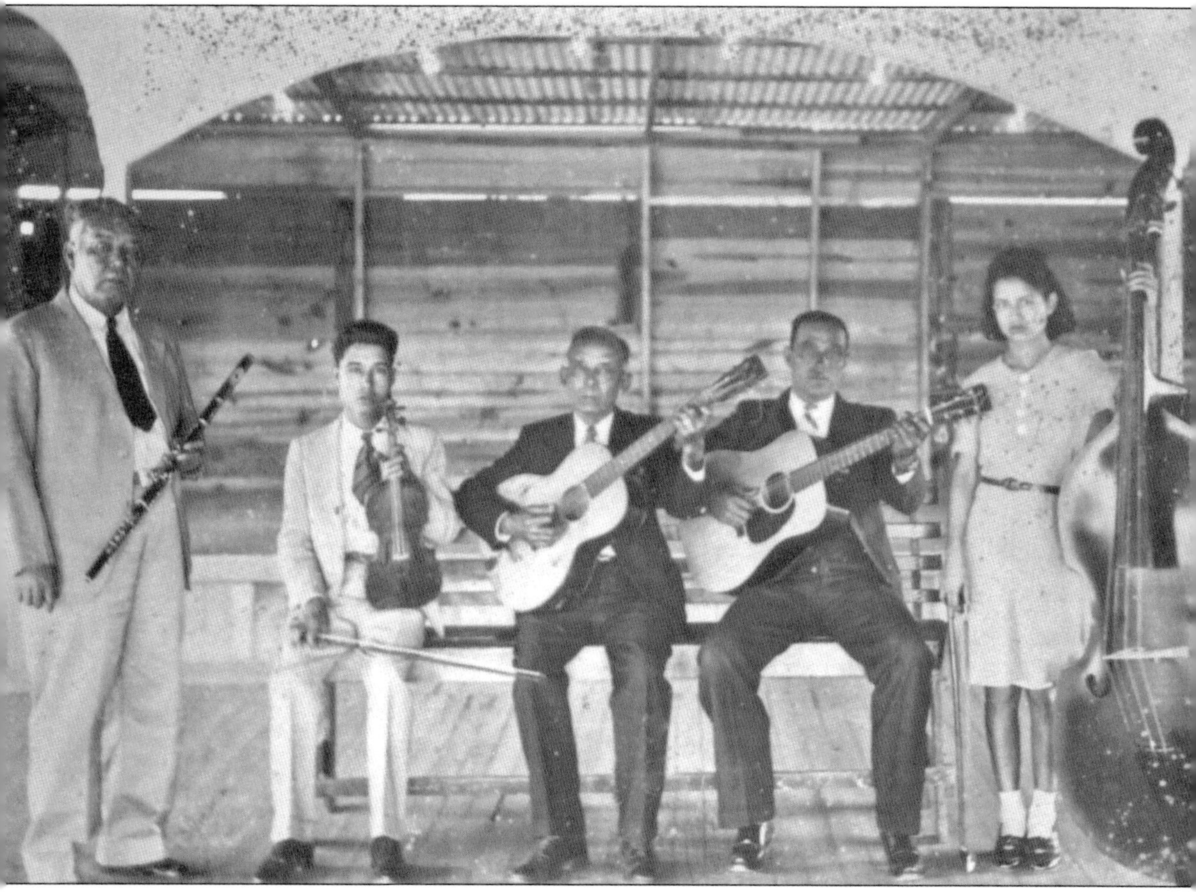

The Perez Orchestra was a major Goliad institution. Organized in 1893 by Hipolito, Esteban, Domingo, and Pedro Perez, it flourished for over 40 years. The group played locally and regionally at dance halls, private parties, weddings, festivals, and for special occasions, such as to serenade recruits leaving for the war or for Eleanor Roosevelt. This 1939 picture shows, from left to right, Pedro, Domingo, Estevan, Luis, and Maria Perez in Perez Hall, located in La Bahia. Maria was the daughter of Pedro, and both played piano and bass and sang. Pedro led the Orchestra from the 1920s until he went off to World War II. Domingo was killed during the war, and the family was so devastated that the orchestra ceased to exist in the 1940s. The wooden frame music hall, which the Orchestra built in La Bahia, served for years as a community meeting place for the residents of the neighborhood.

The Goliad County Courthouse took a beating in 1942 when a hurricane inflicted serious damage to the building. It knocked down most of the towers and turrets, which were an important part of the building's Second Empire architecture. Afterwards, the county chose not to replace those features but repaired the building (at a cost of $6,525) without them. It did keep as many original decorative features as possible. This left a much less distinguished building than the original. After a row over whether to raze or expand the courthouse in the early 1960s, the county remodeled and enlarged the building at a cost of $289,500.

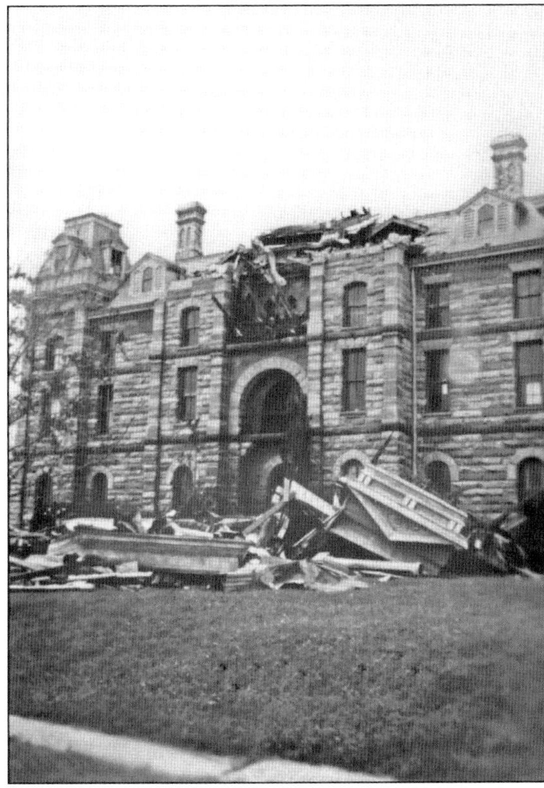

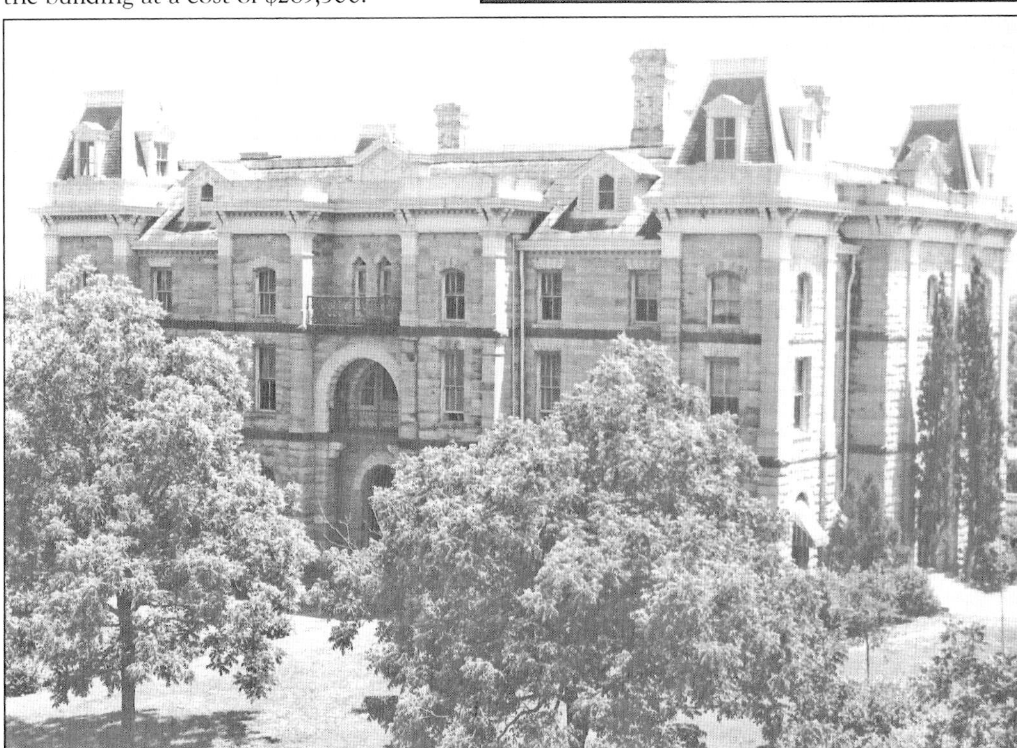

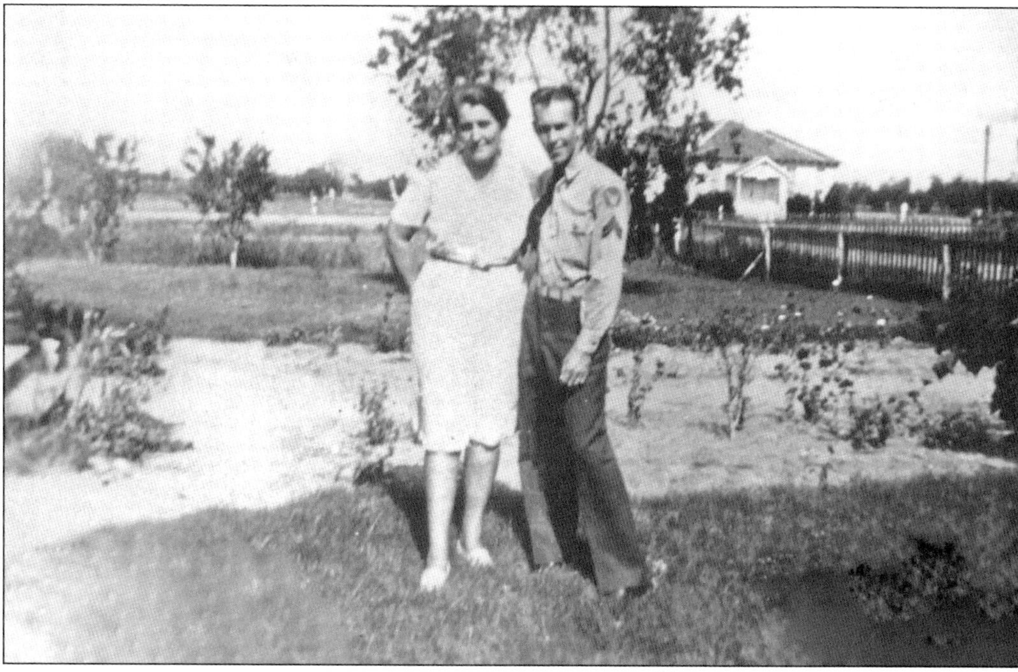

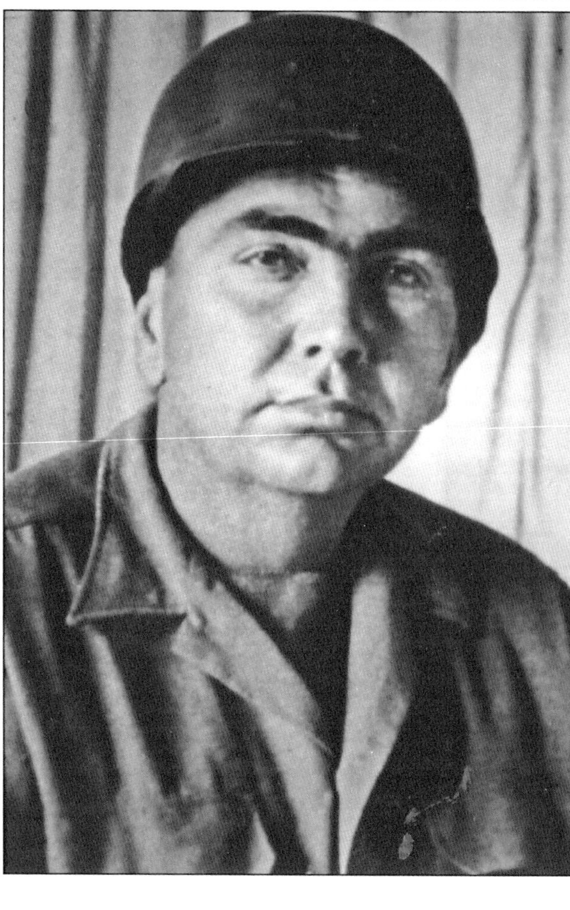

World War II had an immense impact on Goliad. Many Goliad men served in the war; the monument on the courthouse lawn honoring them lists 32 who died in battle. The photographs above shows Myron Reuter of Fannin in 1942 with his mother, Mellie Reute. At left is Cyrus White of Judge White's family, in uniform. Both men survived the war. (Left, courtesy of Goliad County Library.)

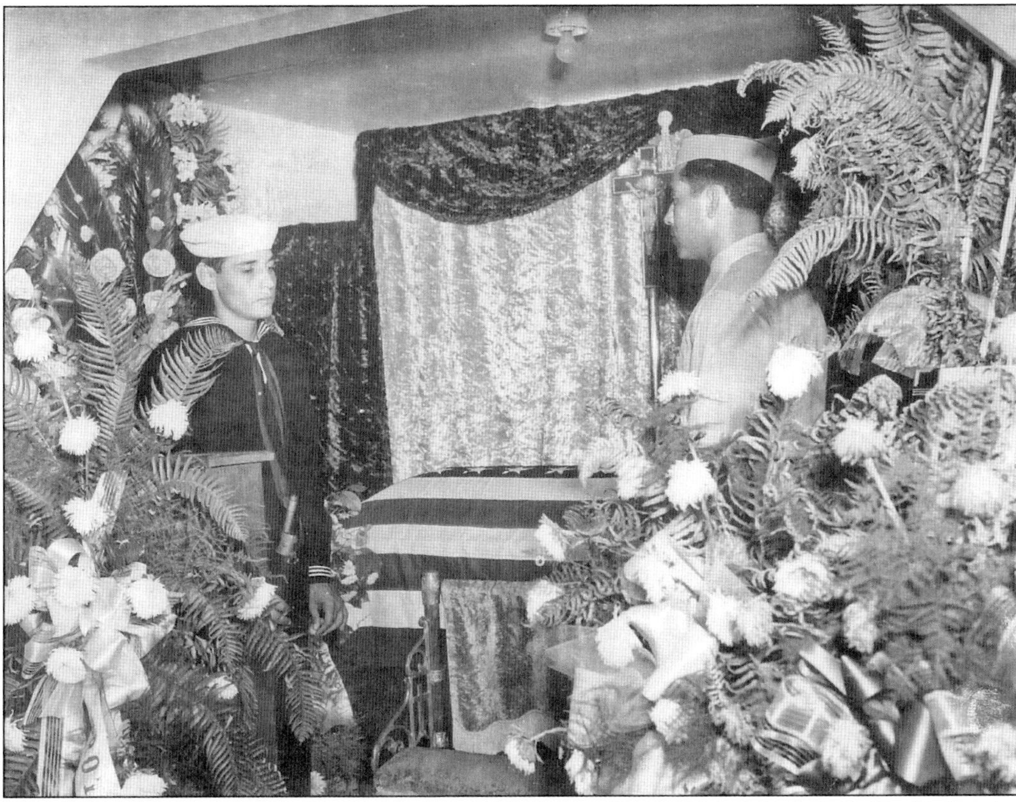

The Carbajal family of La Bahia lost much in the war. Gilberto Carbajal was killed in Holland in October 1944. His remains were not located and returned home until 1949. Above, his casket lies in state in the home of his parents, Anastacio and Pomposa A. Carbajal, with an honor guard of Victor Guzman (left) and Alfred Rubio. Later, his very elaborate funeral was held at Our Lady of Loreto chapel of Presidio La Bahia, as seen below. (Above, courtesy of Estella Zermeno.)

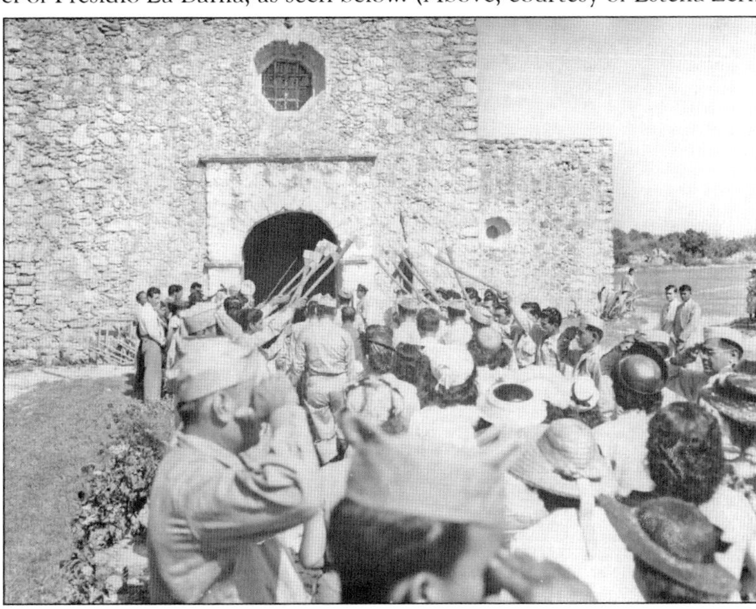

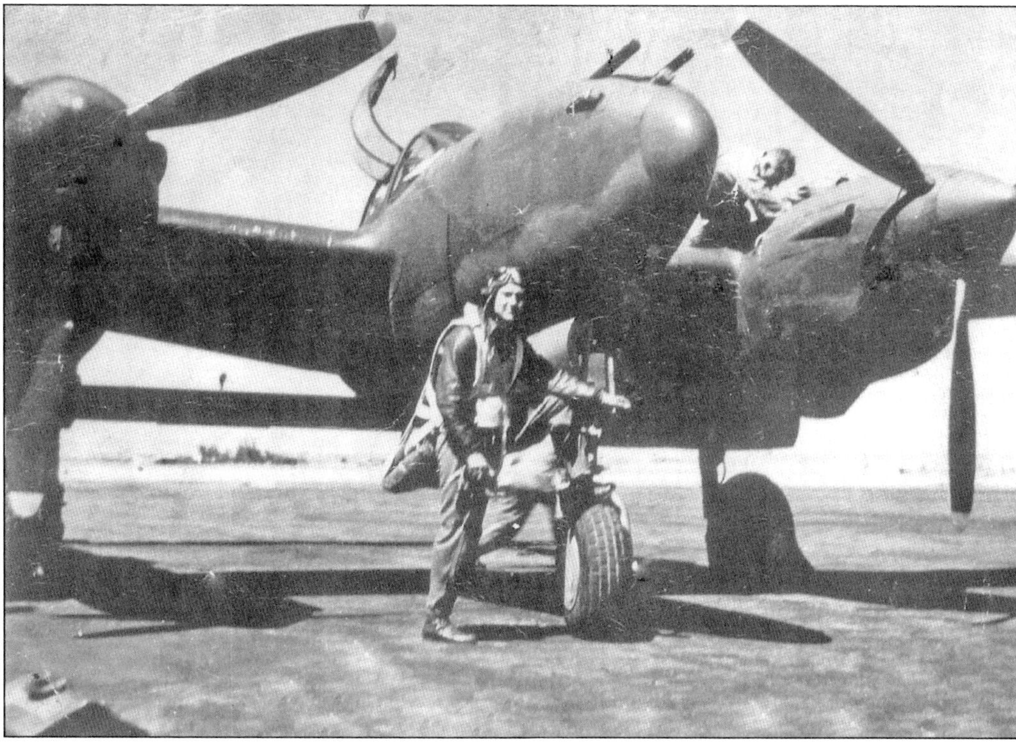

Gilberto's brother Benny Carbajal was a flyer. He is shown with his plane at Kingscliffe, England, where he was stationed. Gilberto was shot down over Germany in January 1944, but his remains were not found until 1951. He was only identified by his dog tags. His remains were not returned home but are buried in Europe. (Courtesy of Estella Zermeno.)

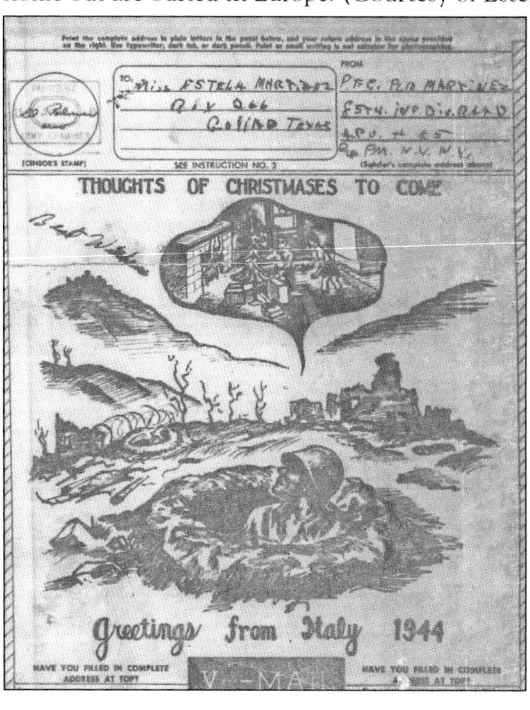

Soldiers in World War II often communicated with family back home through "V-Mail." This is an example of a Christmas letter sent from Polo Martinez to his sister Estella Martinez of Goliad, whose name is misspelled on the form. He was with the 85th Infantry Division of the 5th Army and served in the African and Italian campaigns. (Courtesy of Estella Zermeno.)

Six

The Rural Communities of Goliad County

Since Goliad County was created by the Republic of Texas, the town of Goliad has always been the center of the county. As county seat, it has been the legal and administrative center. It has been the chief commercial focus of the county. Goliad town has also been the social, educational, and cultural leader of the area, but the majority of the people of Goliad County have never lived in the town and still do not. Most have lived in a large number of small rural communities scattered throughout the county. No history of Goliad would be complete without consideration of those rural communities.

The towns were established at various times between the 1840s and the 1890s. They universally included churches and schools, and the larger ones had a sizeable array of commercial and service businesses. All the towns had a strong sense of identity.

They flourished, for the most part, until the World War II era. Some declined after major fires; others declined because paved roads made it possible to shop in larger stores in Goliad and Victoria. The decline of such industries as cotton farming and cotton gins hurt many of the towns. The consolidation of all the schools into a Goliad county system in the 1940s did much to erode the towns. World War II and post-war prosperity pulled people out as they sought better jobs.

Today many of the towns—Angel City, Riverdale, Cummingsville, Dobskyville, and Tusselville—have completely disappeared; often all that is left is a cemetery. Others—Ander, Weser, Charco, and Schroeder—are mere shadows of their previous selves. The largest rural communities left are Berclair, which still has around 250 residents; Weesatche with over 400; and Fannin with about 350 residents, and none of them have the wide array of stores and services they once harbored. They are now essentially bedroom communities for Goliad or neighboring towns.

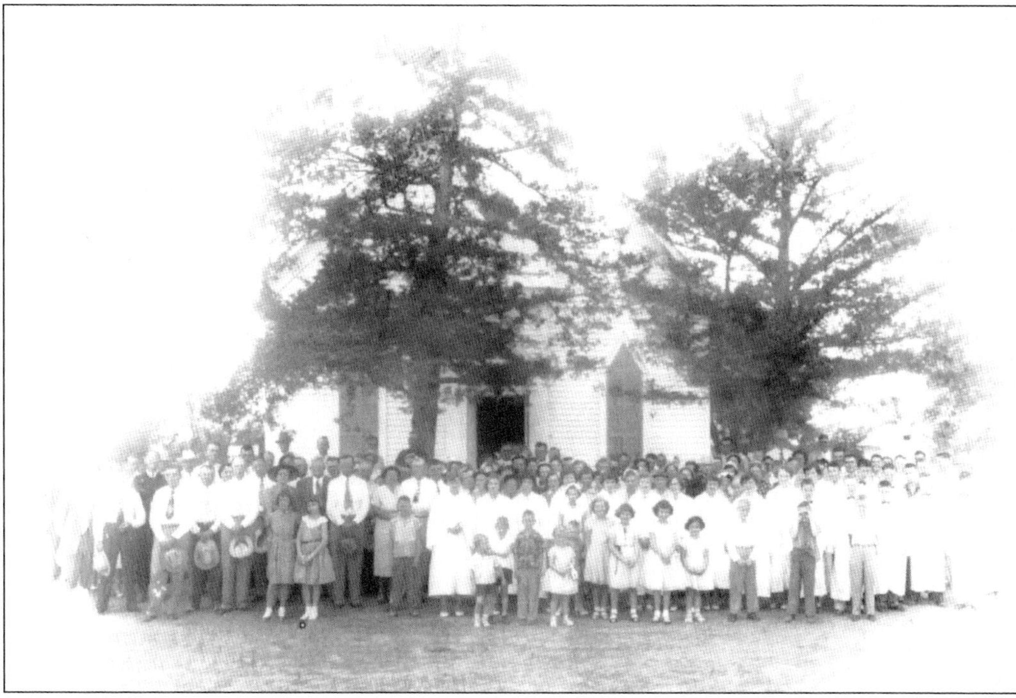

Ander, like most of the northern county towns, was originally settled by people from Germany; in fact, its first name was Hanover. Because of that German background, its church was Lutheran. St. Peters was founded in the 1870s and was the first Lutheran church in Goliad County. For some time, the pastor also acted as a schoolteacher for the town.

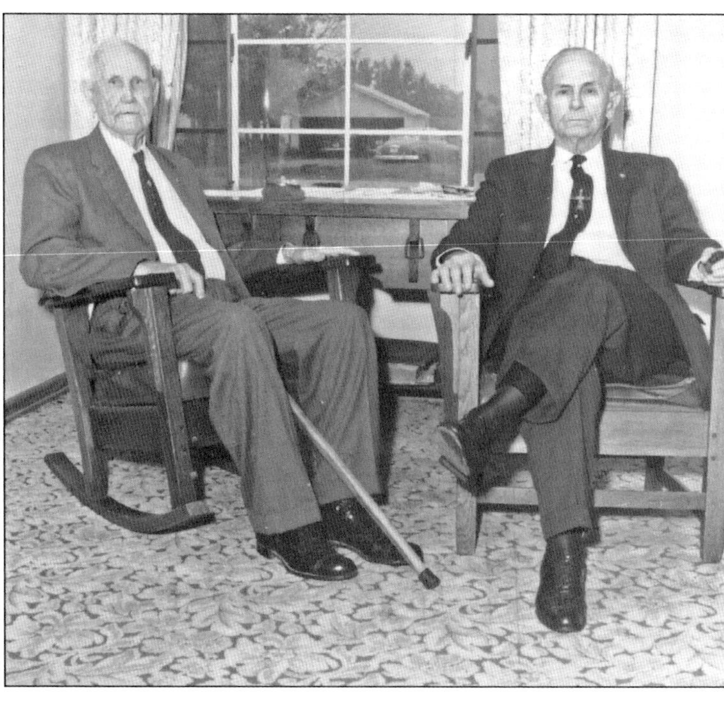

Most of the small towns in the county were full-fledged communities. Ander, for example, had a saloon, a cotton gin, a store, and a blacksmith shop. For most of its history, it also had a doctor. The first was a Doctor Hooper, followed by Dr. Henry Abel, Doctor Yates, Doctor Robertson, and finally Dr. Nathan Elder (right). He is shown with community leader Fred C. Albrecht.

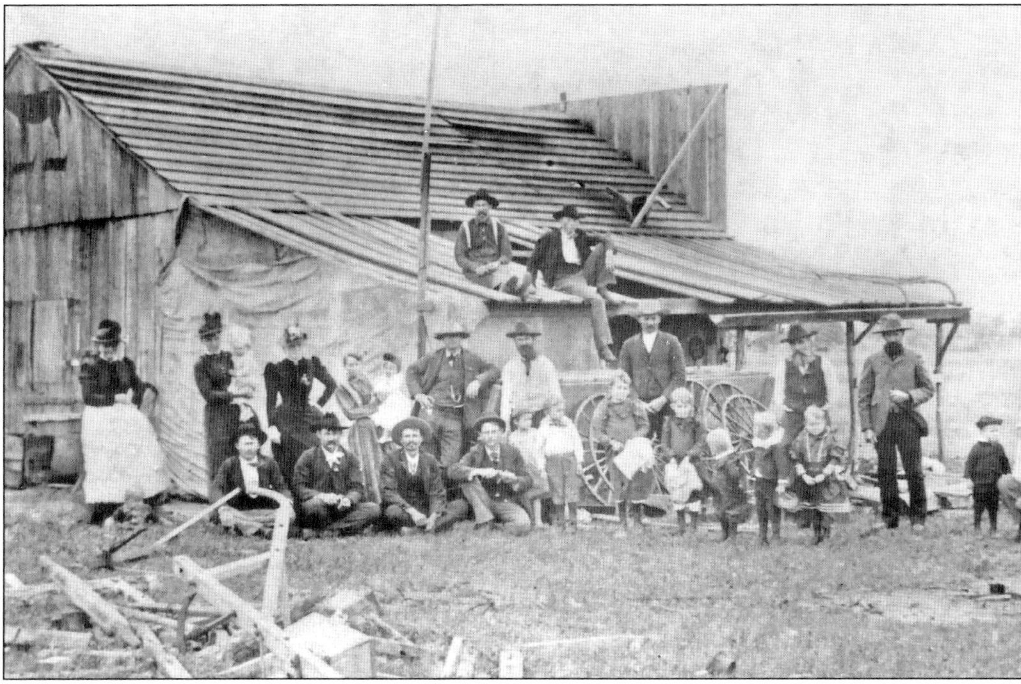

The blacksmith shop was a major part of the Ander community. It was located between the Ander store and the Lutheran church. After the arrival of automobiles, the blacksmith shop became a garage and filling station. This picture from the late 1800s shows owner Louis Jacobs standing fourth from the left. Mrs. Jacobs is the first person standing.

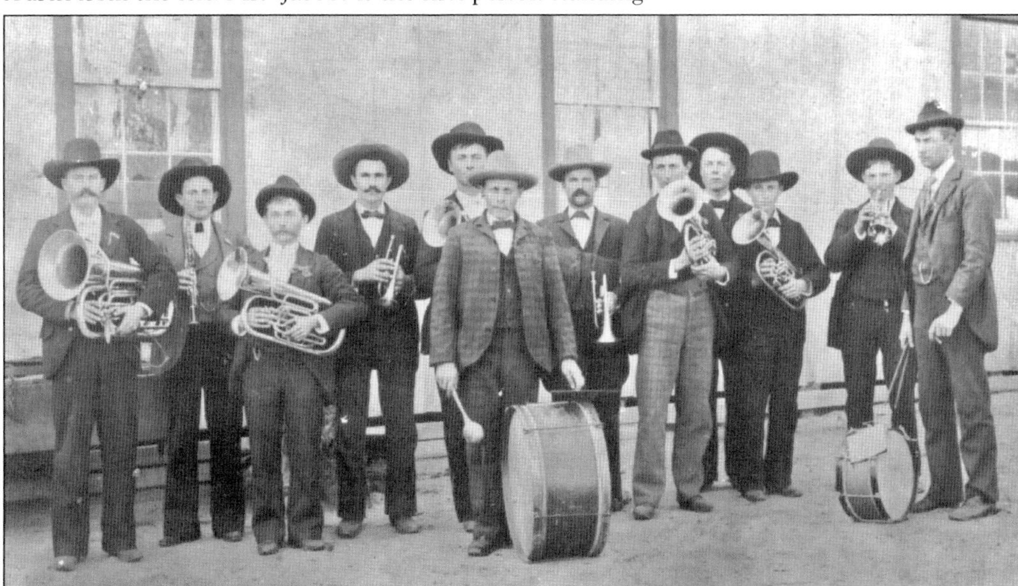

The nearby town of Weser was also settled by mostly German and Eastern Europeans. It, too, was a full-fledged town with a wide range of stores and a post office. One of Weser's main focuses was music, as was common with German communities. It had a round dance hall and, in the early 1900s, a brass band. The names of its members show the ethnic makeup of the community: Albrecht, Arnold, Pfenniger, Dohman, Loeste, Gudat, Arnecker, and Boehl.

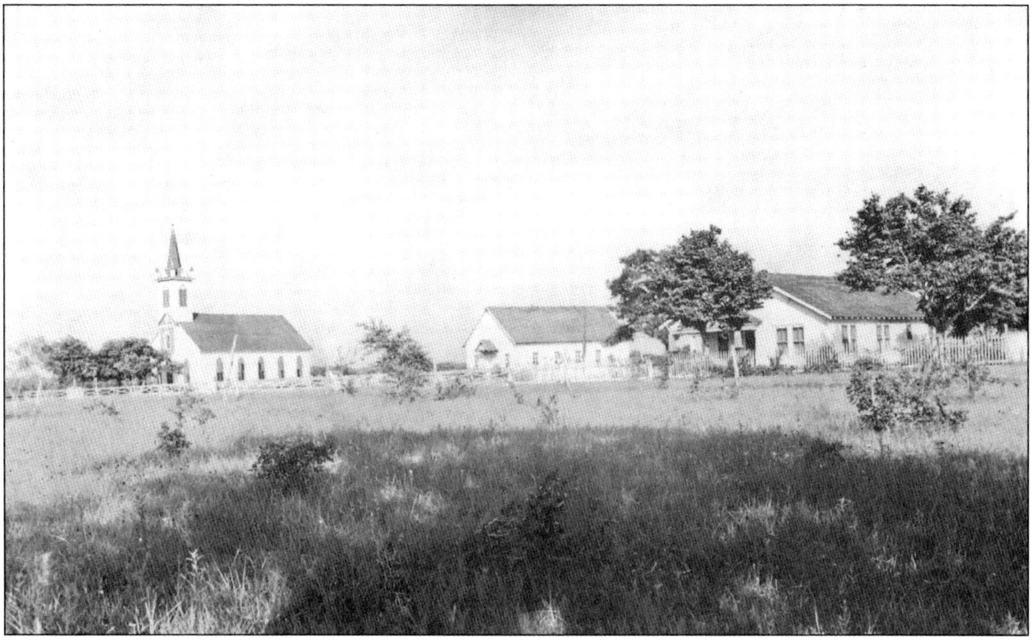

Yet another town in the north county with a primarily German population was Germantown. The town had been settled in the 1840s. In time, it also had a full array of businesses and services. Like most rural communities, the church was the core of the community; in this case, it was St. Luke's Lutheran Church. Because of the hostility to Germans during World War I, the town was renamed Schroeder after Paul Schroeder, the first man from the town killed in that war.

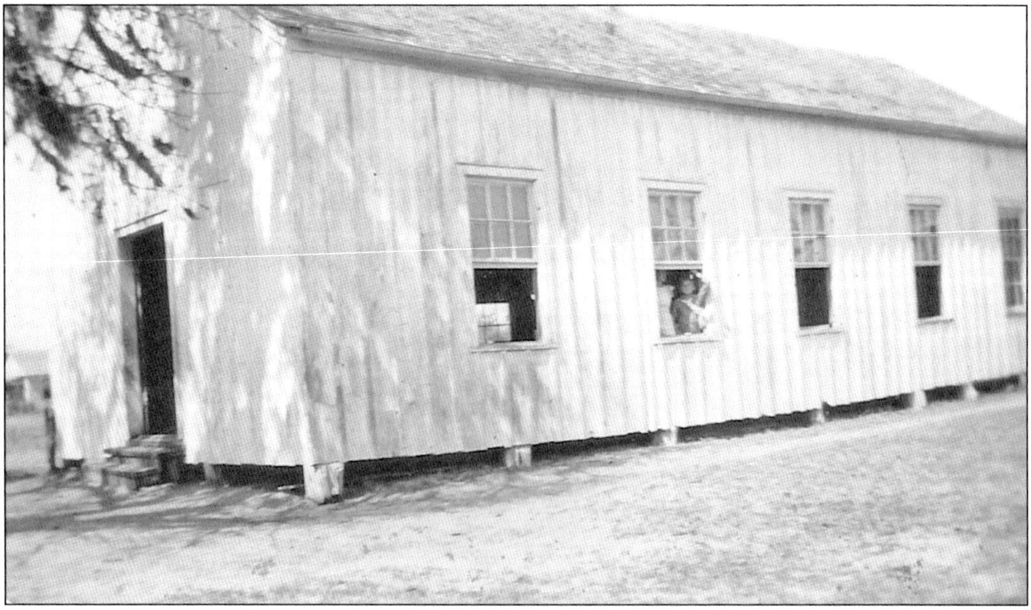

Schroeder had its own public school, like most of the rural towns prior to the consolidation of schools in the 1940s. It was called Germantown School. Its building was used as a school until 1950, when it became a community center.

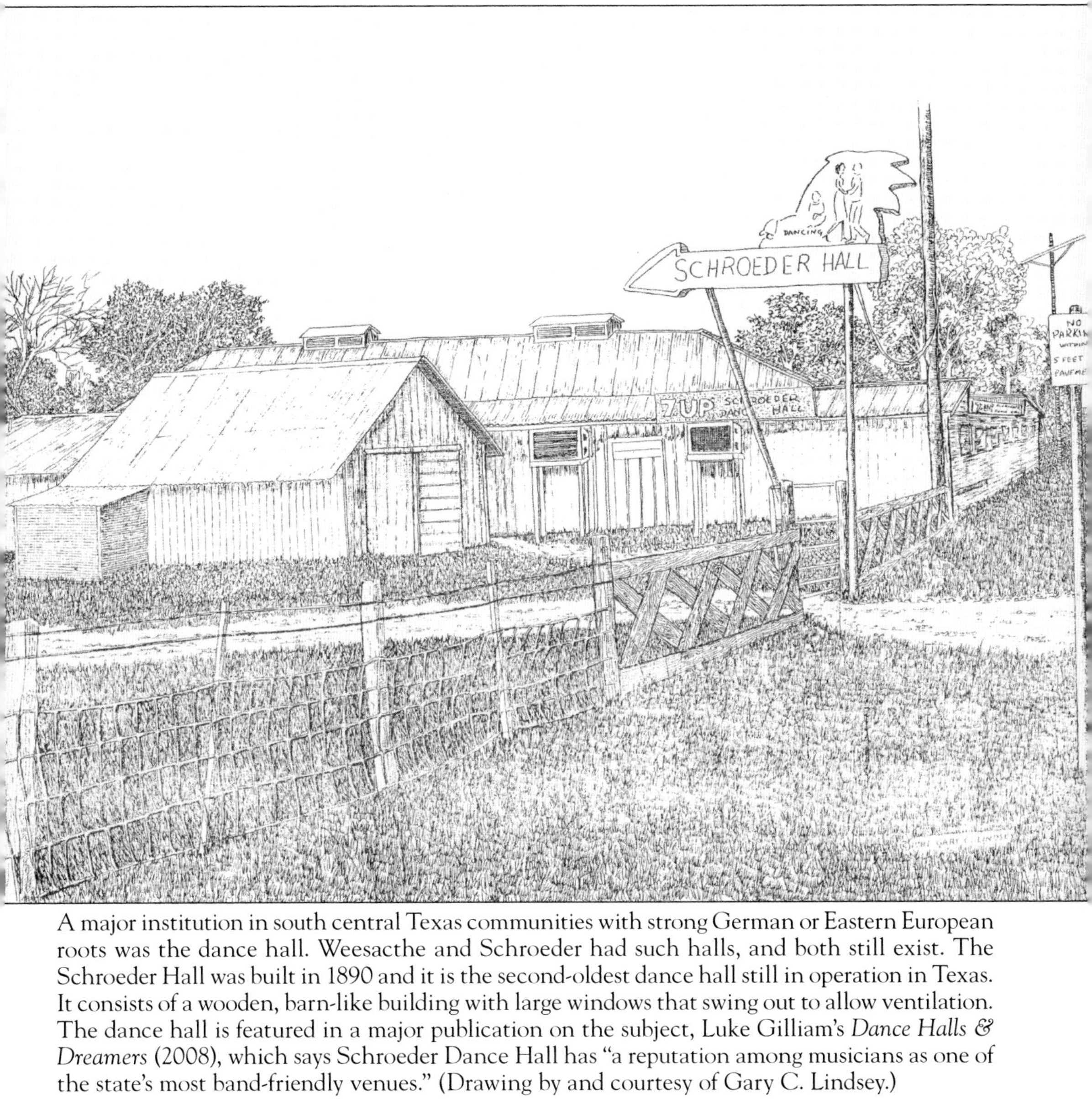

A major institution in south central Texas communities with strong German or Eastern European roots was the dance hall. Weesacthe and Schroeder had such halls, and both still exist. The Schroeder Hall was built in 1890 and it is the second-oldest dance hall still in operation in Texas. It consists of a wooden, barn-like building with large windows that swing out to allow ventilation. The dance hall is featured in a major publication on the subject, Luke Gilliam's *Dance Halls & Dreamers* (2008), which says Schroeder Dance Hall has "a reputation among musicians as one of the state's most band-friendly venues." (Drawing by and courtesy of Gary C. Lindsey.)

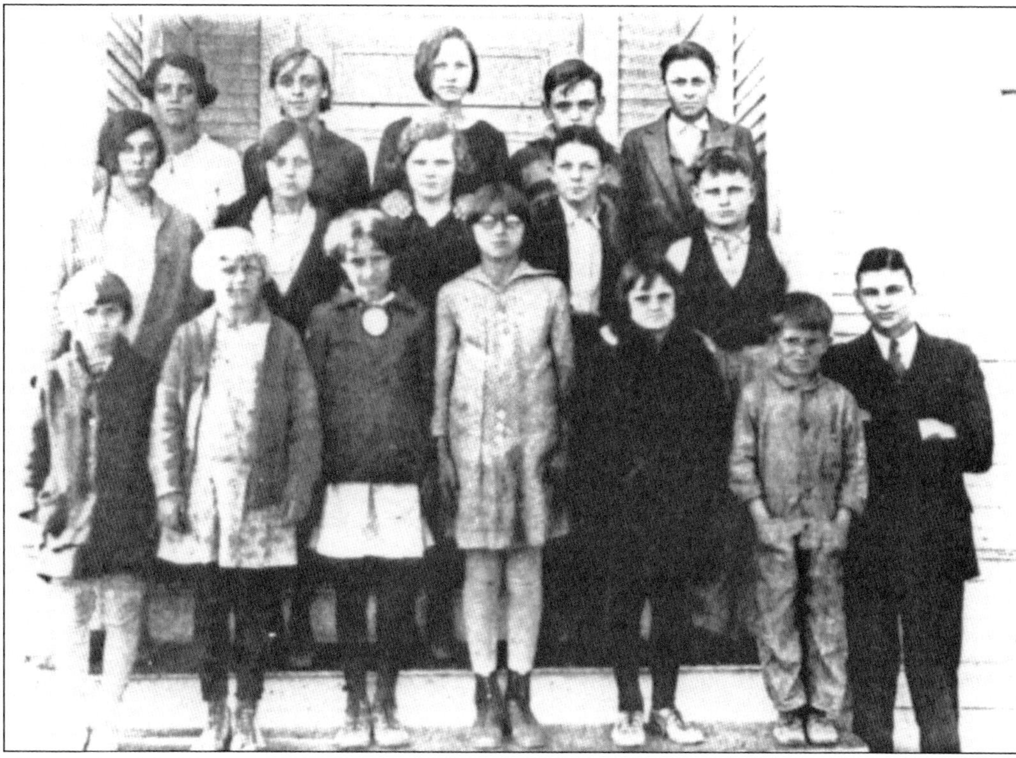

These schoolchildren represent yet another community with strong German ties—Weesatche. Settled in the 1840s, it was originally called Middletown. In 1859, the post office decided it needed a new name since there were other towns called Middletown, so the community chose to name itself after a local plant, the huisache. The post office, however, spelled the word phonetically as Weesatche, which it has been ever since.

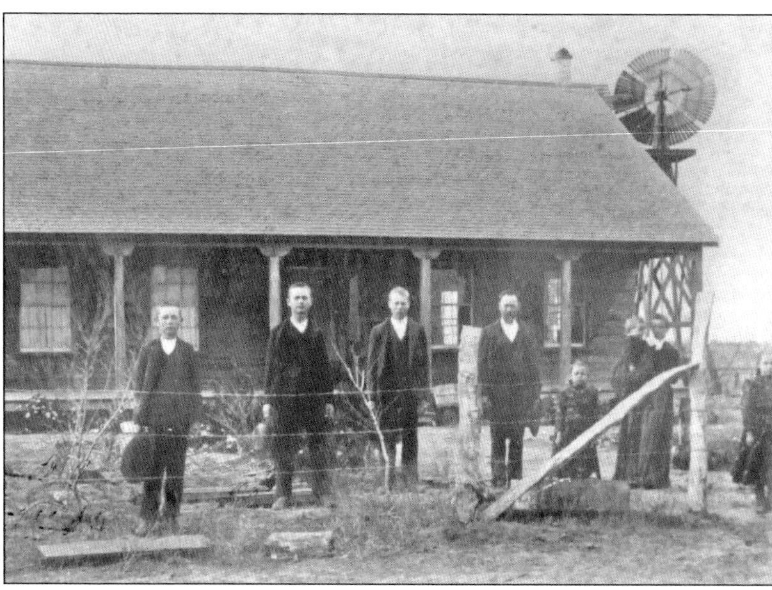

The Dohmann family, lined up in front of their house in 1894, illustrates the German roots of Weesatche. They are, from left to right, Otto; Ferdinand; Werner A.; Werner F., the father; Almeda; baby Norman, being held by Isabel, the mother; and Anna Dohmann. The family is still prominent in the county.

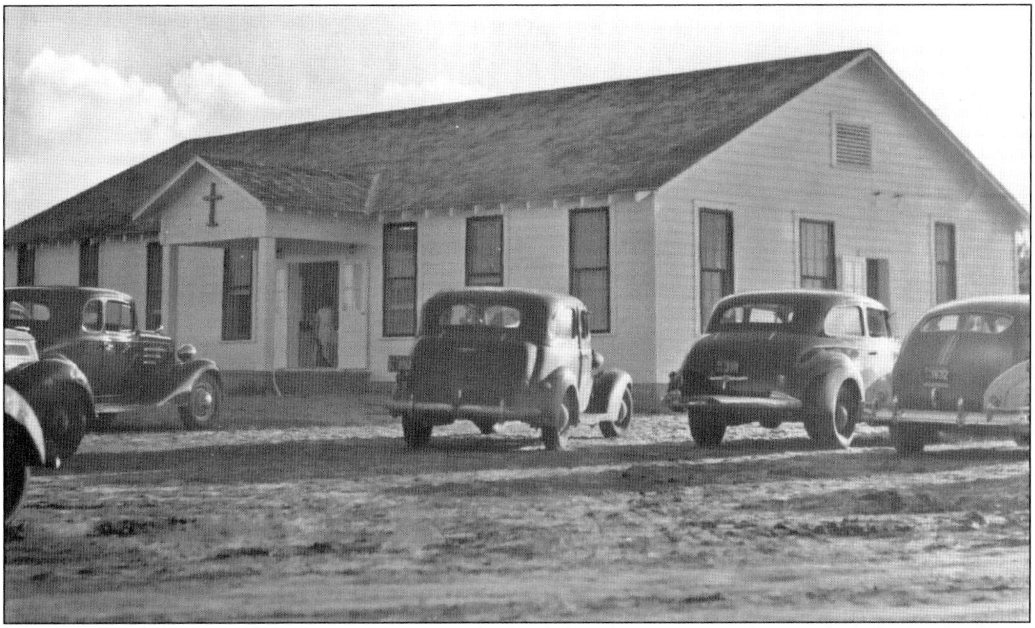

Although it had other churches too, Weesatche had the ubiquitous Lutheran church. St. Andrews was not organized until 1891. It erected a building in 1893, which was replaced in 1929. They also had an educational building and parish hall, shown here in the 1940s.

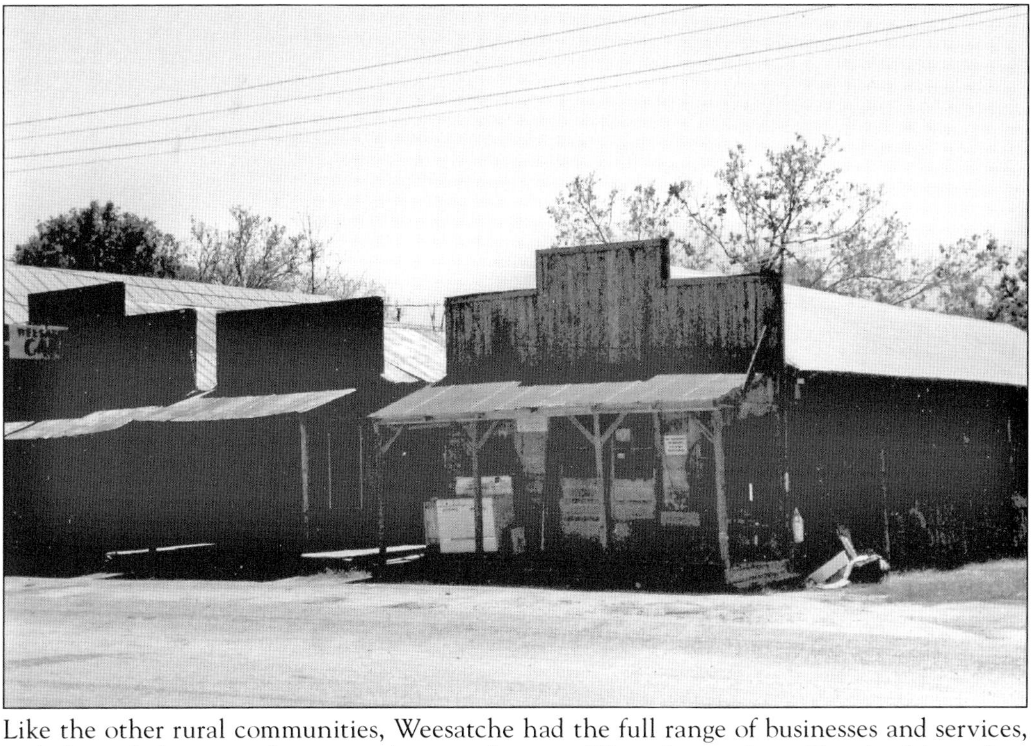

Like the other rural communities, Weesatche had the full range of businesses and services, including a lightning rod agent, a photographer, a saddle maker, and a miller. As this modern photograph of an old business shows, most of the businesses have closed, and the main street is almost a ghost town. (Photograph by Olen Klump; courtesy of Goliad County Library.)

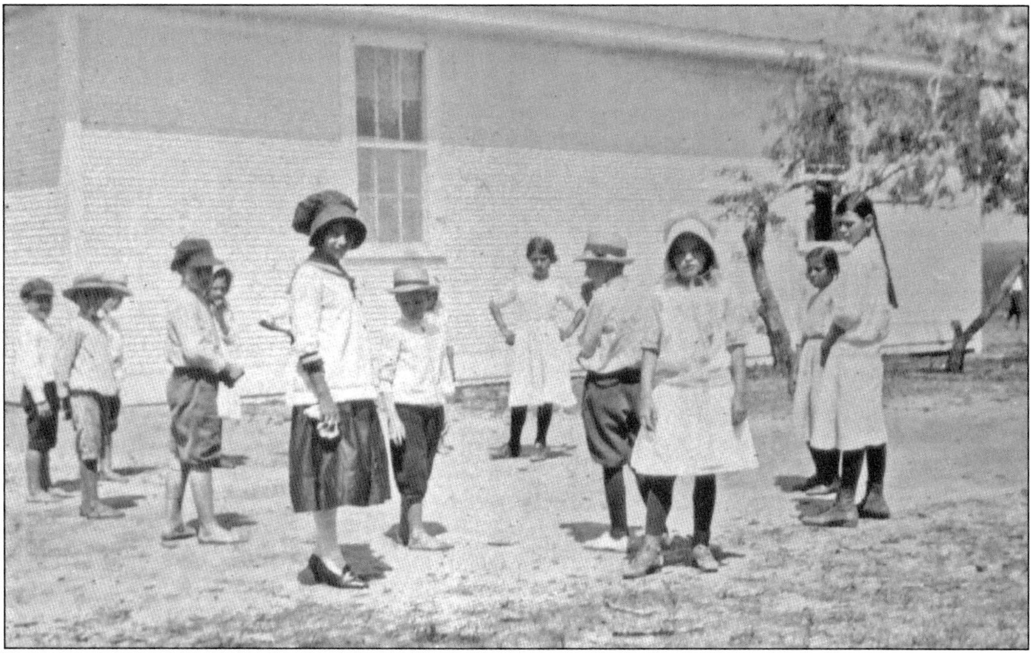

Angel City was unique among Goliad rural towns. It was a "company town" designed to serve the needs of tenant farmers on the Ramsey and other lands. There were several stores, which operated on a credit basis with bills paid at harvest time. There were two schools, one for Anglos and another for Spanish-speaking students. With the decline of cotton farming, tenant farming ended and the town has disappeared.

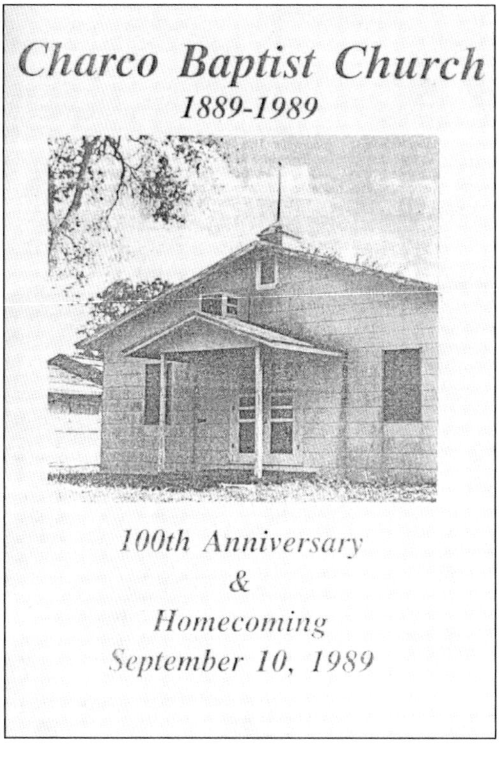

This faded picture of the Charco Baptist Church at its centennial parallels the town's fate. Charco began on the site of an Indian settlement and was a significant center for farming and ranching families until the boll weevil attacked cotton, sharecropping ended, and people began to leave the town. The Baptist church had been founded in 1889, at the peak of Charco's existence. Today there is almost nothing left of the town.

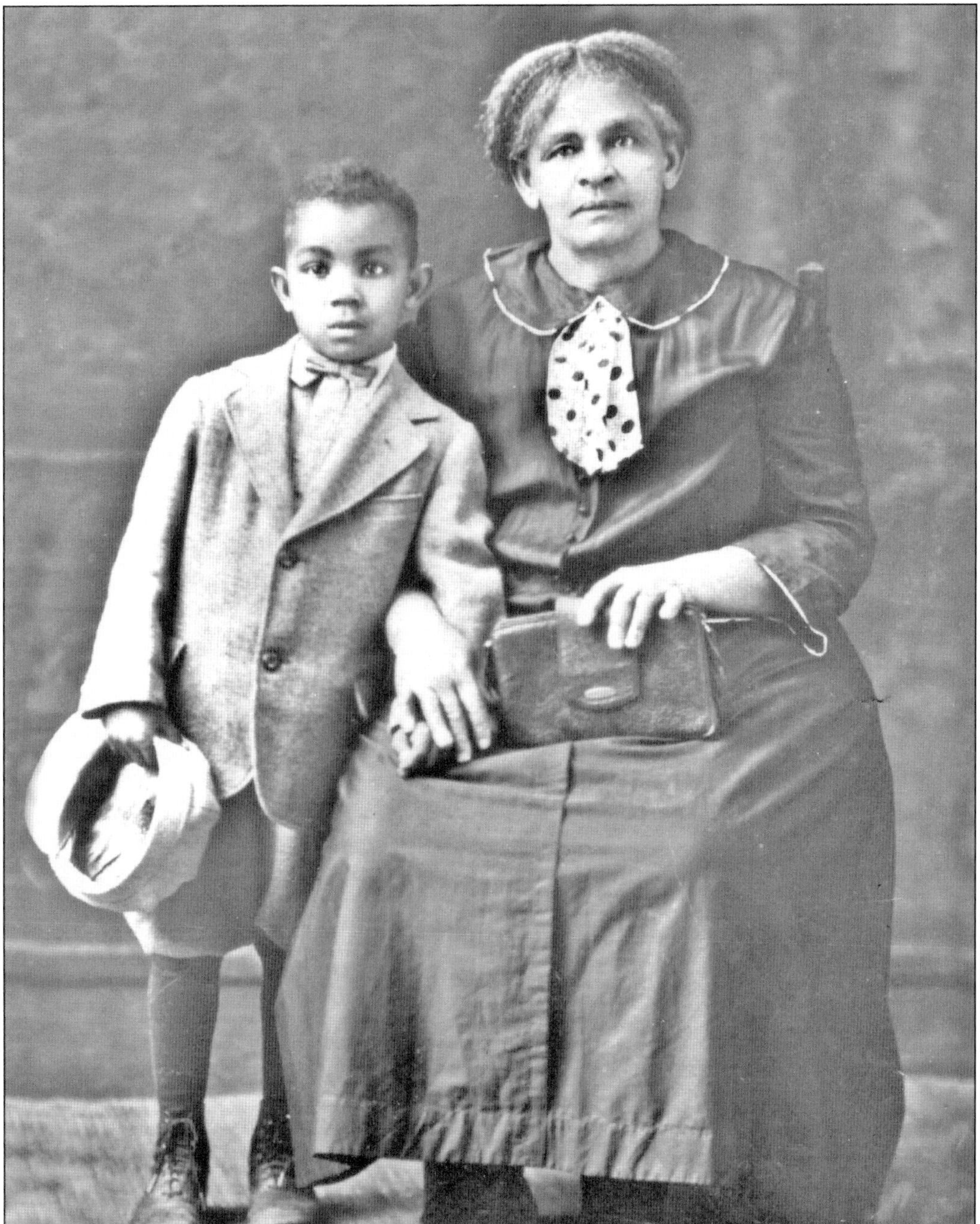

The most unique community in rural Goliad was Cologne. In 1877, African Americans, mostly freed slaves, purchased land and established a town in order to provide themselves security and prosperity in the face of the tremendous hostility they faced in Texas after the Civil War. The town flourished with a railroad depot (the only unsegregated one in Texas), a post office, school, churches, a cemetery, and a store. Lavelle Wesley and Lara Lott are descendents of town founders; this image shows the level of prosperity the town achieved in the decades before its post–World War II decline, when jobs and the automobile caused Cologne, like many small towns in rural Texas, to disperse. (Photograph by Barbara Young; courtesy of UTSA Institute of Texan Culture.)

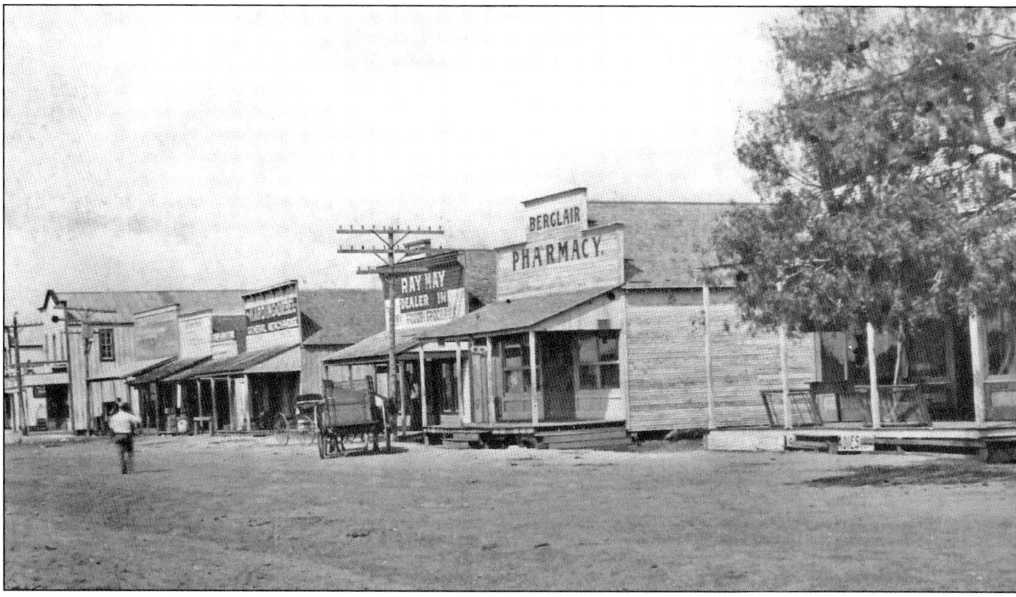

Berclair was different from most other rural towns. It was established late, after 1889, and it was created as a result of the railroad. The western part of the county was mostly occupied by large ranches, and Berclair became important when shipping pens were built alongside the railroad. The town developed a large array of businesses to serve the rather considerable population of that part of the county. As can be seen in the above 1914 photograph, most of the stores were built in a row on one side of the street, across from the railroad tracks. There was an array of businesses: a post office, a telephone office, a doctor's office, a shoe repair shop, and a lumber yard. One of the most significant businesses was the Berclair Mercantile Company, whose wares were touted in this 1909 advertisement.

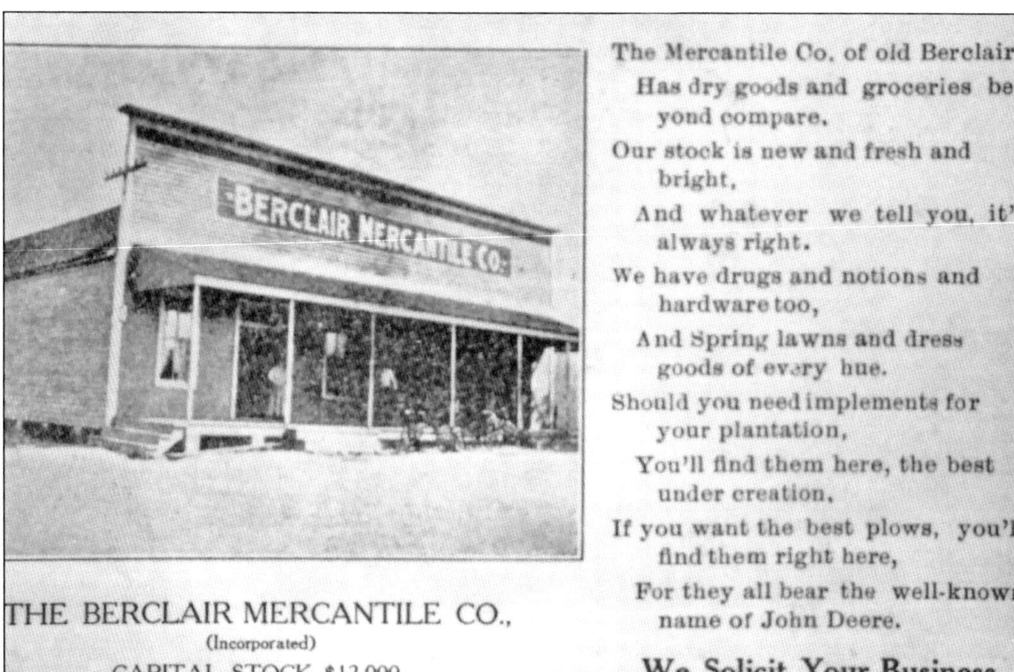

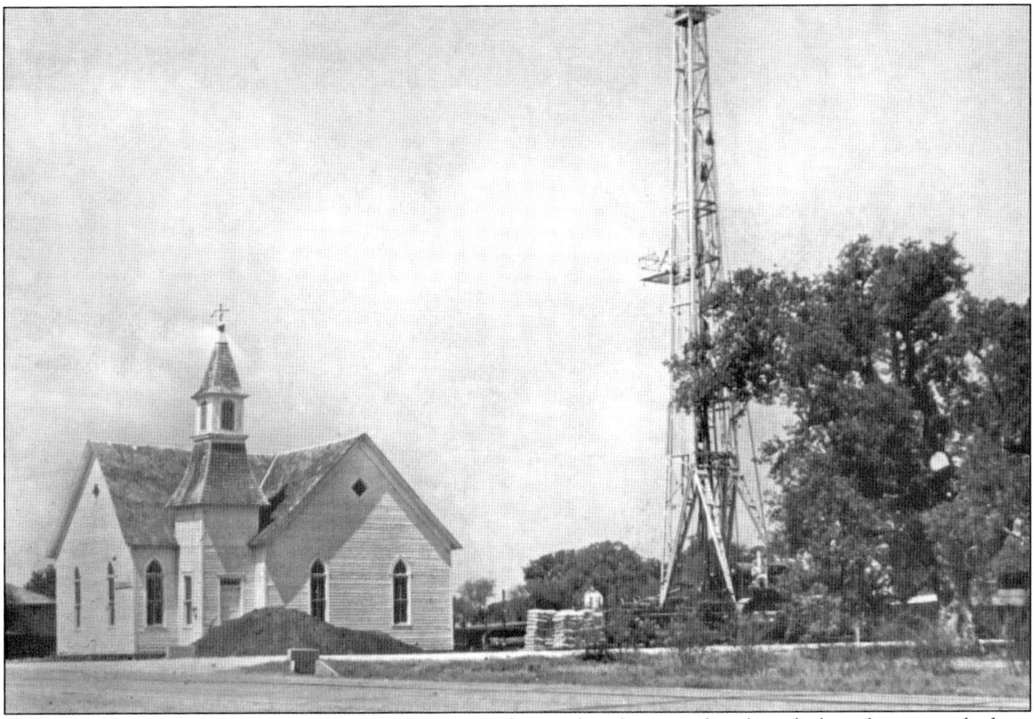

Like the other small towns, Berclair was bound together by its school and churches—including Baptist and Catholic churches, an African-American church, and the Methodist church, shown here with an adjacent drilling rig. The church was destroyed by fire in 1942.

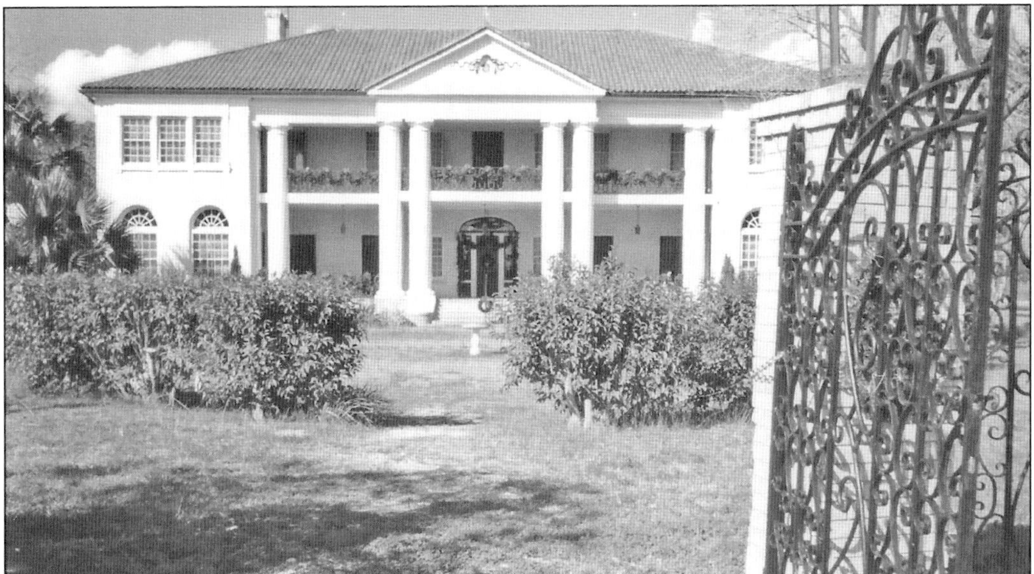

One structure still standing in Berclair is the Berclair Mansion, a 22-room, 10,000-square-foot residence built in 1936. It is considered the largest steel strand house in the nation and was constructed with over 60 tons of concrete and steel. The mansion was built by Etta Terrell, a descendant of Robert P. Wilkinson who came to Goliad County from Matagorda Island after it was bombed during the Civil War. (Courtesy of Beeville Art Association.)

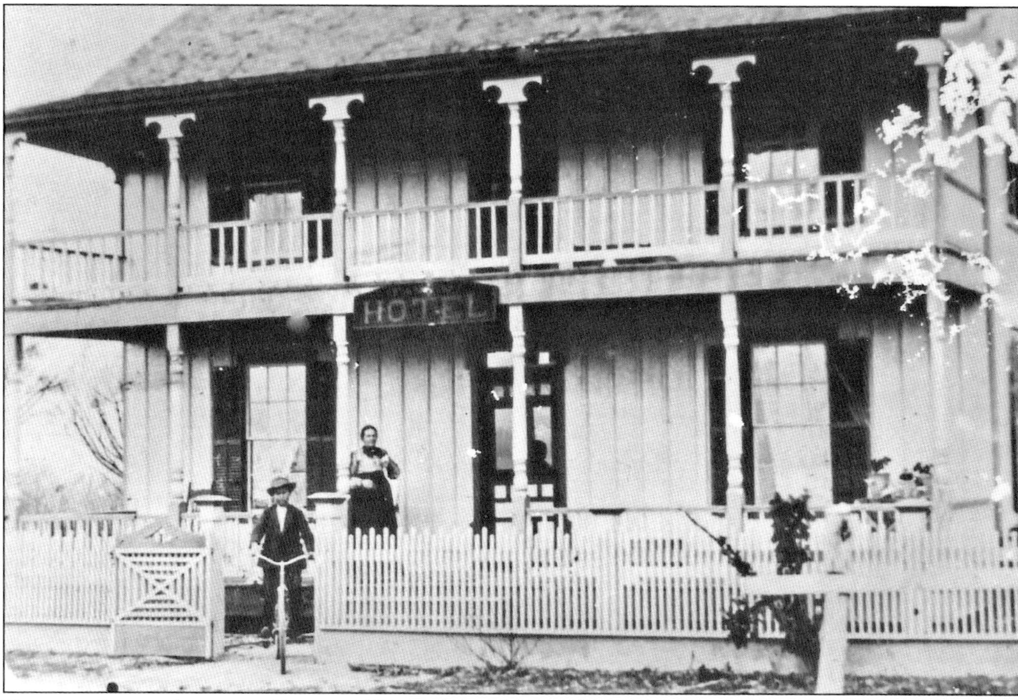

Fannin obtained a post office in 1873 and was first called Perdido after a nearby creek. After the railroad came through, the town moved southward and, in 1890, was renamed Fannin. As the town grew, it acquired a number of establishments including the Hanley Hotel, which operated from the 1890s to the 1950s. Ross C. Hanley is on the bicycle, and Claudia Goff Hanley is on the porch.

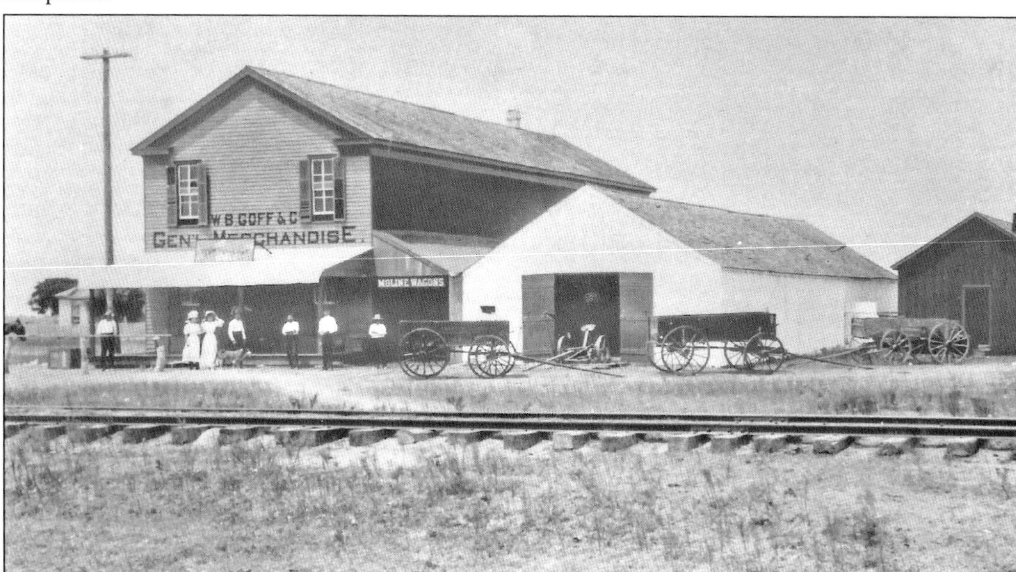

The most prominent establishment in town was the Goff general merchandise store, known to carry everything "from cradle to grave—from safety pins to coffins." There were also many other business establishments, including many saloons. The Goff store housed the post office, and Benson Goff served as postmaster until he was murdered in 1898.

Grocer Charlie Hanley is seen with his famous "Old Blue." Having a gun was probably a good idea, as Fannin was an extremely violent town with many murders, as well as a host for the questionable activities expected in a town with hustlers, prostitutes, saloons, and a dance pavilion. Frederick Douglas Young, a resident of neighboring Cologne, wrote in his reminiscence of life in the area, *From These Roots: Cologne—one hundred years (1870–1970)*, that he blamed Fannin for corrupting the morals of the town's youth.

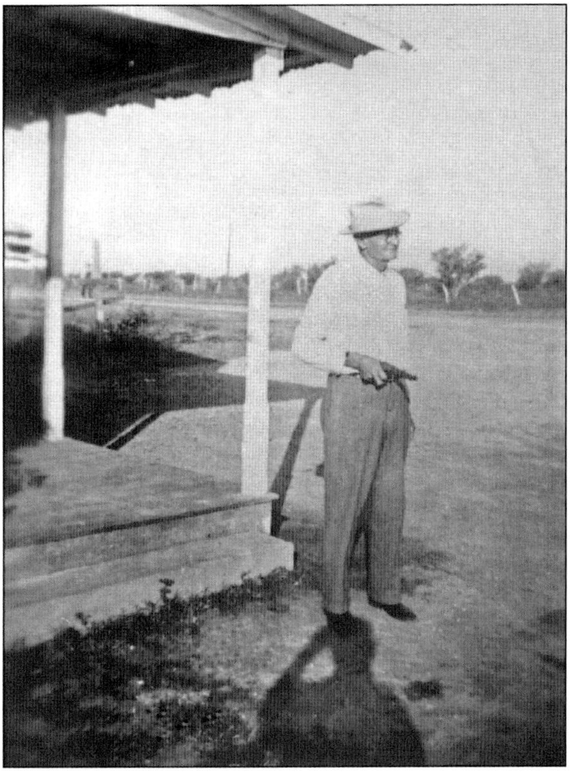

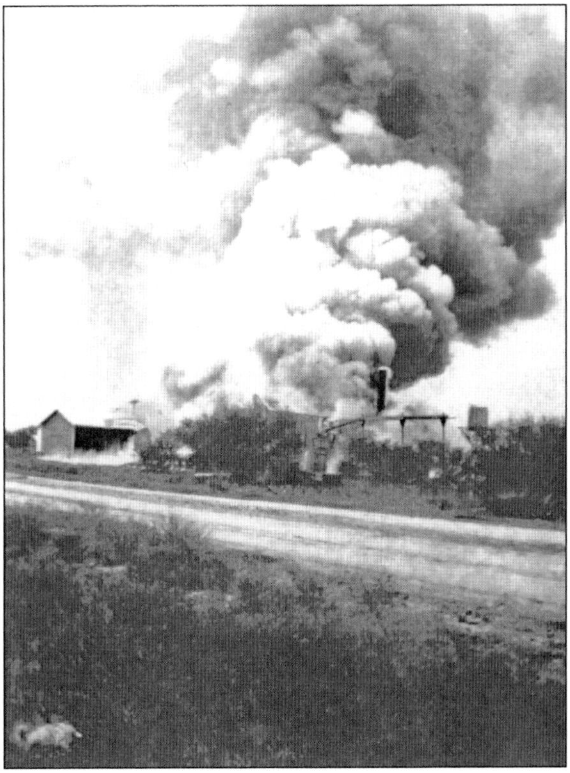

This dramatic picture of the Fannin cotton gin burning illustrates the Fannin fire of 1911. It began when a bullet from a gunfight outside a saloon was shot into the saloon, ignited oil on a cooking stove, and caused a conflagration that burned most of the buildings in town. Most of Fannin was never rebuilt.

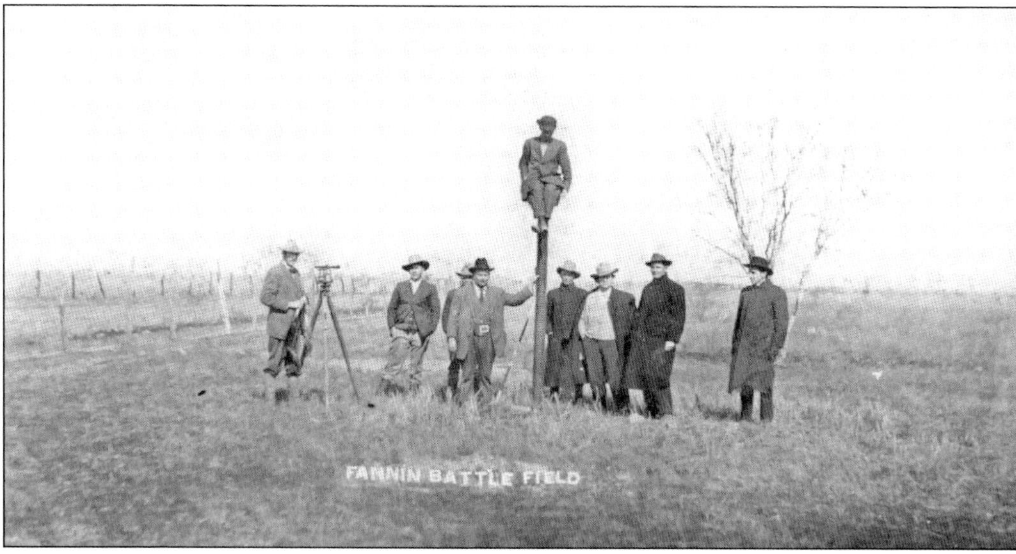

Fannin is primarily known as the site of the Battle of Coleto Creek, where Fannin's army was defeated in 1836. The site was preserved by local residents like Sol Parks Sr. who, in 1891, took an iron screw from the drive mechanism of a grist mill and had it placed where an observer claimed the battle had occurred. The man in this photograph is sitting on the screw, which is still in place.

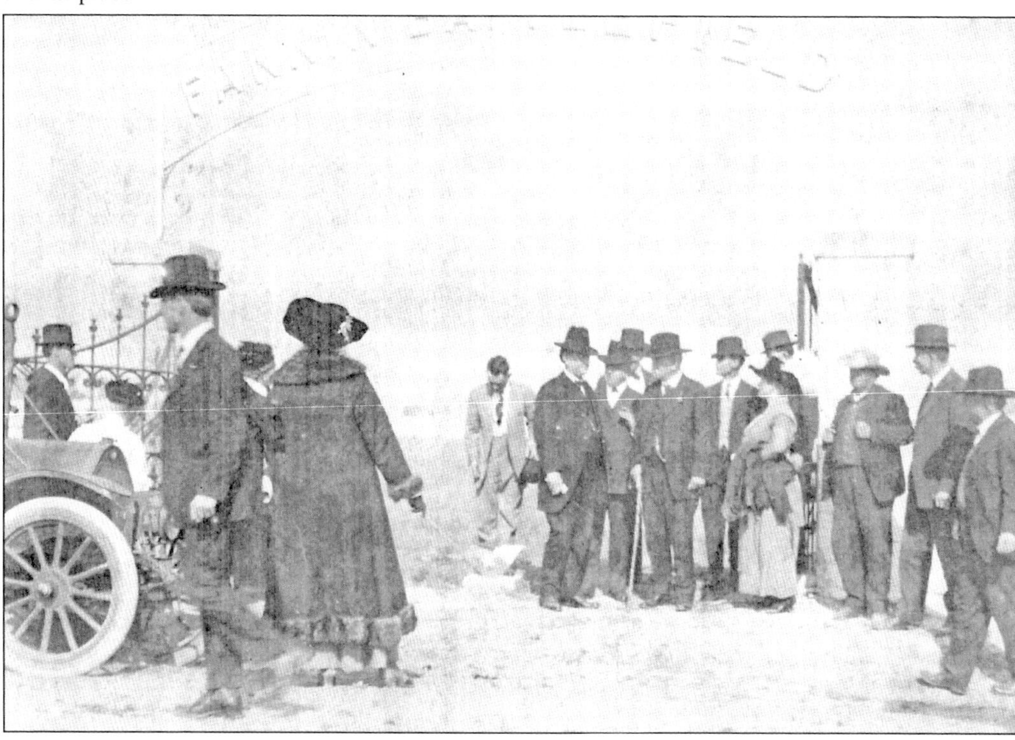

In 1913, another local resident, Hugh B. Hanley, donated the site to Texas. In 1914, a monument was built, and the site of the battle became a state park. (It has recently been transferred to the Texas Historical Commission.) Gov. James Ferguson came to visit on March 8, 1916. Donor Hugh Hanley is in the white hat.

Seven
Goliad Since World War II

After World War II ended, Goliad flourished briefly in the glory days of the 1950s and early 1960s but soon began the decline that other nearby communities experienced. Better roads and automobiles made it desirable to shop and patronize services in larger towns. Although there were many major developments after the 1950s—a new city hall, a hospital, a race track, a military airport, and new school buildings—the fact is the town began to decline. Population declined, many stores closed, and the area around the courthouse square began to look shabby.

In the 1970s, citizens began to fight back. They created a historic district to preserve the older buildings around the courthouse square. Goliad was accepted into the Main Street program, the smallest town ever accepted. This led to a revitalization of the town square. The town developed many activities and programs to invigorate the town. Most of them related to Goliad's past, including restoration of the Presidio La Bahia in the 1960s, institution of an annual longhorn stampede, and a major conference on Goliad's ranching past. Although there was a move in the 1960s to destroy the 1894 courthouse, the building was saved and restored 40 years later. Other activities and groups, such as the Presidio La Bahia's Living History programs, the Zaragoza society, Cinco de Mayo, and the Goliad County Historical Commission's Christmas in Goliad joined monthly market days and long-running attractions like the County Fair to bring life into the community and to make it an inviting place to visit. At the same time, ranching and oil continued to be important to the local economy, along with heritage tourism. At the beginning of the second decade of the 21st century, Goliad is a thriving, lively town beloved by many of its residents and by visitors from all over the country.

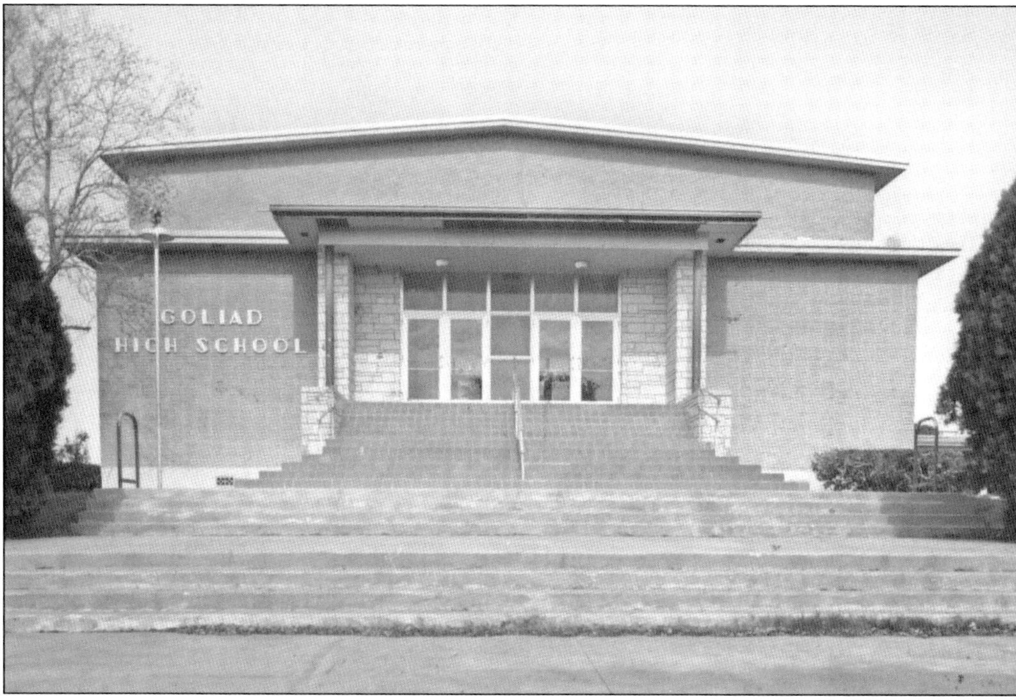

As was typical in a small town in the 1950s, the local high school was a focal point for many community activities. Immediately after the war, students continued to attend school in a building constructed in 1914, but in 1957 the school district constructed this new building. In time, the old building was destroyed and replaced by new elementary and middle school structures.

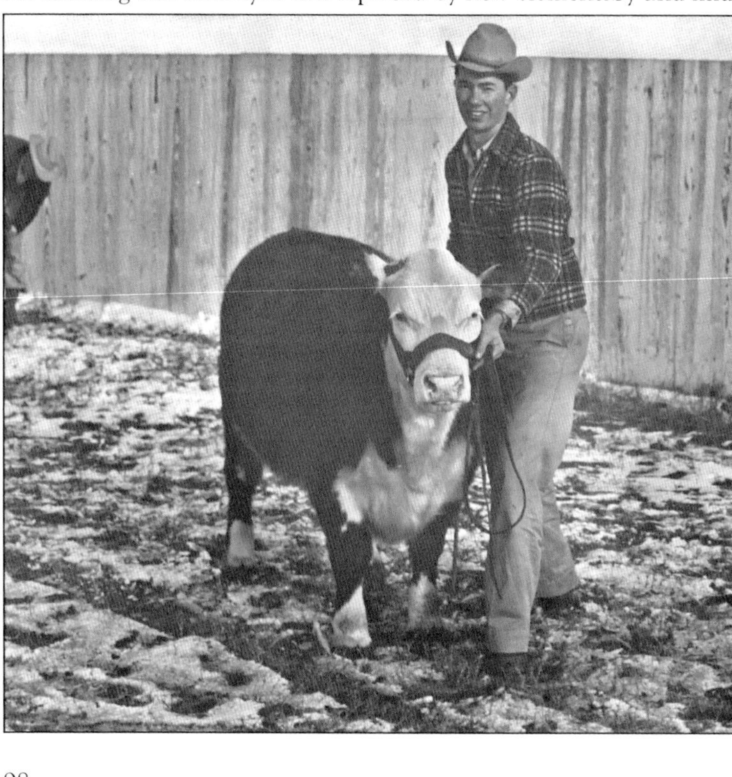

As a rural community, agricultural activities played a large part in school life. An example would be Eugene Hennig and his 1950 Future Farmers of America entry. There were both formal classes and student activities devoted to agriculture.

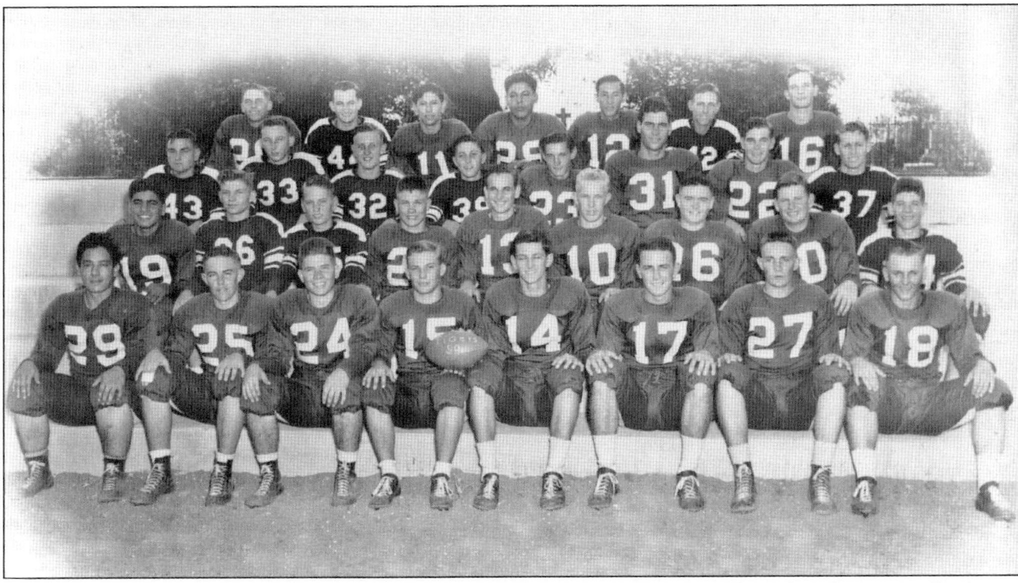

This being Texas, football was king. This is the 1950 Goliad High School team, which was coached by University of Texas graduate John Peacock, who promised to use the "T" formation for exciting, winning football. He was not entirely effective as that team (and the next year's) only went 5-4-1.

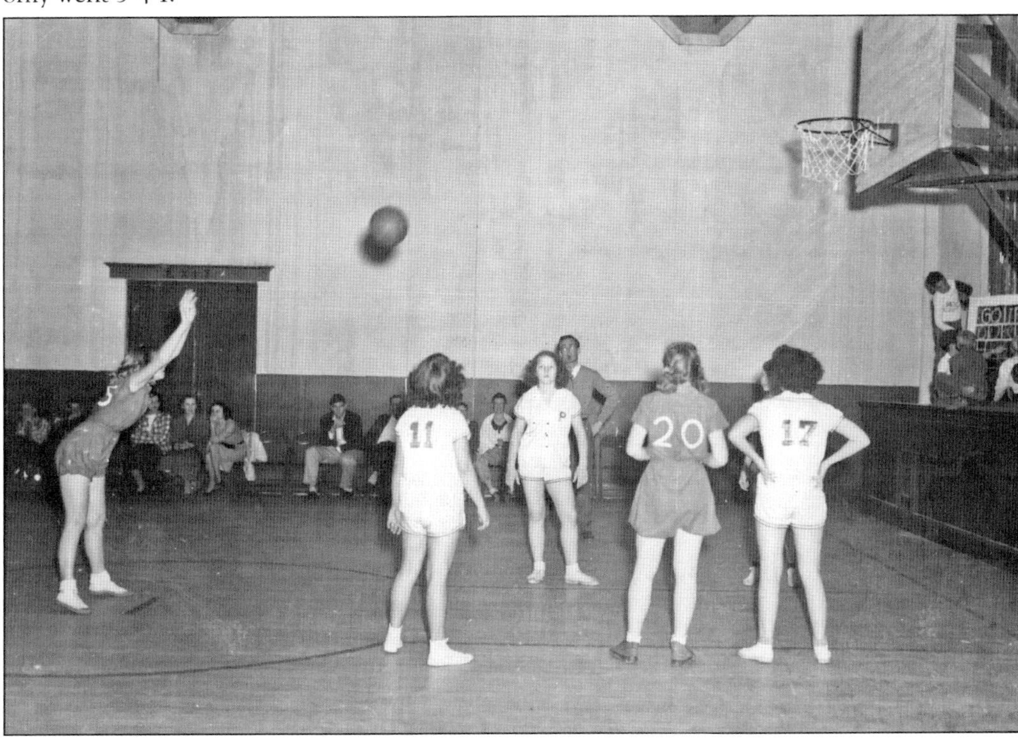

In the post–World War II era, women's athletics did not receive the attention they do now. For a long time, the only varsity sport was women's basketball, depicted by this 1950 game in the Goliad High School gym. Over the next several years, female teams were added in tennis, volleyball, and softball.

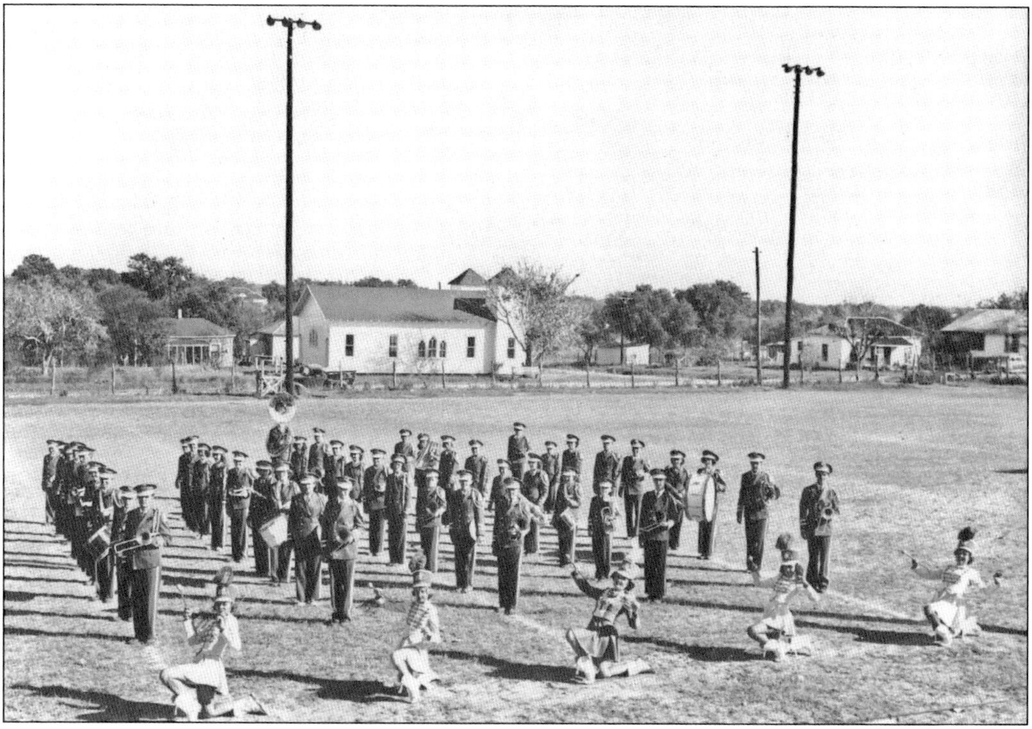

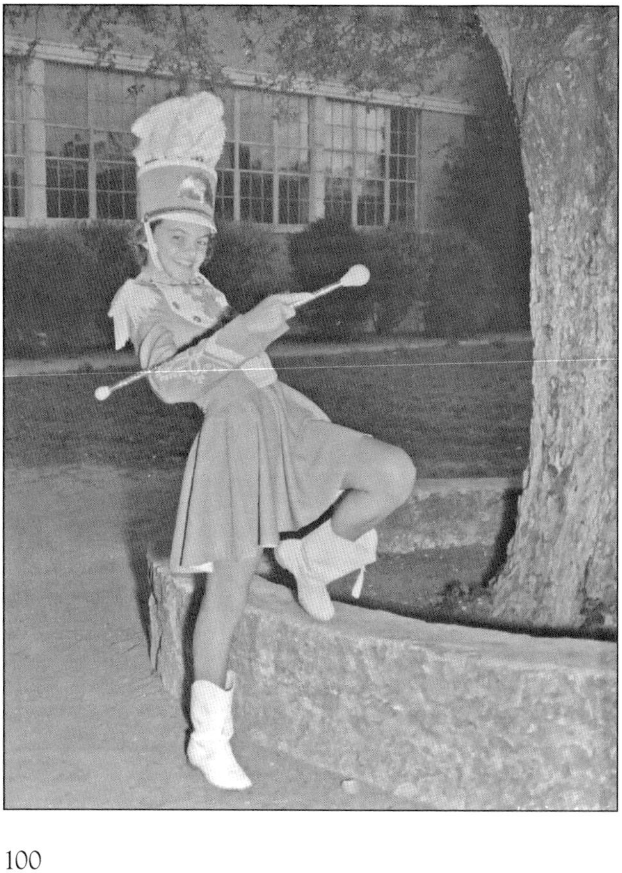

What would high school sports be without a band? In this picture, the band is dressed to perform and is lined up on a school field next to the old high school and across from the Mount Moriah Church. The band's drum major every year, until she graduated in 1954, was Claudette von Dohlen (Billo). She was the most prominent band member of her era, serving on the band council and, in 1953, as the Band Sweetheart.

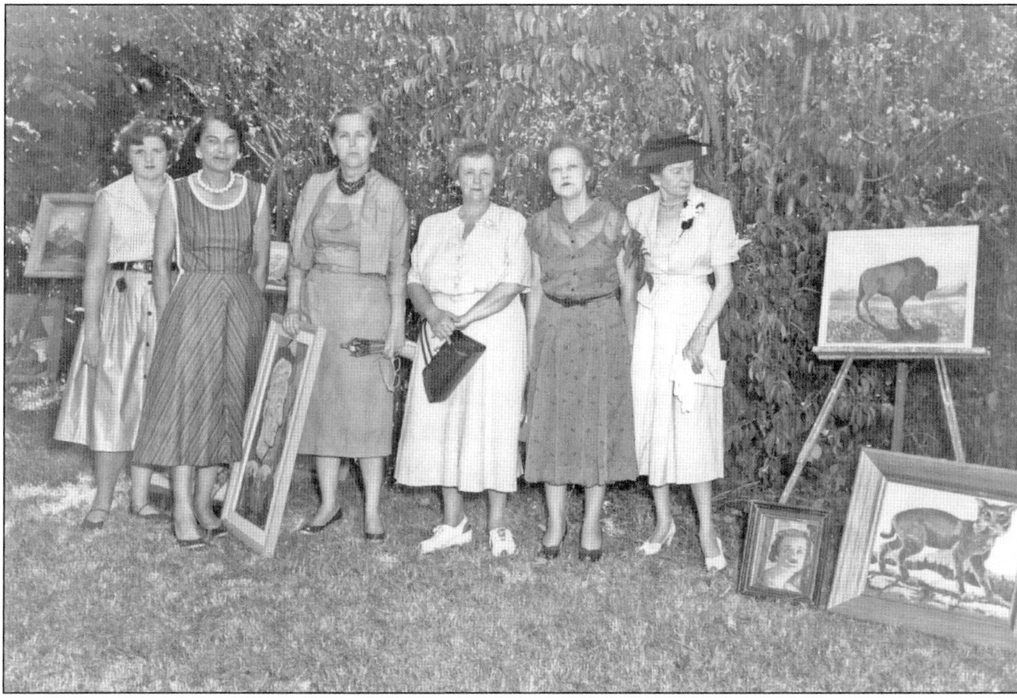

After the War, Goliad had a thriving small-town cultural life. For example, there was the Brush and Gush Art club. This gathering included, from left to right, Idella Bridges, Gladice Martin, Sallie G. Pettus, unidentified, Irene Courtret, and Helen McCampbell.

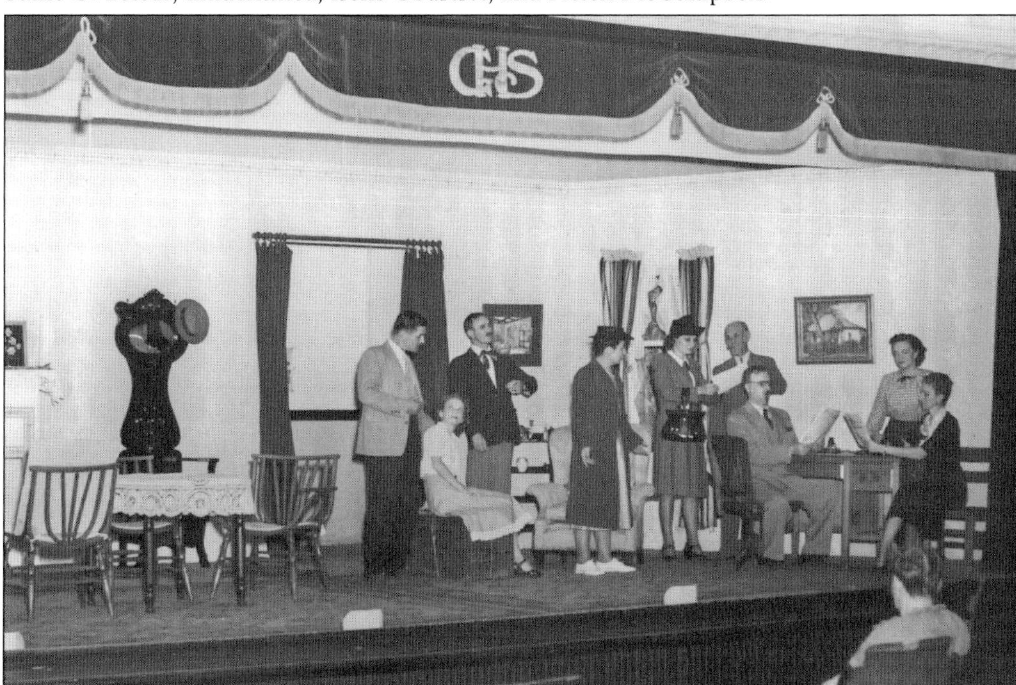

Likewise, there was interest in drama. The Goliad Community Adult Theatre was active, producing plays in the high school auditorium

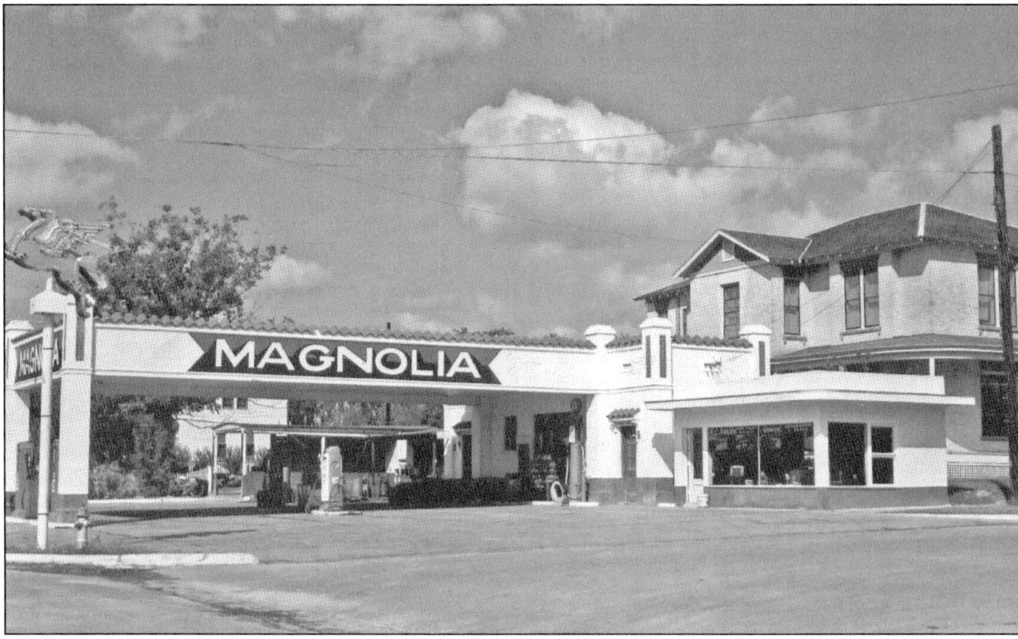

The generation after the Second World War was the heyday of the automobile in America. This was evident by Goliad's Magnolia service station, with its iconic flying horse sign. There were other service stations, repair shops, and new car dealers for Ford, Chevrolet, and Pontiac.

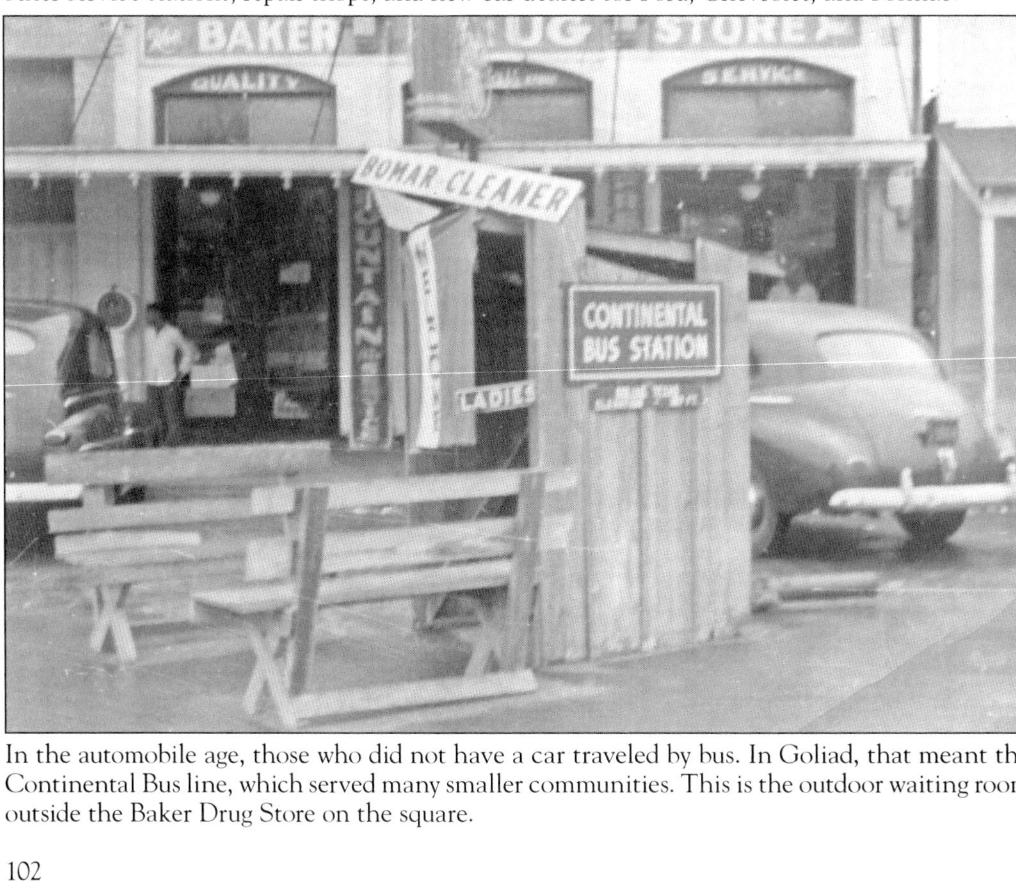

In the automobile age, those who did not have a car traveled by bus. In Goliad, that meant the Continental Bus line, which served many smaller communities. This is the outdoor waiting room outside the Baker Drug Store on the square.

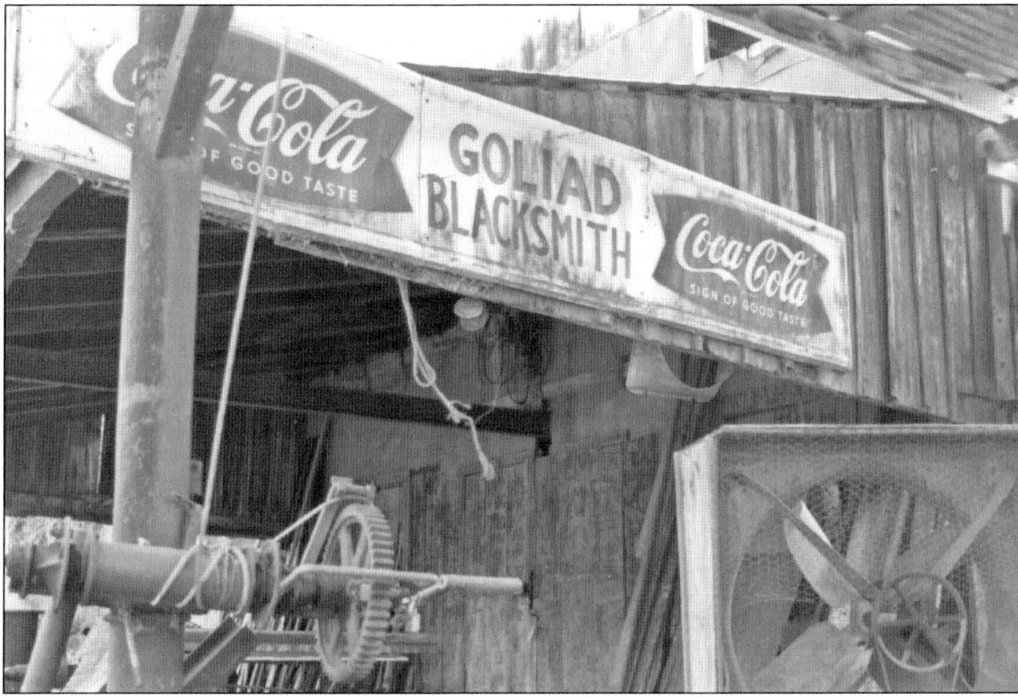

There has been a Goliad blacksmith for many decades. Since 1960, the shop has been run by Jim Young. A Goliad native, he learned his welding and cutting skills at the high school. Young has made thousands of branding irons and has repaired hitches, bumpers, trailers, and all types of farm or ranch equipment. For his contributions, the Chamber of Commerce awarded him its Lifetime Achievement Award in 2009.

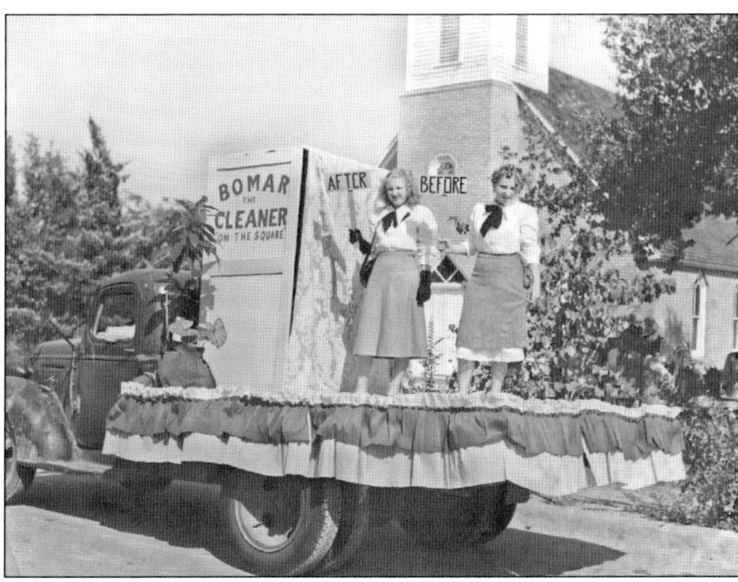

This float in one of Goliad's ubiquitous parades advertised Bomar the Cleaner. The business began years earlier with one galvanized tub, a clothesline, and an ironing board. In 1945, N. A. Bomer bought the property and immediately modernized it. The company prospered, but in 1973 was sold to the Troy family, who still operate the business.

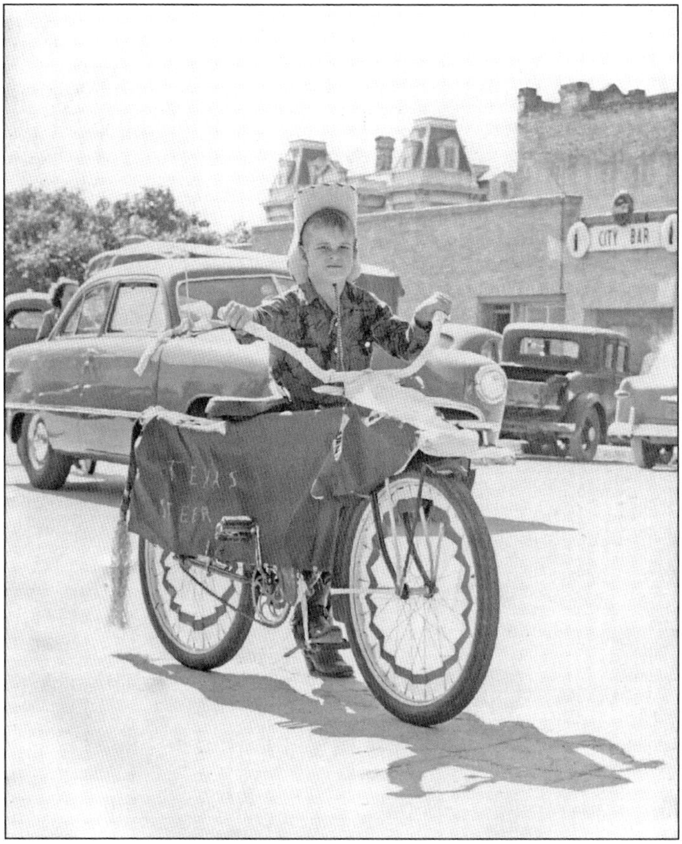

Goliad parades usually featured lots of local children and still do. The photograph on the left shows Jerry Harvey and his decorated bicycle, probably around 1950. The bottom picture from May 1967 shows both the streamlined fashions of the 1960s and how Goliad harkened back to its historical roots.

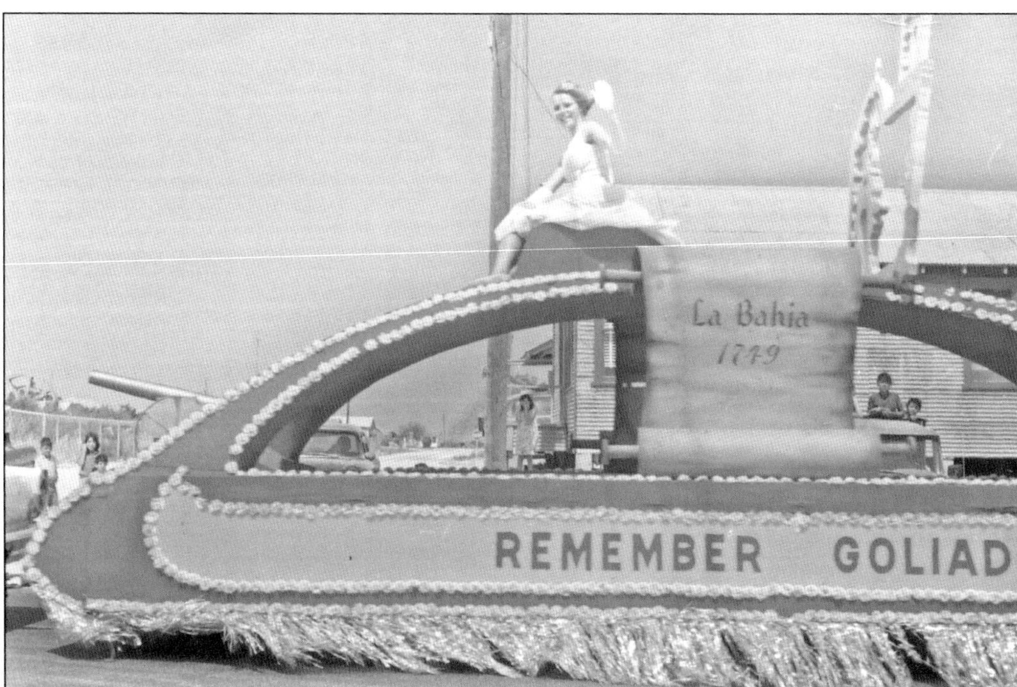

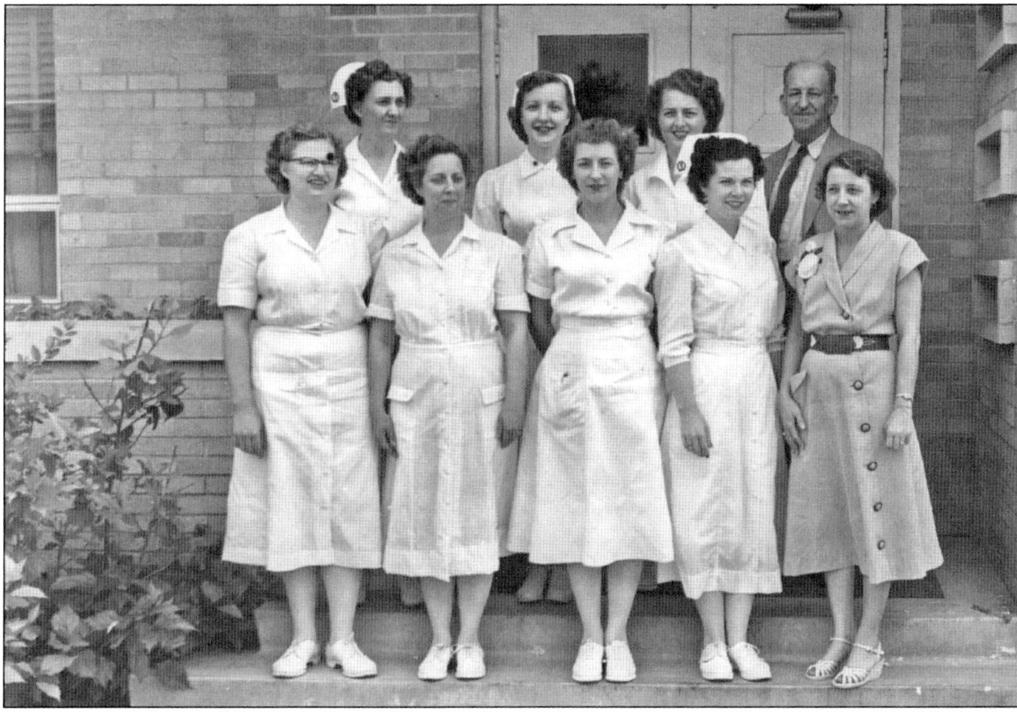

These nurses and Dr. L. W. Chilton Jr. are standing in front of the new Goliad County Hospital, which was dedicated on May 7, 1950. There had previously been small private hospitals, but this was the first major public facility. Financed by a bond issue, a federal grant, and a voluntary subscription, it was so successful that it had to be expanded in 1965.

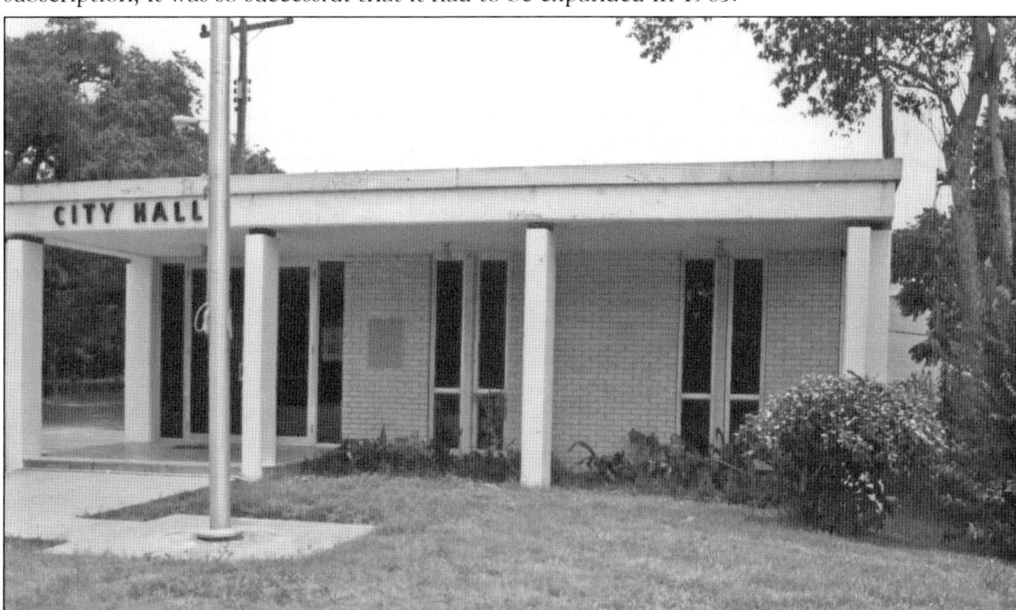

On May 15, 1964, the community dedicated a new city hall and fire station. By moving the fire station out of the market house, that building was freed up to be restored in 1967 by the Goliad Art Guild and to be listed on the National Register of Historic Places in 1972.

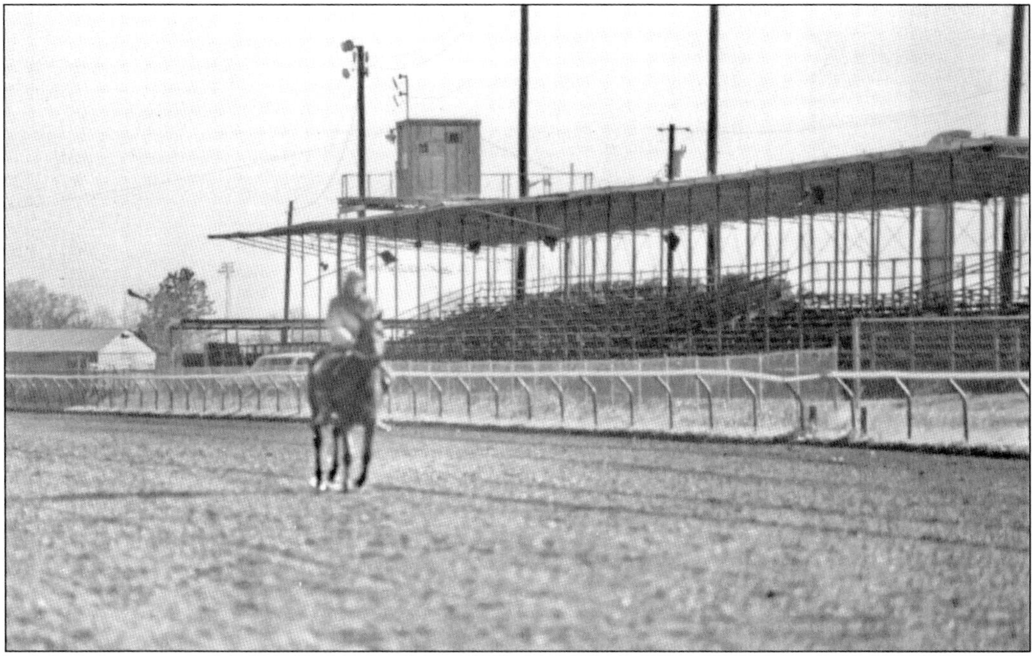

Prior to its closing in 1990, La Bahia Downs was a major attraction in Goliad. Featuring quarter horse racing, the South Texas Race Association, formed in 1961, scheduled races from 1962 until its close. In 1969, it opened the complete facility shown here, with barns, grandstand, offices, and other services. Some of the fastest sprint horses in the nation raced there, usually to capacity crowds.

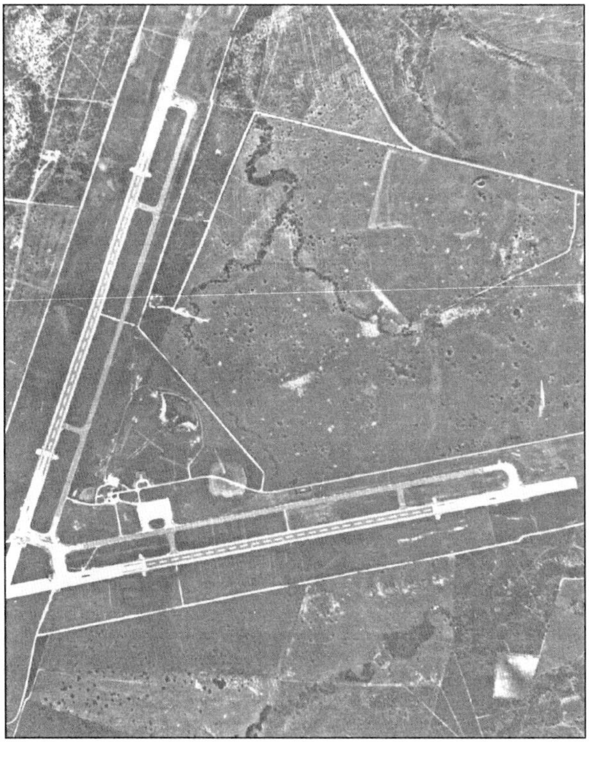

Goliad benefitted from the military buildup of the Cold War when the U.S. Navy built the Goliad Naval Auxiliary Landing Field in 1969. Designed for use by navy fliers for touch-and-go landing and carrier landing practices, the navy acknowledged that the noise could bother local residents and their livestock. The facility was eventually turned over to the county. (Courtesy of Goliad County.)

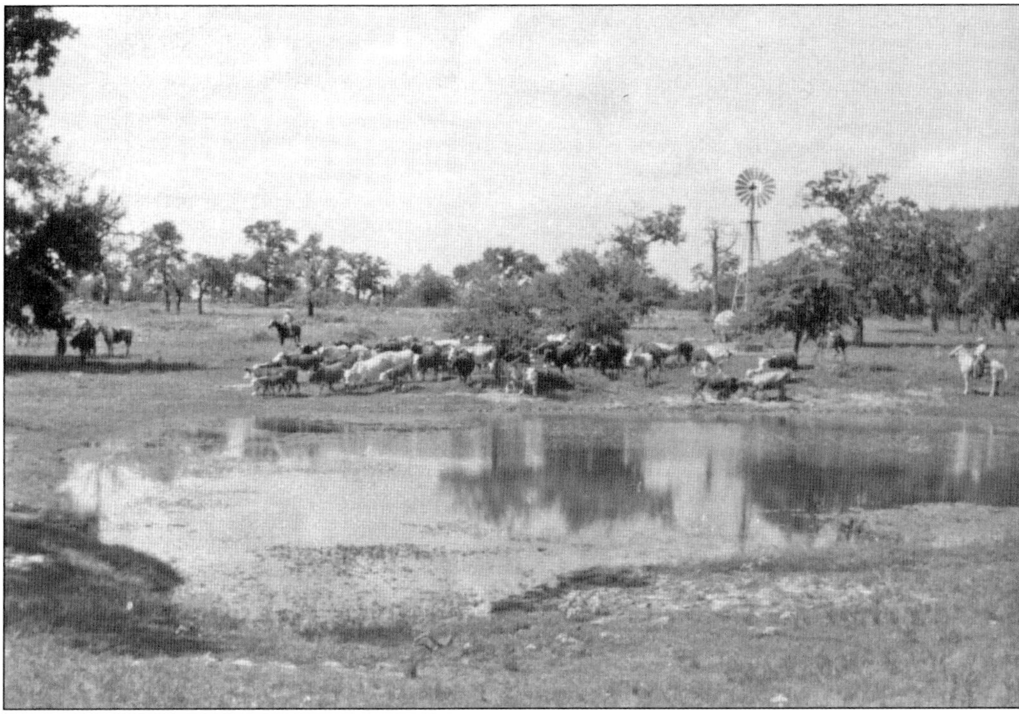

Cattle ranching has continued as a major facet of Goliad life. This 1950s photograph shows cattle on the Hoff Ranch being held at the Kinney Mill Pond until they were driven to the cattle pens for marketing.

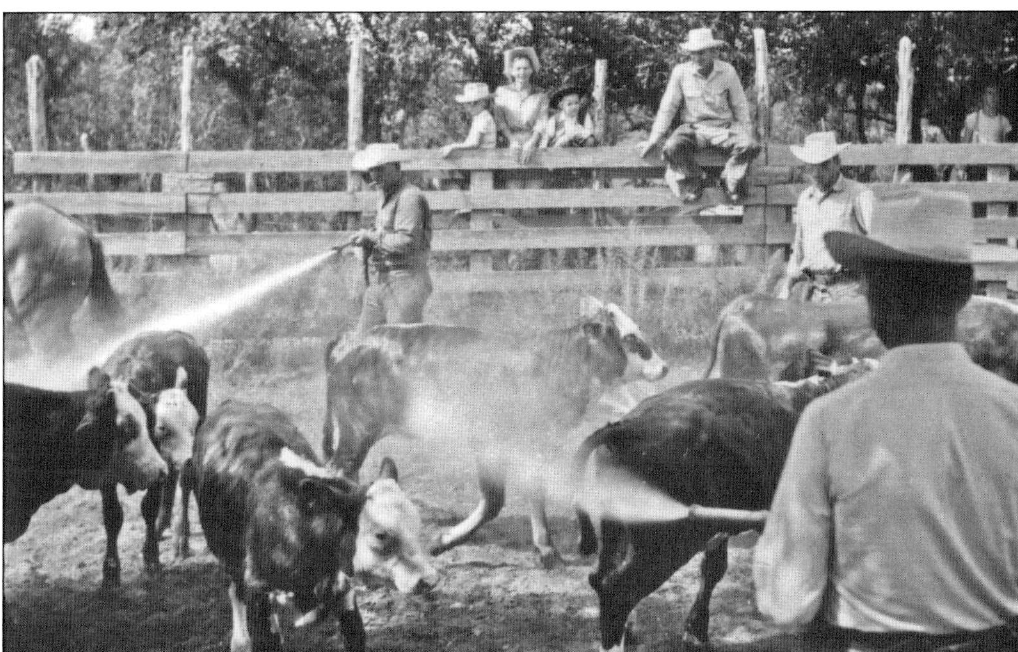

Gene and Cammie Hoff are shown spraying cattle for lice and flies during the summer. Along with fever ticks and screwworms, these were major pests ranchers had to contend with.

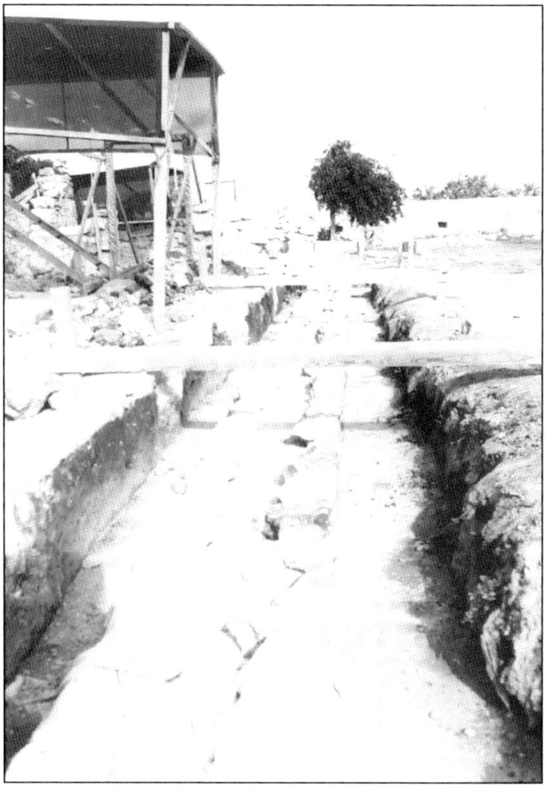

The Presidio La Bahia was relocated here in 1749, along with the Mission Espiritu Santo, to begin what eventually became Goliad. It was a major administrative and military center during the Spanish and Mexican eras and played a significant role in the Texas Revolution. Yet in the 1930s, when the mission was restored and other work was done during the Texas Centennial years to preserve Goliad's past, almost nothing was done to the presidio. Some believe it was because it belonged to the Roman Catholic Church. In the 1960s, devoted friend and benefactor of the presidio Kathryn Stoner O'Connor spearheaded the fund-raising and restoration of the facility, and work began in 1964. The four photographs on these two pages show the work in progress. The two on this page show some of the extensive archaeology—under the leadership of Roland E. Beard—which laid the foundation for the rebuilding and created a major collection of artifacts for the presidio. (Both courtesy of Kyle Boyd-Roberton.)

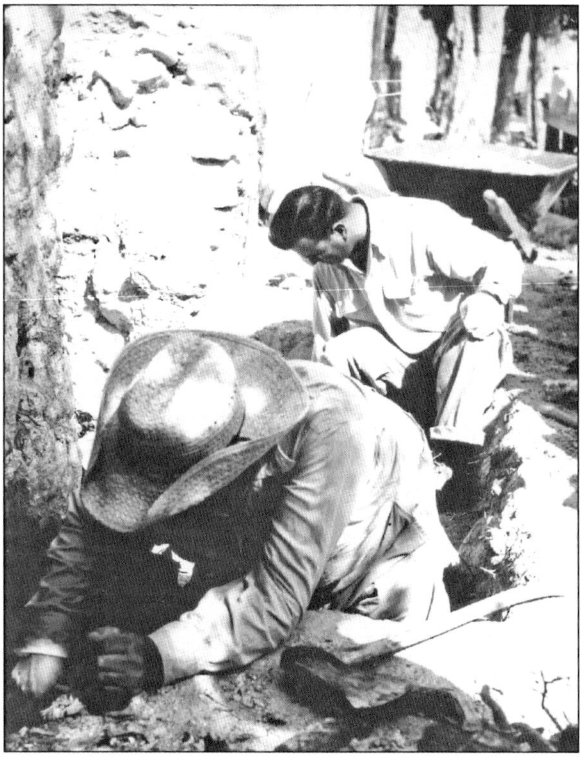

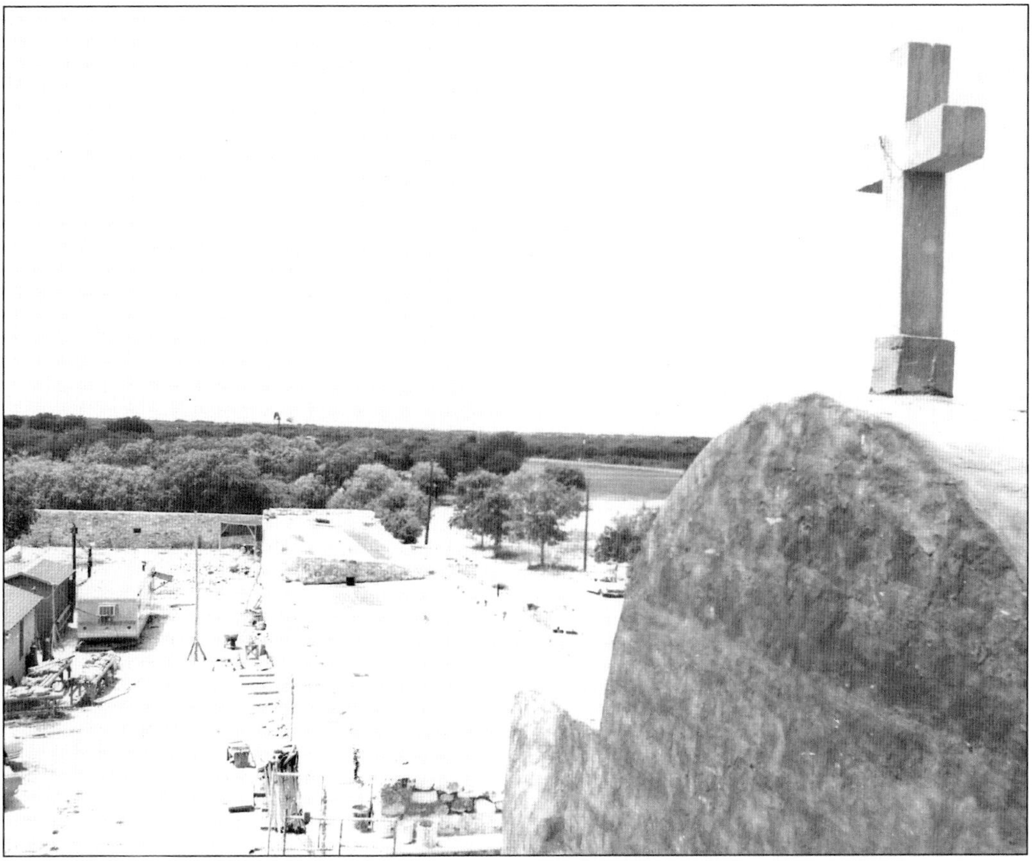

Visible here is the presidio as a construction site and a workman (part of a crew of 40 local artisans) installing the new floor in the commandant's quarters. (Both courtesy of Kyle Boyd-Robertson.)

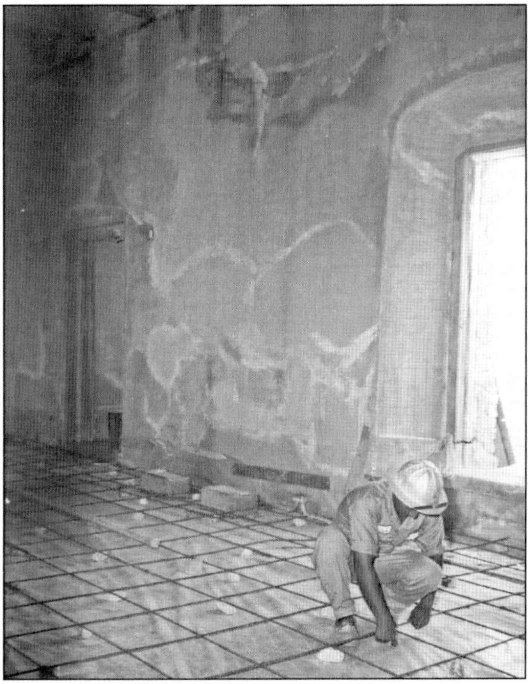

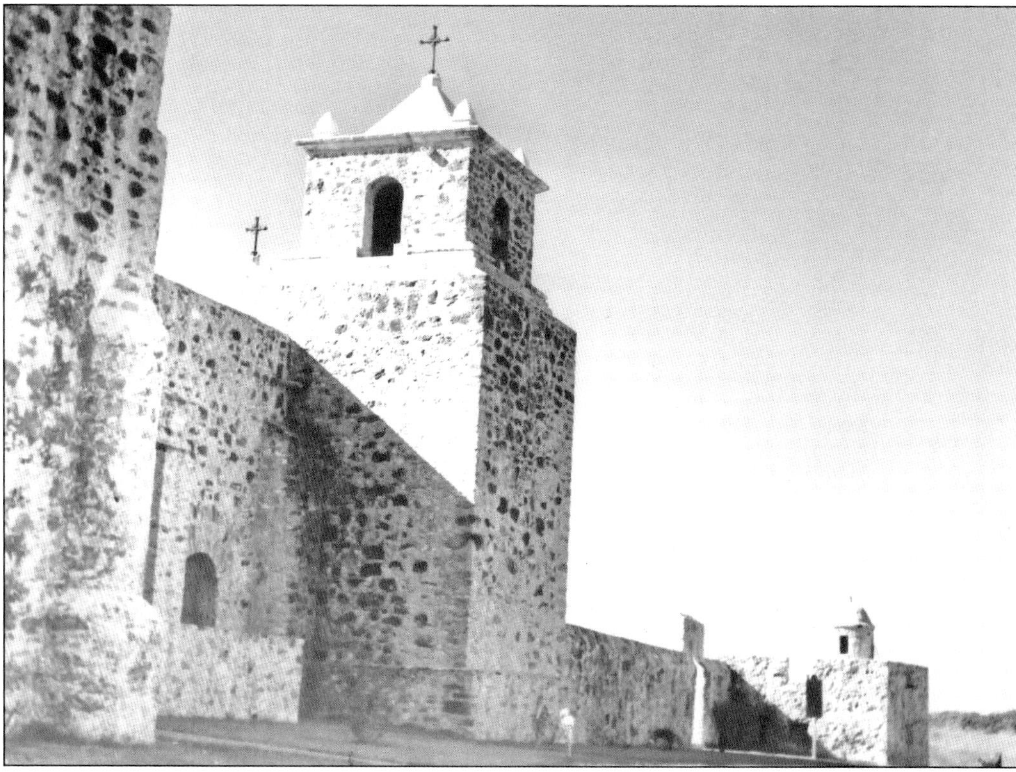

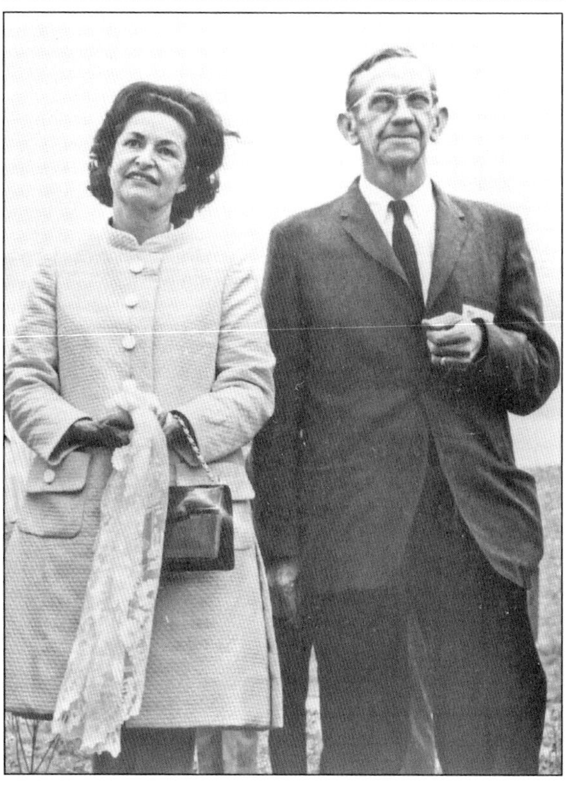

The reconstructed Presidio La Bahia was finished in 1967 at a cost of over $2 million, made possible mostly through Kathryn Stoner O'Connor's efforts. This photograph shows the completed reconstruction. In a later 1968 ceremony, U.S. secretary of the interior Stuart Udall called the restoration "the finest example in the United States of a Spanish presidio." (Courtesy of Kyle Boyd-Robertson.)

The restored Presidio La Bahia was officially dedicated on October 8, 1967, before a crowd of 4,000 including many distinguished guests. In April 1968, Secretary of the Interior Udall and the president's wife, Lady Bird Johnson, came to Goliad and unveiled the plaque designating the structure as a national historical landmark. Lady Bird Johnson is shown with the architect of the restoration, Raiford Stripling, who was well-known to Goliad (see page 71). (Courtesy of Kathryn Stoner O'Connor Foundation.)

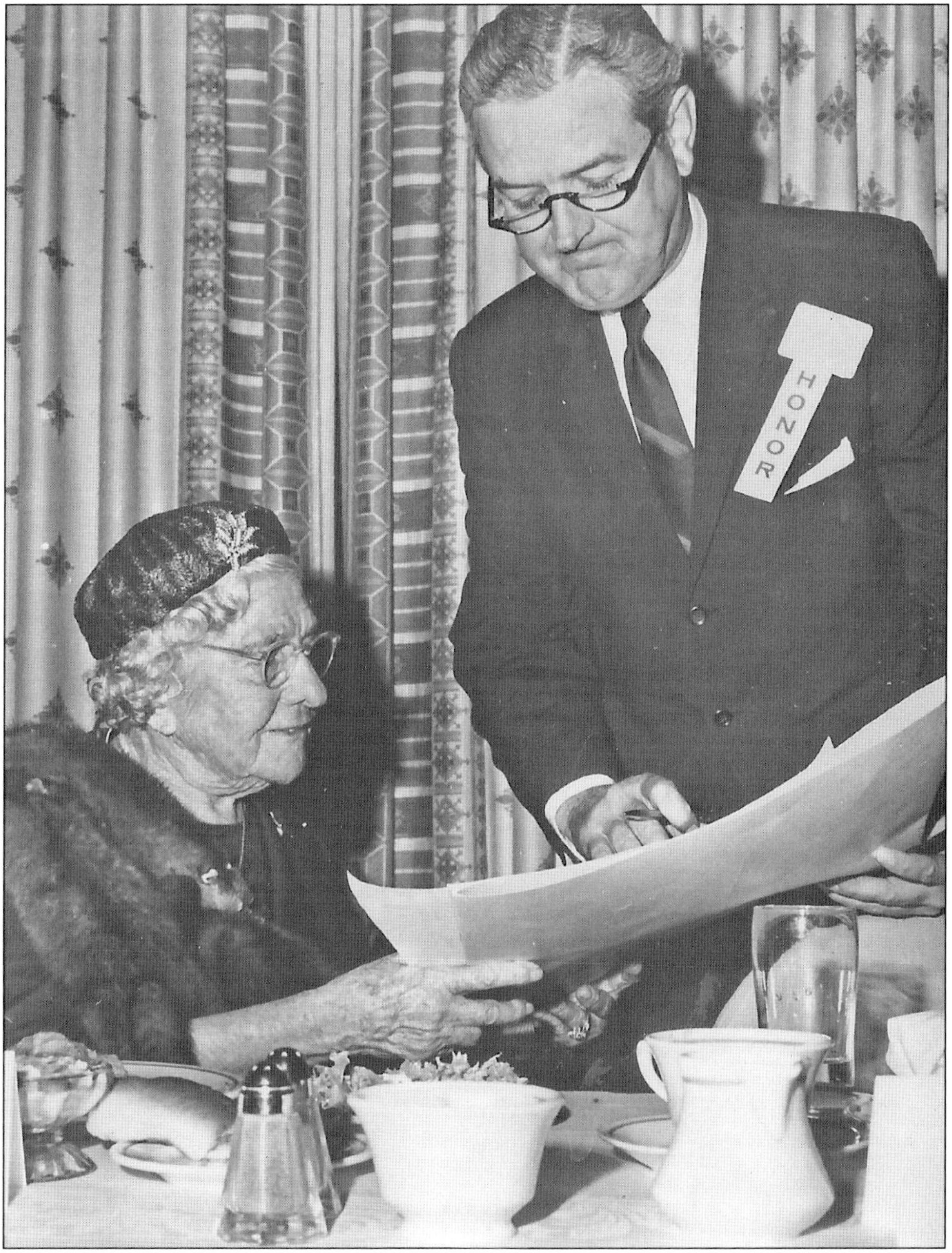

The angel behind the restoration of the Presidio La Bahia was Kathryn Stoner O'Connor. A native of Victoria, she married Thomas O'Connor III of a local ranching family. She devoted her life to her family, the Catholic Church, and historical preservation, publishing in 1969 *Presidio La Bahia del Espiritu Santo de Zuniga 1721 to 1846,* and spearheading the restoration of the presidio. For those activities, she received many awards. One was the Texas Award of Merit for Preservation, being given to her here by Texas governor John Connolly. In addition, the king of Spain awarded her the Order of Isabel la Católica for her work preserving Spanish cultural heritage in Texas. This was the first time the award had been given to an American. (Courtesy of Kathryn Stoner O'Connor Foundation.)

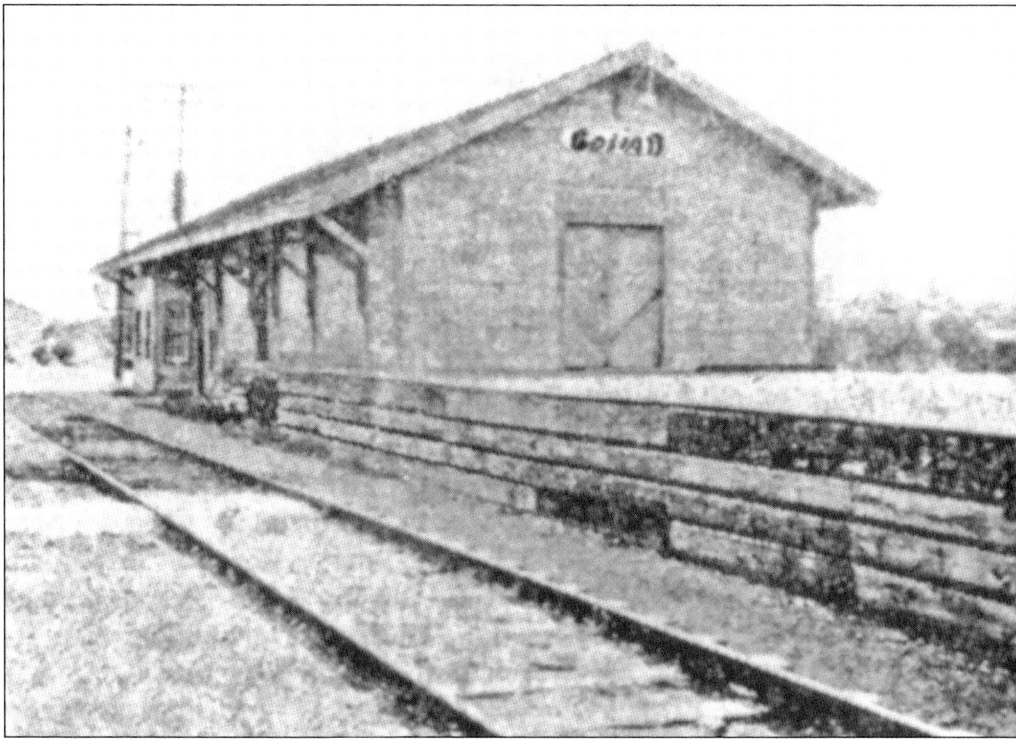

This is not a very good photograph, but it is an important one. It shows the Goliad railroad depot on June 30, 1979, the last day of train service in Goliad. Shortly thereafter, the railroad tracks were torn up. This ended a 90-year era in which the train served Goliad's commerce, passengers, celebrations, and disaster assistance.

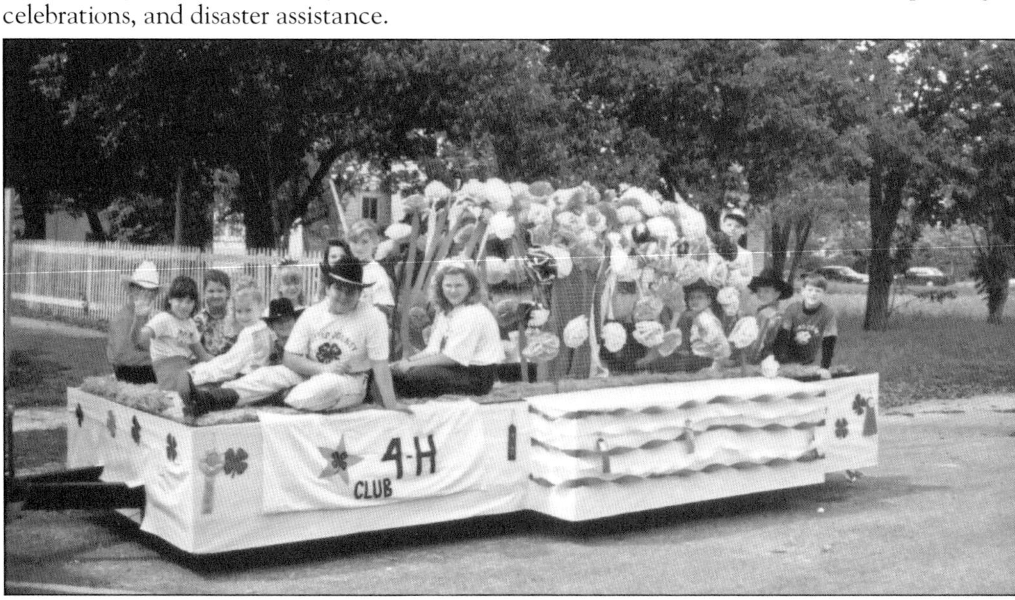

As expected in rural communities, the county fair has always been an important event. Resurrected in 1955 after a brief lapse, the fair features livestock and animal exhibits and judging, household crafts, a major rodeo, a carnival, and other attractions. The Goliad County Fair also hosts one of the town's largest parades each year, featuring floats such as this 4-H Club entry.

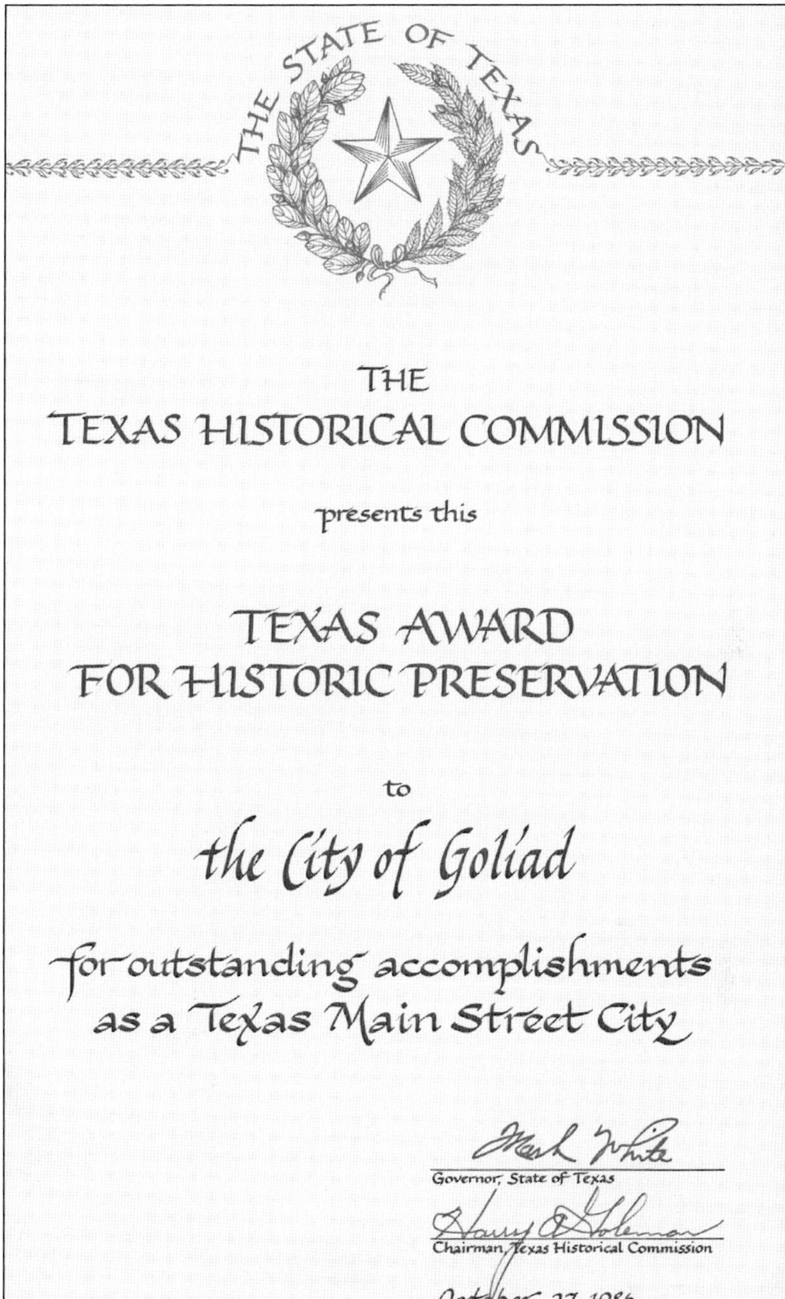
THE STATE OF TEXAS

THE
TEXAS HISTORICAL COMMISSION

presents this

TEXAS AWARD
FOR HISTORIC PRESERVATION

to

the City of Goliad

for outstanding accomplishments
as a Texas Main Street City

Governor, State of Texas

Chairman, Texas Historical Commission

October 27, 1986
Date

In order to salvage its increasingly neglected downtown, Goliad took action. In 1976, they created the Goliad County Courthouse Historic District and passed an architectural review process to maintain the historical integrity of the buildings around the courthouse square. In 1984, Goliad became the smallest town to be selected as a Texas Main Street City. In the first 15 months after the program began, $700,000 was invested in the commercial district. The success of Goliad's preservation efforts was recognized in 1986 by the Texas Historical Commission, which presented the city the Texas Award for Historic Preservation. (Courtesy of City of Goliad.)

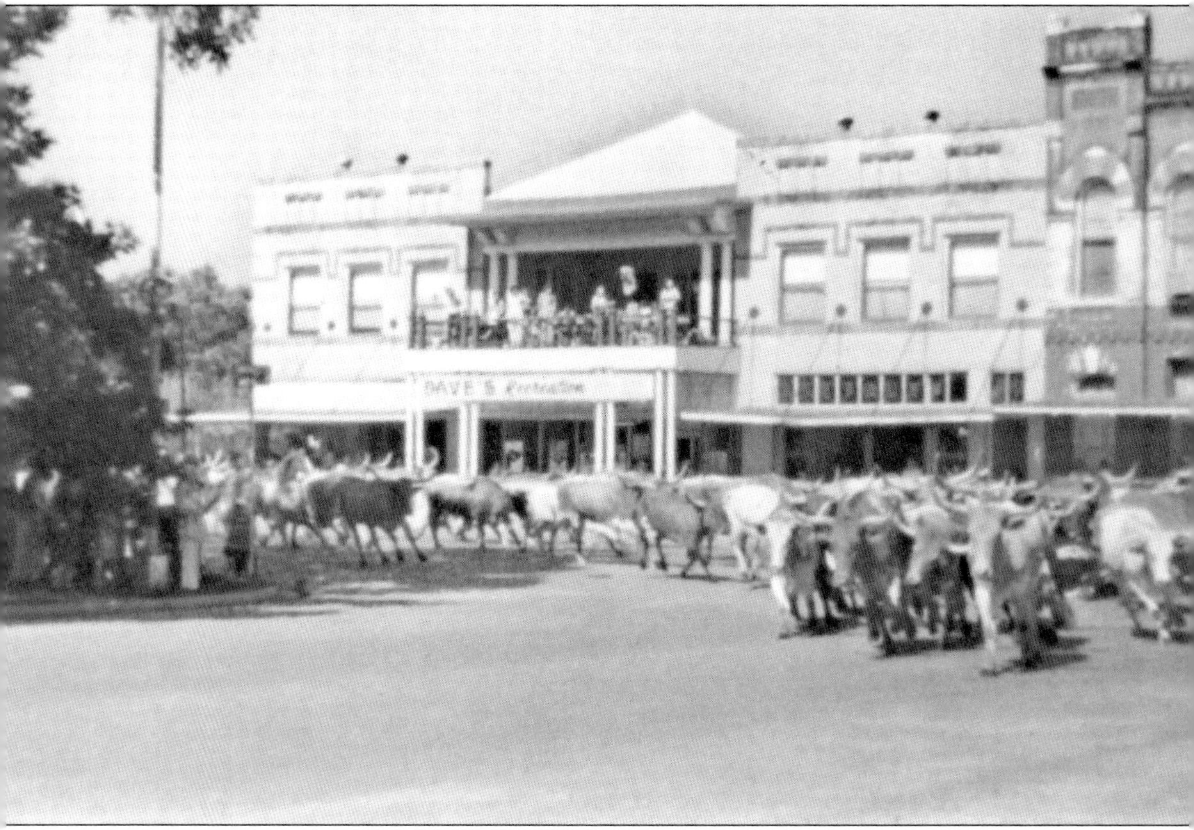

On May 29, 1976, as part of a bicentennial celebration, Goliad decided to celebrate its ranching heritage by driving of a herd of 116 longhorns from Fannin to the Goliad square. As they proceeded around the square, something spooked the animals and the herd stampeded, scattering longhorns, cowboys, and onlookers around the town's center. Although only one person was injured, the county has refused to allow the driving of a longhorn herd around the square ever since. The community continued its annual celebration of ranching until 1992 and called the event The Stampede. (Courtesy of Dorothy Ramsey.)

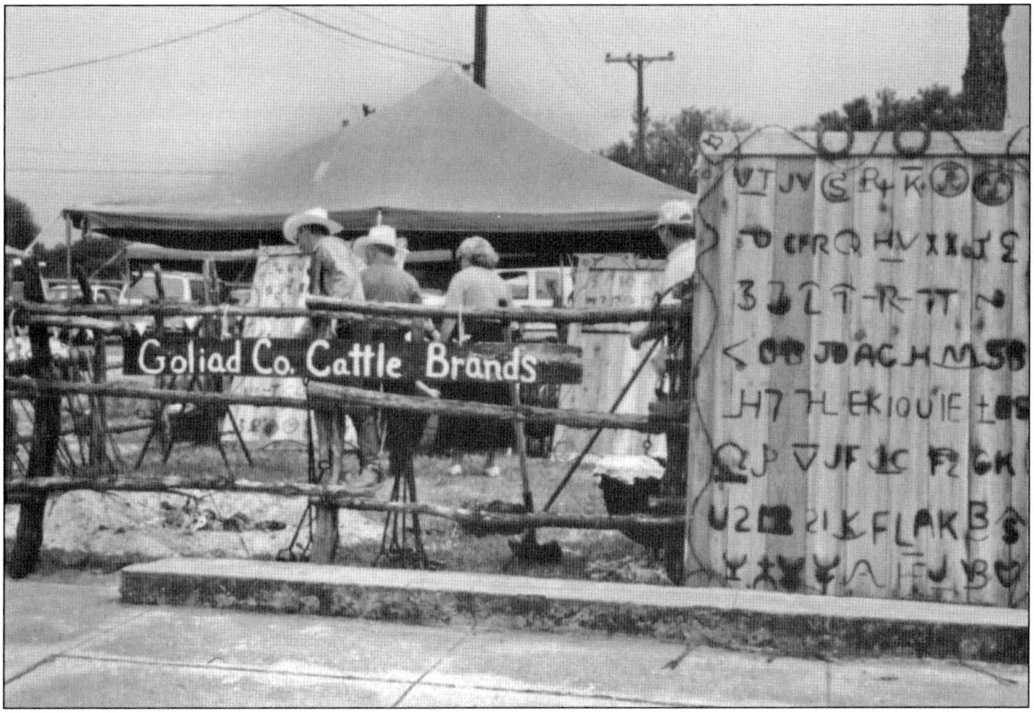

Goliad continued to celebrate its ranching heritage. In the 1990s, it scheduled a number of Goliad Heritage Day programs. This celebration of Goliad County cattle brands is from the 1994 event held at the Hoff Ranch. The board displaying the county's brands can be seen in the Market House Museum.

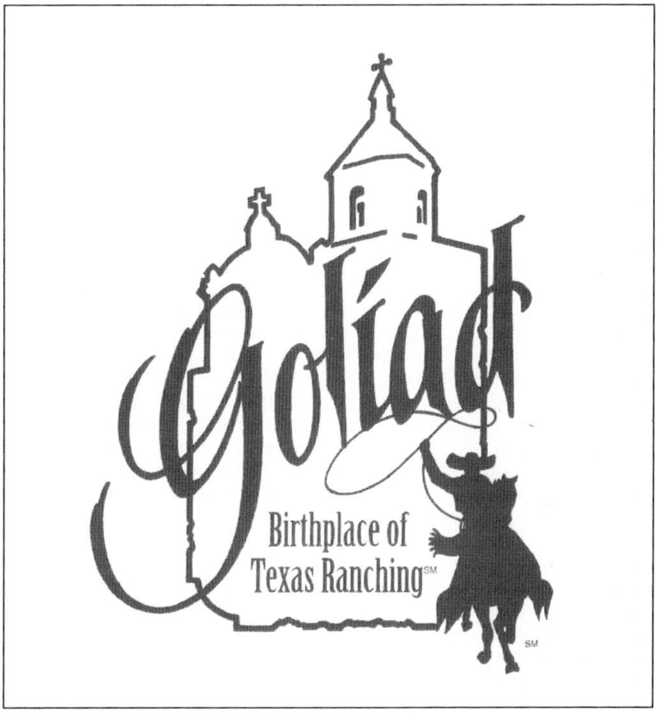

In 1999, the community secured a number of grants to develop a master plan to guide Goliad's future. The report focused almost exclusively on Goliad's heritage and how it could be protected, interpreted, and used to attract visitors to the community. One result of that conference was the logo "to establish a single visual identity for all the sites."

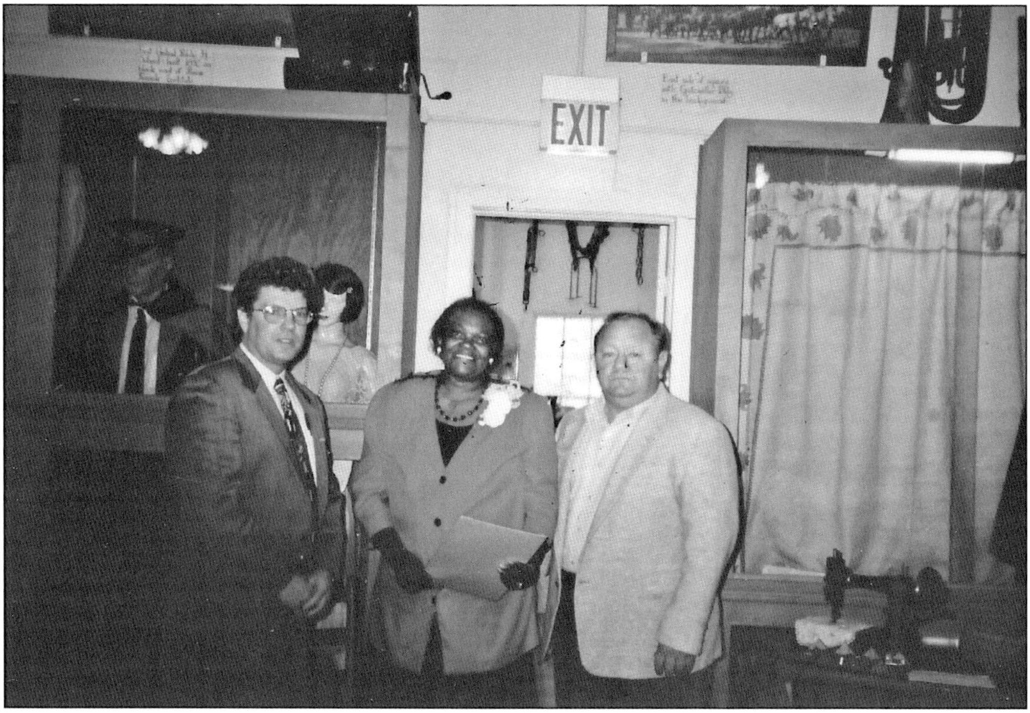

County judge Steven Paulsgrove (left) and Goliad mayor Buddy Zavesky are presenting prominent citizen Ruby Lee Edwards with a joint city-county proclamation establishing "Ruby Edwards Day." She was honored for her leadership in the African American community, Manahuilla Baptist Church, Goliad Senior Center, Goliad County Historical Commission, Goliad Nursing Home, Little League, County Fair Association, the Sapenter Cemetery Association, the Goliad County Library, and many more.

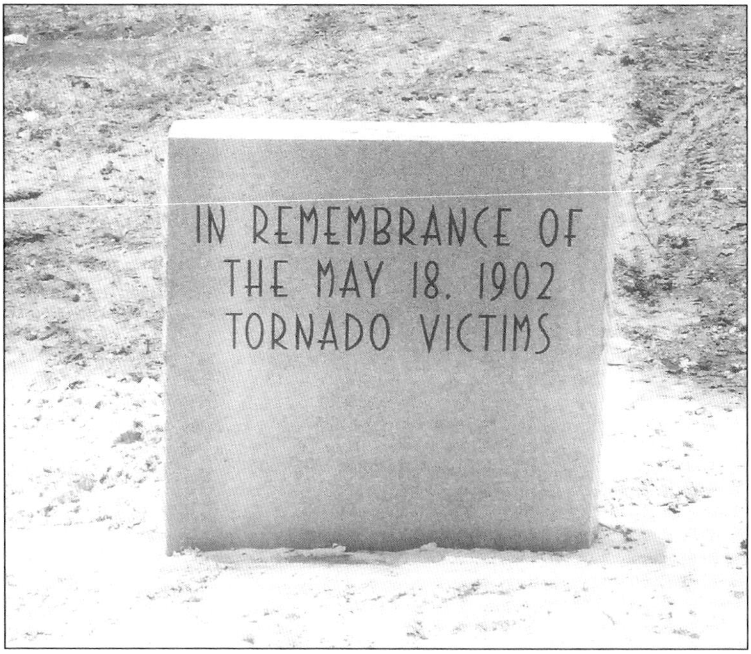

In 2002, the Goliad County Historical Commission sponsored a commemoration of the 1902 tornado's centennial. There were scholarly papers, speeches, memorials to the victims, and the placement of this monument in the Sapenter Cemetery, where the majority of the casualties from the Fannin Street Methodist Church are buried, most in unmarked graves.

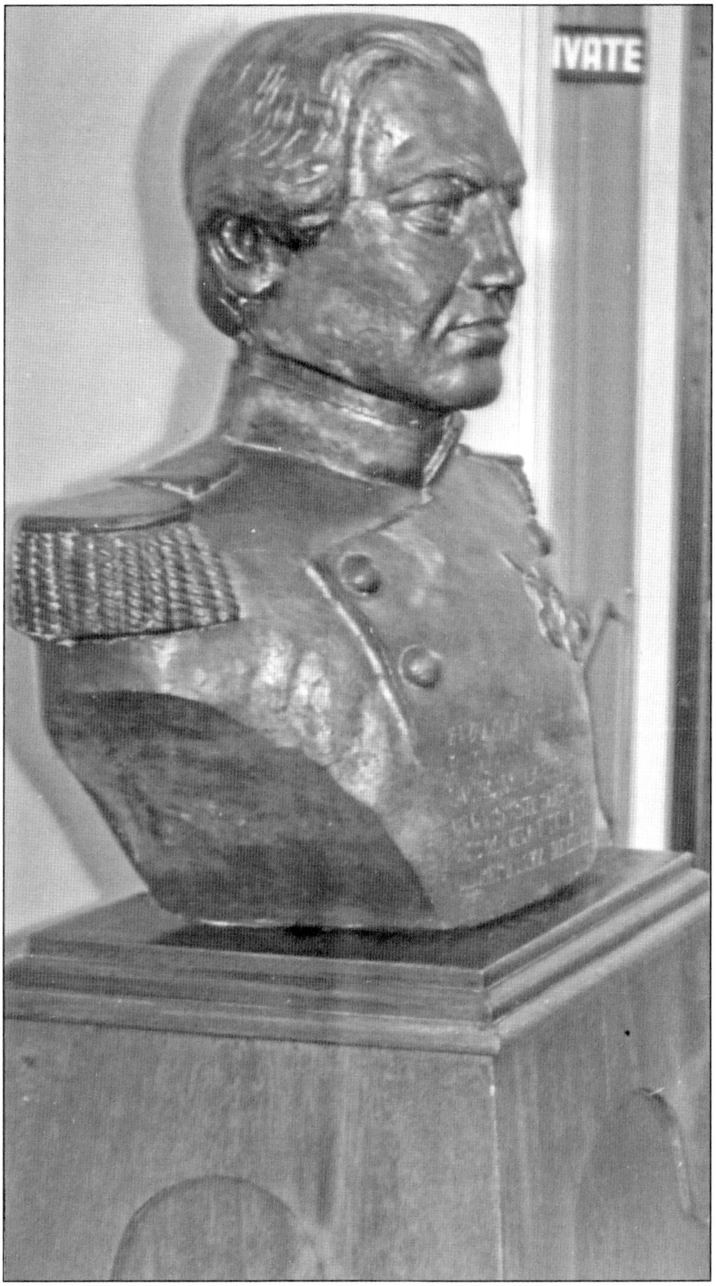

One of Goliad's most distinguished natives was Ignacio Zaragoza, born in La Bahia in 1829. He had a successful military career in Mexico, where he led a Mexican army to victory against a superior-sized and equipped French force in the Battle of Puebla on May 5, 1862. Unfortunately, soon after this brilliant victory, Zaragoza died of typhoid fever. President Benito Juarez declared Cinco de Mayo a national holiday in 1862, and the victory on that date is a major source of Mexican pride. To honor Zaragoza, the Texas Department of Parks and Wildlife built a representation of military housing in the 1960s adjacent to Presidio La Bahia. It is called the Zaragoza House and contains exhibits honoring him. There is also a nearby statue, as well as a bust (pictured) given to Goliad by Puebla, Mexico, in 1962. (Courtesy of Kyle Boyd-Robertson.)

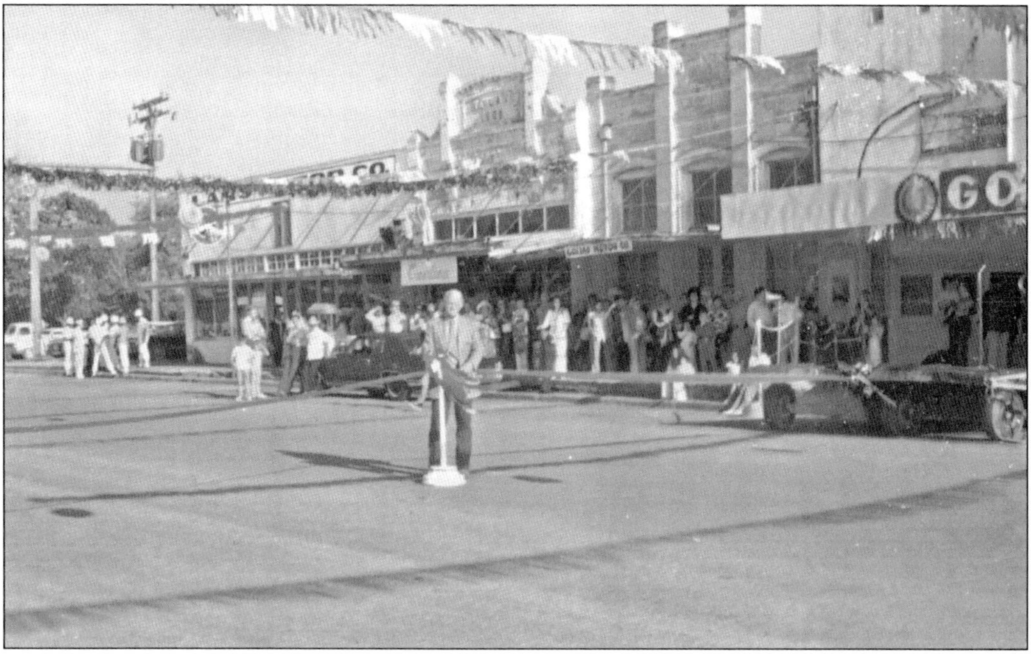

In 1992, the state legislature proclaimed Goliad the official Texas site for the celebration of Cinco de Mayo. Under leadership of the Zaragoza Society, each year the community holds a number of events, including a parade. Here Judge Jack Hayes cuts the ribbon initiating the first Cinco de Mayo parade.

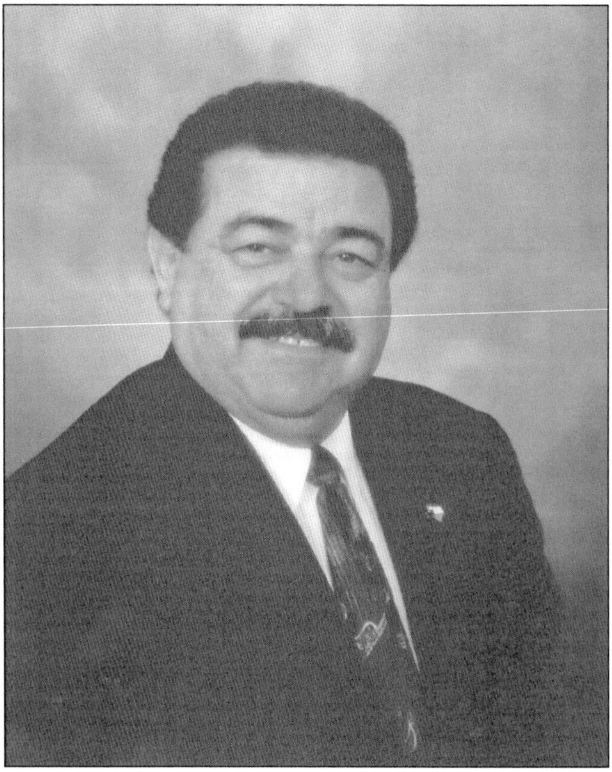

In 1976, Goliad elected its first Tejano mayor, Hernan E. Jaso. Coupled with the election of Robert de la Garza as sheriff in 2000 and the dedication of the U.S. Post Office to Judge Emilio Vargas in 2005, this represented a significant move of Mexican Americans into Goliad leadership positions. (Courtesy of Estella Zermeno.)

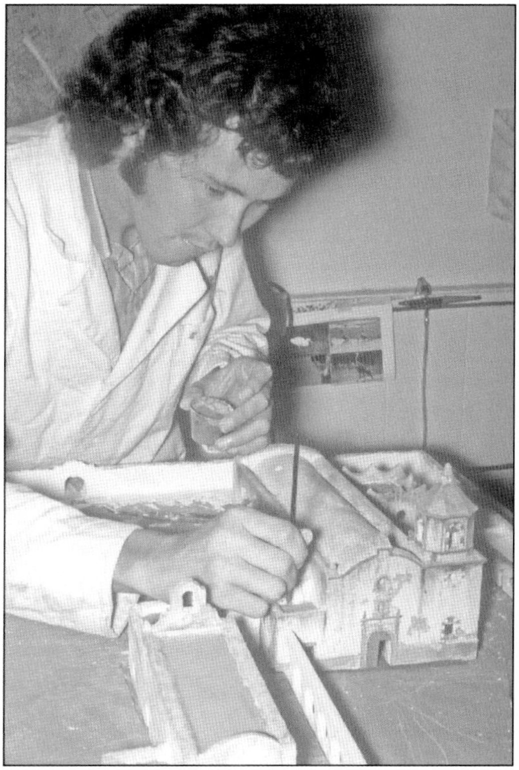

Since the creation of Goliad State Park and the restoration of Mission Espiritu Santo in the 1930s, the park has worked hard to preserve and interpret Goliad's past. In the 1970s, Texas Parks and Wildlife created a museum interpreting the significance of the mission. The photograph at right shows George Nelson working on a model for that exhibit. The photograph below shows the parks department painting the reconstructed chapel in 2005. Since most Texas missions were plastered and whitewashed, the painted building is probably an accurate depiction of its appearance during the colonial period. (Both courtesy of Texas Department of Parks and Wildlife.)

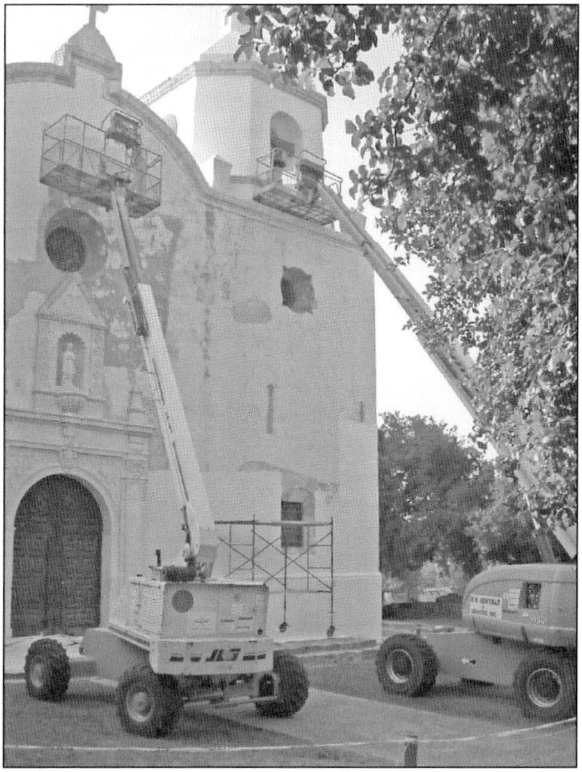

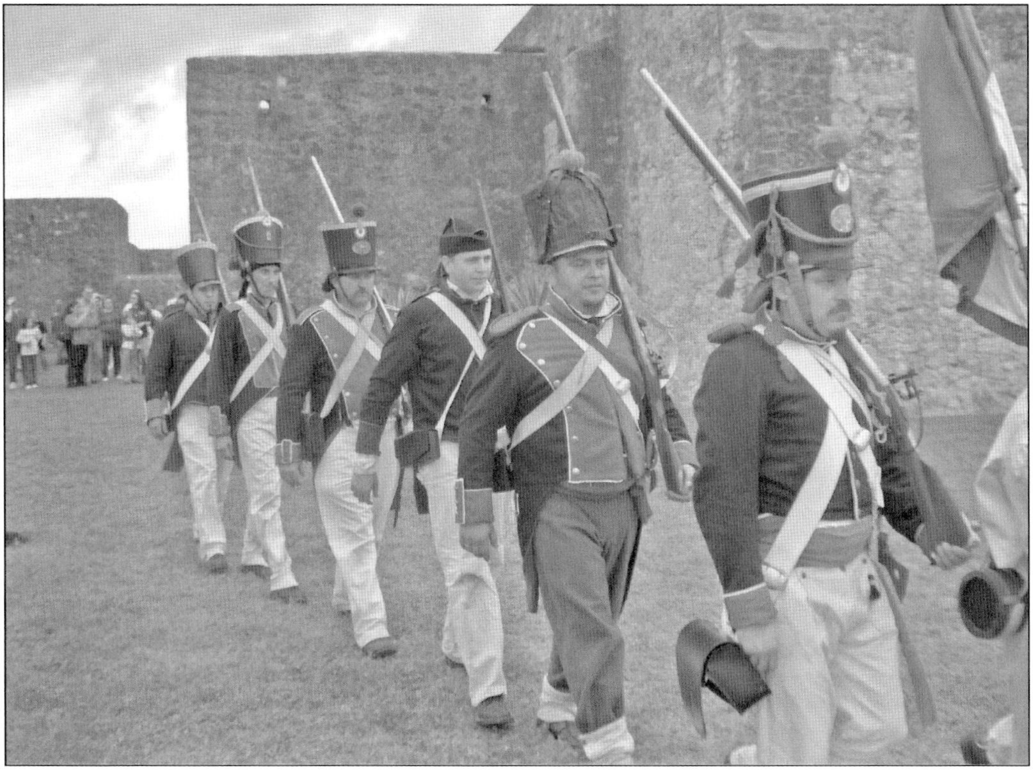

Each year, the Crossroads of Texas Living History Association presents a two-day reenactment of the Goliad Massacre at the Presidio La Bahia. Since it began in 1986, the program has grown into one of Goliad's major events, drawing over 4,000 visitors a year. The reenactors re-create a military camp; there are lectures, a candlelight tour of the presidio, and reenactments of skirmishes and the massacre. These photographs by Jim Wilson show reenactors costumed as Mexican officers (above) and Texan soldiers leaving the presidio to be executed (below). (Both courtesy of Jim Wilson.)

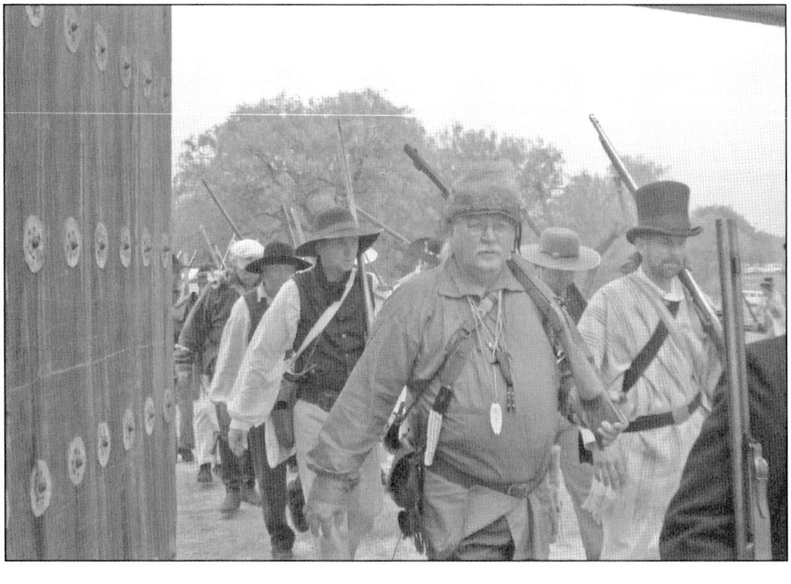

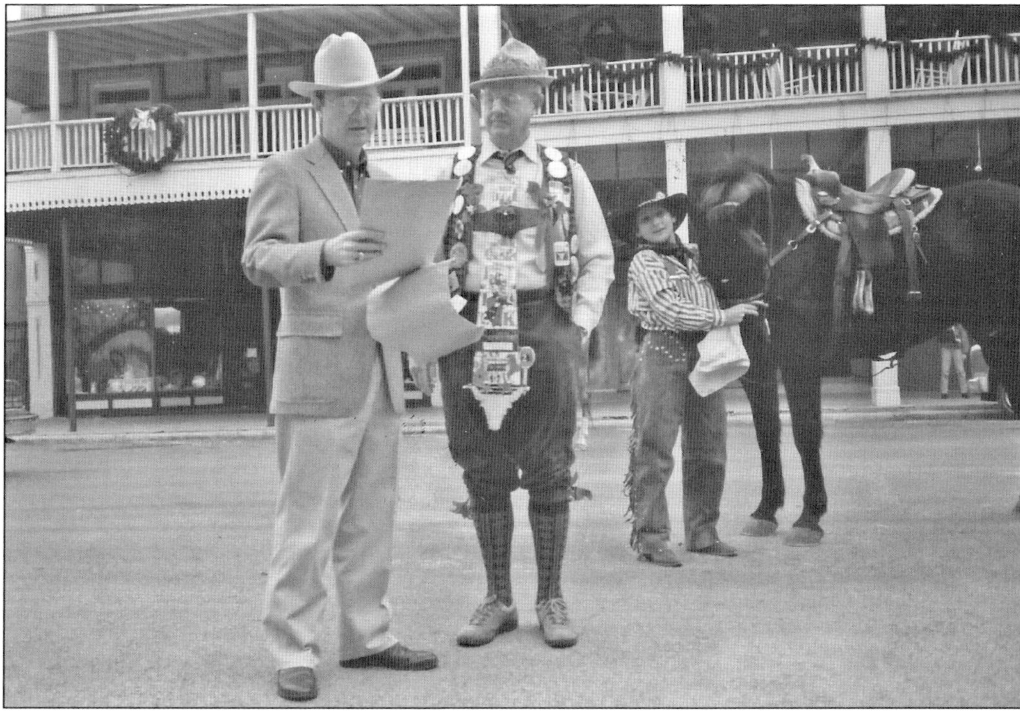

Since 1983, the Goliad County Historical Commission has conducted Christmas in Goliad. Begun primarily as a fund-raiser for the commission, the event has become one of the community's major annual events. It features a juried craft show, a lighted night parade, music and dancing, food booths, a posada at the Presidio La Bahia, and a Christmas concert at the Goliad State Park. One feature every year is the re-creation of a pony express ride from Goliad to San Antonio; the photograph above shows Judge John R. Barnhill reading a proclamation to that effect during the 1994 event. The highlight each year is Santa Claus riding into the square on a longhorn (called a reinsteer), as illustrated below.

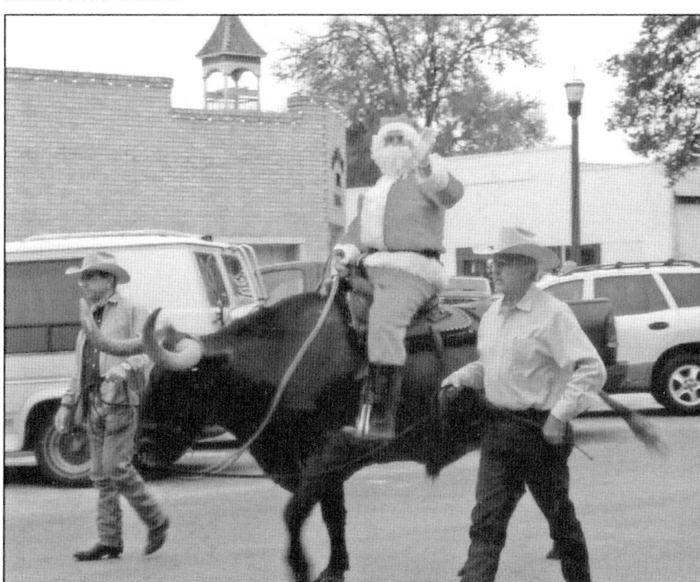

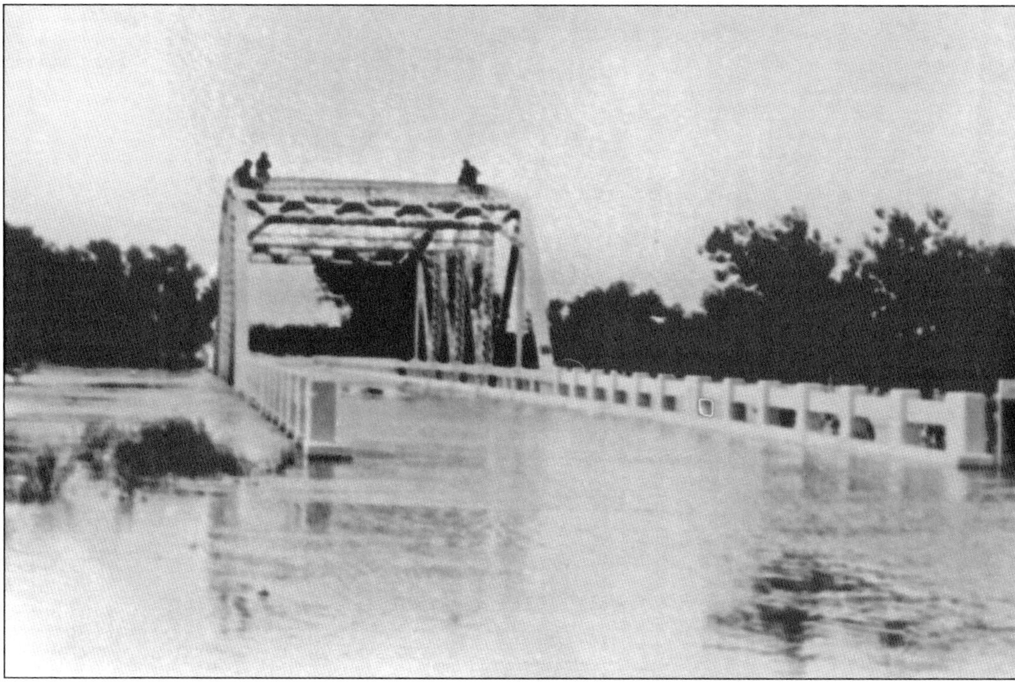

Nature has not always been kind to Goliad. In addition to the deadly tornado of 1902 and the hurricane of 1942 that ripped the top off the courthouse, there have been many San Antonio River floods. The photograph above shows the 1935 flood washing over the White Bridge at the state park; the photograph below shows a higher water level in the 1998 flood, which damaged the bridge, necessitating its replacement.

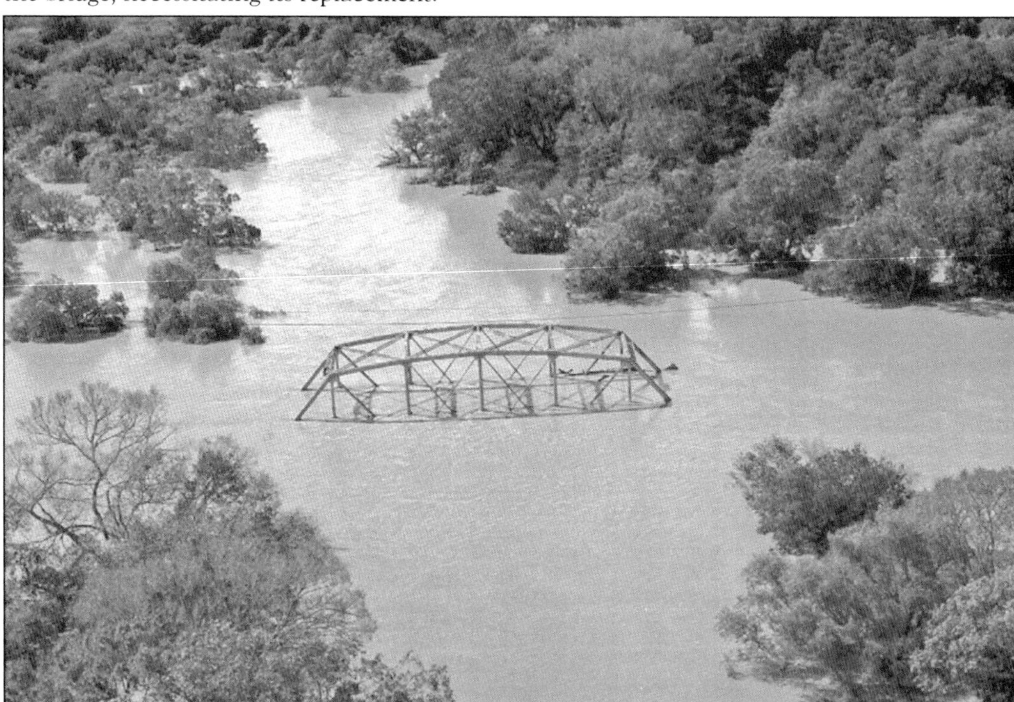

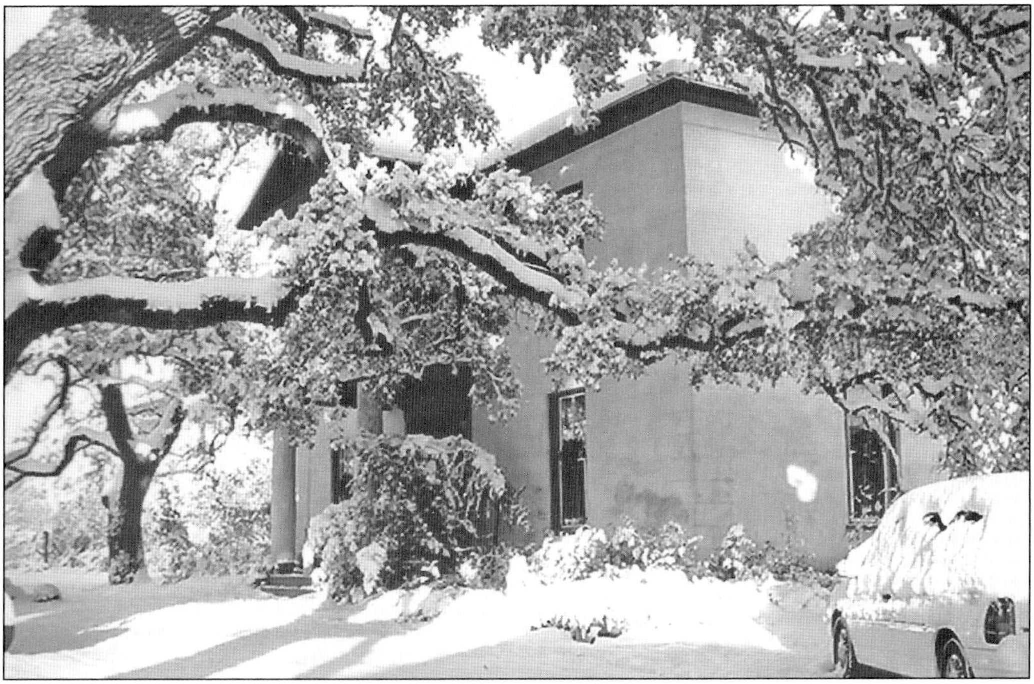

In addition to floods and tornados, nature also occasionally sent snow to Goliad. There have been minor snowfalls and sleet storms over the years but nothing like the "Christmas Miracle of 2004." On Christmas eve, it began snowing, and before it finished, up to 12 inches had fallen in Goliad. The storm was the result of the right juxtaposition of a dry arctic front, an upper level disturbance from Mexico, and just enough Pacific and Gulf moisture to produce snow. It created a winter wonderland in Goliad, with historic buildings (like the Peck Plantation House) draped in snow. It also inspired the irrepressible urge to build snowmen, such as these by the Billo family (From left to right are Cristy, MacKenzie, and Cory.) The snow on their mailbox gives a good idea of the depth of the snowfall. (Both courtesy of Cristy von Dohlen Billo.)

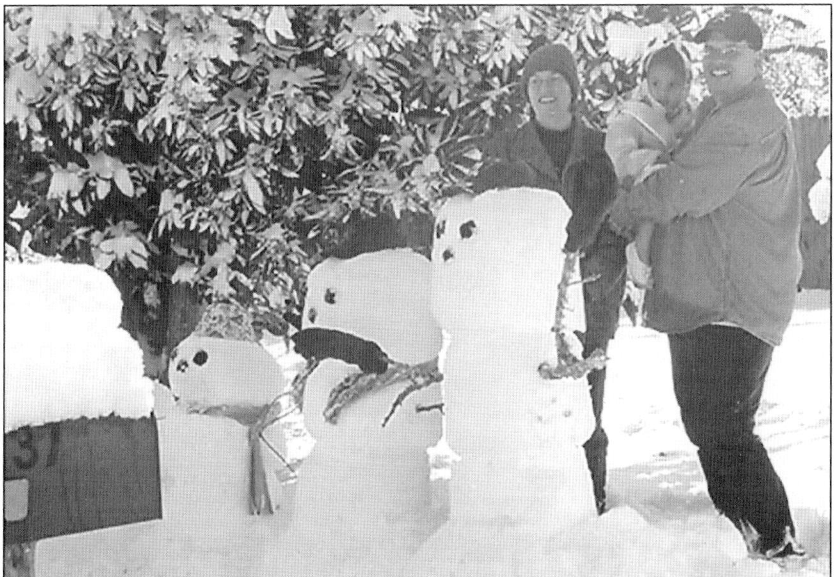

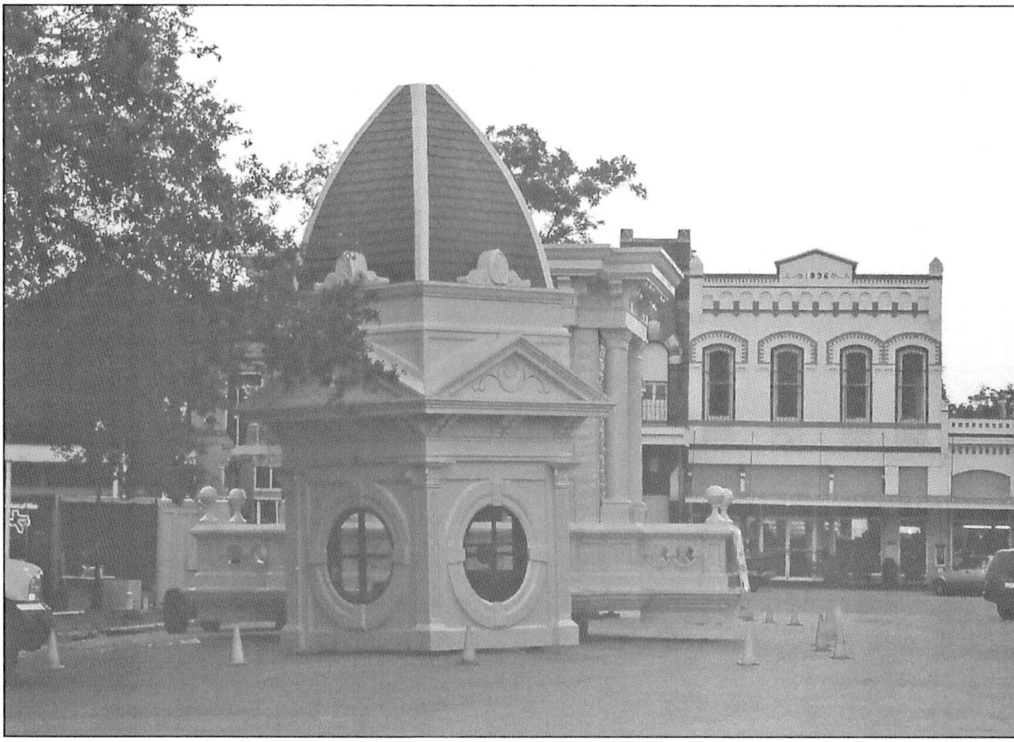

The restoration of the Goliad County Courthouse began in 2001 and included full repairs of the exterior and replacement of the original towers. In addition, there was work done on the site, remedial structural work, safety upgrades, restoration of two small balconies in the courtroom, and some reallocation of space. For most people, the most exciting part of the rebuilding was the replacement of the towers and turrets, which had been destroyed in the hurricane of 1942 (see page 79). The tower replacements were constructed on the ground and were built of heavy steel so they would not blow away again. The photograph above shows them on the ground prior to being lifted to the roof. The second photograph shows the addition of the wind vane, the final touch. (Both courtesy of Goliad County Chamber of Commerce.)

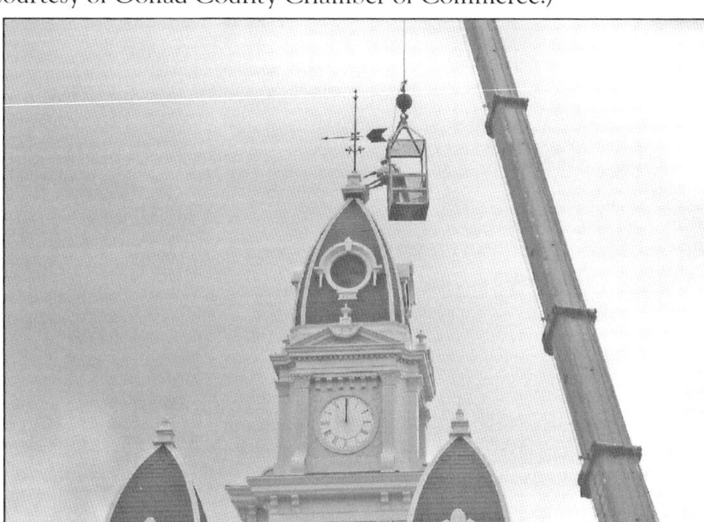

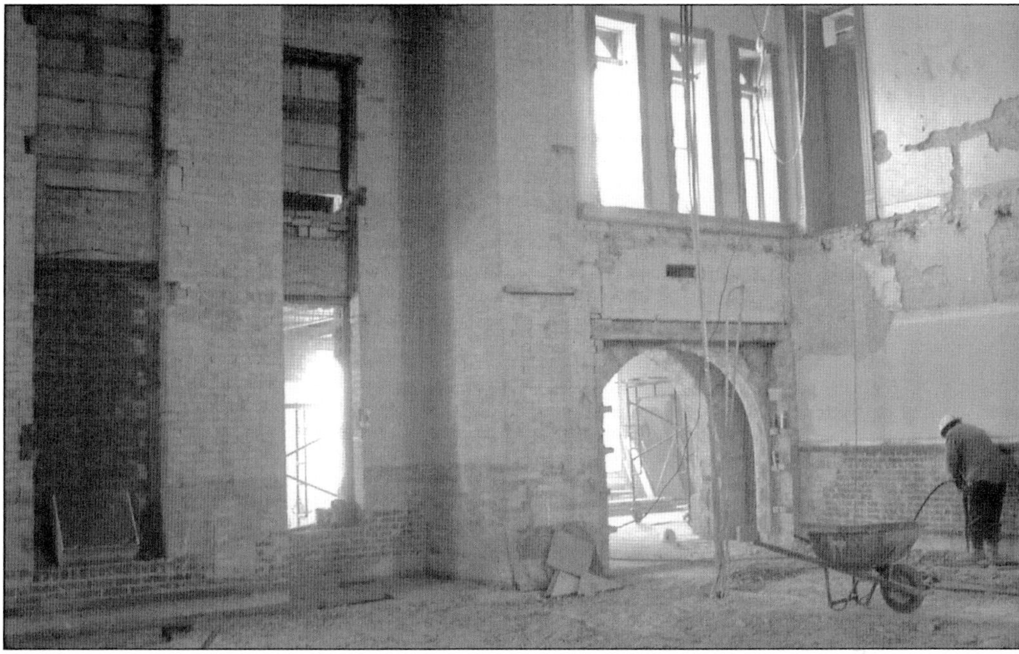

The restoration of the courthouse was done on its interior and exterior. This shows the courtroom, gutted and ready to be rebuilt. The county and its contractor went to great lengths to restore the interior authentically. They brought in highly skilled craftsmen and worked hard to match woods and finishes in order to re-create the interior's 1894 appearance.

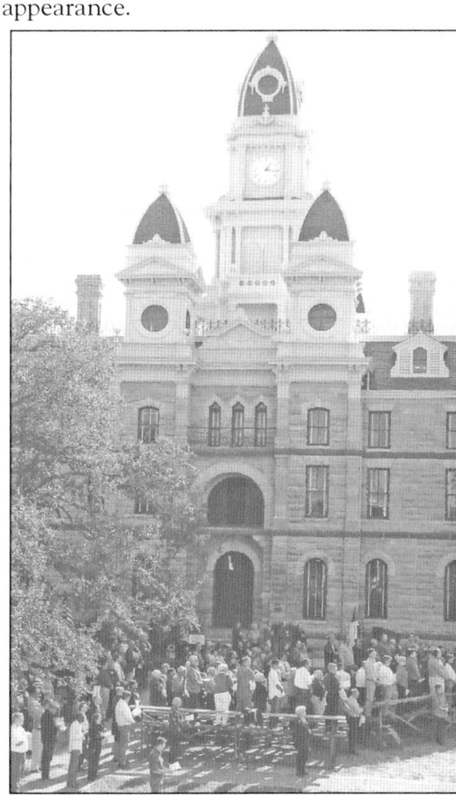

On December 4, 2003, Goliad dedicated its completely restored courthouse. Made possible by the Texas Historical Commission's Texas Historic Courthouse Preservation program and state legislation, the state provided $3.7 million, and Goliad covered $800,000 of the cost. The project was launched under the leadership of Judge Steven Paulsgrove and was finished in 2003 under Judge Harold Gleinser, who declared at the time, "You are looking at the proudest judge in Texas." (Courtesy of Goliad County Chamber of Commerce.)

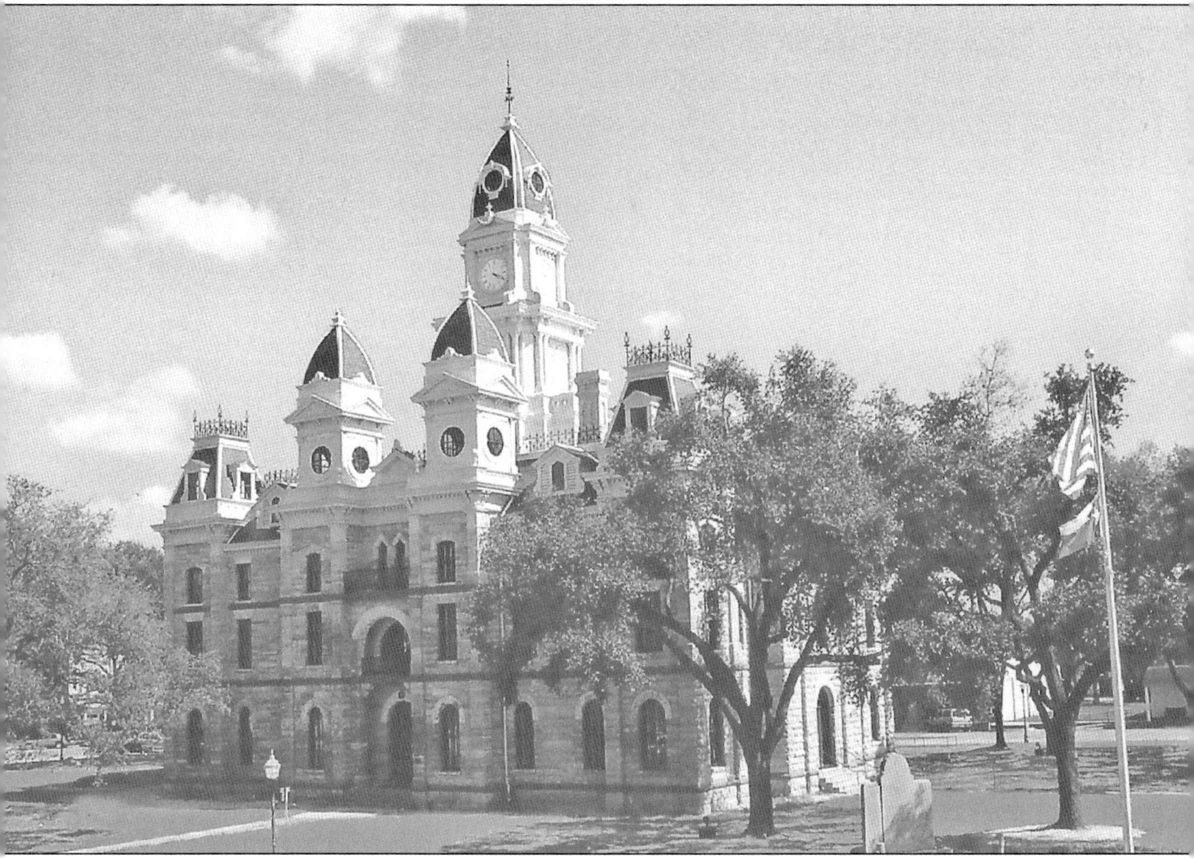

The 1894 courthouse is seen here in 2003, after its restoration. The building, a magnificent example of Second Empire architecture, has had its towers replaced and has been restored inside and out. It maintains its place as the spiritual, visual, and physical center of Goliad, ready for another century of service. (Courtesy of Goliad County Chamber of Commerce.)

BIBLIOGRAPHY

Bradle, William R. *Goliad: The Other Alamo*. Gretna, LA: Pelican Publishing Company, 2007.

Brown, Gary. *Hesitant Martyr in the Texas Revolution: James Walker Fannin*. Plano, TX: Republic of Texas Press, 2000.

Davis, Joe Tom. *Historic Towns of Texas, Vol 3: Nacogdoches, Goliad, San Felipe*. Austin, TX: Eakin Press, 2001.

Fox, Anne A., Samuel P. Nesmith, and Daniel E. Fox. *Silent Witness to Texas History: Archaeology and Artifacts of Goliad's Presidio La Bahia*. Victoria, TX: Presidio La Bahia, Catholic Diocese of Victoria, 2009.

McLean, Malcolm, translator, and John R. McLean, ed. *Voices from the Goliad Frontier: Muncipal Council Minutes: 1821–1835*. Dallas, TX: William P. Clements Center for Southwest Studies, Southern Methodist University, 2008.

O'Connor, Kathryn Stoner. *Presidio La Bahia: 1721–1846*. 3rd ed. Austin, TX: Wexford Press, 2001.

O'Connor, Louise S. *Cryin' For Daylight: A Ranching Culture in the Texas Coastal Bend*. Austin, TX: Wexford Publishing, 1989.

Pruett, Jakie L., and Everett B. Cole, eds. *The History and Heritage of Goliad County*. Goliad, TX: Goliad County Historical Commission, 1983.

Stout, Jay A. *Slaughter at Goliad: The Mexican Massacre of 400 Texas Volunteers*. Annapolis, MD: Naval Institute Press, 2008.

White, Beth. *Goliad Remembered, 1836–1940*. Austin, TX: Nortex Press, 1987.

White, Nell. *Goliad in the Texas Revolution*. Austin, TX: Nortex Press, 1988.